The Money Pit

THE MONEY PIT

The Story of Oak Island and The World's Greatest Treasure Hunt

D'Arcy O'Connor

Coward, McCann & Geoghegan, Inc.

New York

Copyright © 1978 by D'Arcy O'Connor

SBN: 698–10877–9

Library of Congress Cataloging in Publication Data

O'Connor, D'Arcy.
  The world's greatest treasure hunt.

  Bibliography: p. 247
  Includes index.
  1. Oak Island treasure site, N.S.—History. I. Title.
F1039.5.015026 1978 917.16'23 77–21882

Printed in the United States of America

For my father

List of maps and diagrams

"It may well be doubted whether human ingenuity can construct an enigma of the kind which human ingenuity may not, by proper application, resolve."

Edgar Allan Poe
"The Gold Bug"

Acknowledgments

I am indebted to the following people for supplying valuable information pertaining to their involvement in the search for the answer to the riddle of Oak Island: George Bates, Dan Blankenship, Charles Brown, Claude Chappell, Mel Chappell, Bob Dunfield, Kerry Ellard, Arnie Gilson, Johnny Goodman, Marguerite Hedden, Dunbar Hinrichs, Lavern Johnson, Parker Kennedy, Thomas Leary, Eugenia Macer-Story, Amos Nauss, Fred Nolan, Bill Parkin, Sr., Mildred Restall, Charles Roper, Louise Ruth, Bill Sobey, and David Tobias.

I am also grateful to the following persons and organizations who provided me with research assistance: Ray Joseph, Andy Kopkind, Zabé Rothschild, Bobbie Stein, the American Geographical Society, Francis Bacon Society, Franklin D. Roosevelt Library, Public Archives of Nova Scotia, Smithsonian Institution, and Triton Alliance Ltd.

For their guidance and encouragement I want to thank Blanche Boyd, Joan Peters, Roberta Pryor, and Frank Wilkinson.

Many thanks also to Gerrie Grevatt who transcribed the taped interviews, Ty Grevatt who took some of the photographs and developed and printed many of the others, and David Moore who did the artwork.

Finally, but most importantly, there is Kathryn Kilgore who somehow managed to put up with two years of my obsession with Oak Island.

Introduction

Nova Scotia's Oak Island contains one of the world's most baffling mysteries. Who constructed the labyrinth of tunnels and chambers deep beneath the island? When and how was it done? And most important, why was it done? After almost two hundred years of searching, none of these questions has been satisfactorily answered. The island has been investigated by scientists, engineers, and psychics; and by ordinary people with dreams of sudden wealth. They have uncovered tantalizing clues and formed many theories, but the solution has always eluded them.

While the existence of the man-made underground workings has been firmly established, a system of ingeniously designed flood tunnels from the sea has thwarted a complete investigation of the island's subterranean secret. Nevertheless, there is one general assumption that can be made about Oak Island. The workings, which may have taken several years to complete, were designed to hide something of great value. No other explanation makes sense. But what is the nature of the treasure; why was it so elaborately concealed, and is it still down there? All of this remains to be seen.

Meanwhile, the search has killed six men and left dozens of others with frustrated hopes and lost fortunes. Some say that more money—about $2 million to date—has been poured into the island than will ever be recovered. Yet the search undoubtedly will continue until the riddle has been solved.

Perhaps a reader of this book, using the documented history of the exploration and the evidence that has been discovered, will realize a truth about Oak Island that has escaped previous investigators.

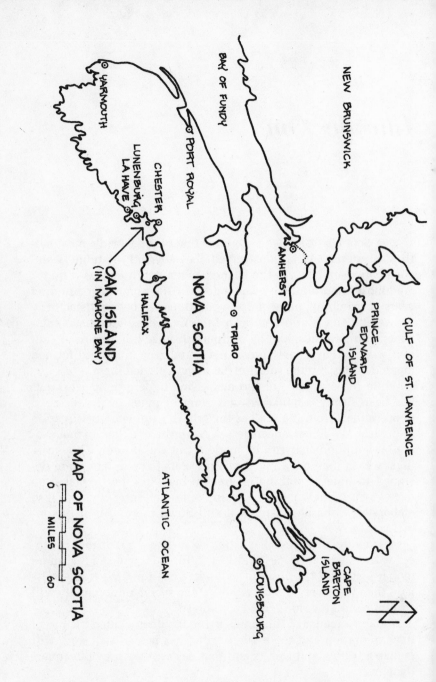

MAP OF NOVA SCOTIA

NEW BRUNSWICK

BAY OF FUNDY

GULF OF ST. LAWRENCE

PRINCE EDWARD ISLAND

CAPE BRETON ISLAND

NOVA SCOTIA

ATLANTIC OCEAN

YARMOUTH

PORT ROYAL

LUNENBURG
LA HAVE
CHESTER

OAK ISLAND
(IN MAHONE BAY)

HALIFAX

TRURO

AMHERST

LOUISBOURG

0   MILES   60

Chapter One

September 25, 1976. A clear, warm autumn afternoon on Oak Island. But 160 feet underground Dan Blankenship shivers in the clammy darkness as his pneumatic drill bites through the rusted ¼-inch steel casing of Borehole 10–X. Today, he hopes, will be the day he has been waiting for these past eleven years.

On the surface another man, Mel Chappell, also waits. But his anticipation began in 1897 when, as a boy of ten, he was told that a great treasure lay somewhere in the depths of Oak Island. With him are a handful of people who also wonder if today is the day: Bill Parkin, an engineer and inventor from Boston, whose specially designed sonar equipment detected several cavities, possibly man-made, far below the earth behind the casing of Borehole 10–X; Bill Sobey, chairman of a large supermarket chain, whose personal funds are helping finance this venture; David Blankenship, Dan's twenty-seven-year-old son, who will go down to cut entrances into the chambers with an acetylene torch once Dan has made sure there is no deadly methane gas seeping through the holes he's drilling; Janie Blankenship, Dan's wife, who watches nervously, aware that eleven years ago another woman lost her husband and son in a gas-filled pit only 300 feet away from this spot. They too had thought they were close to the treasure.

A mining safety engineer, linked to Blankenship by a headset telephone, instructs him on the use of the gas detector. The test is negative, and Dan signals to be winched up through the 27-inch-diameter tube. He emerges several minutes later, squinting against the bright sunlight, and David begins suiting up in preparation for his descent. Last-minute instructions are being shouted over the din of the compressor supplying air down the hole and the roar of two large pumps that are sucking up 800 gallons of water each minute in order to keep down the water level in Borehole 10–X. The water is no geological accident. It comes through a network of artificial underground drains leading from the surrounding ocean; a booby trap that was built to prevent the work that's going on today.

As David with his cutting torch, tools, and emergency oxygen supply is carefully lowered into 10–X, a pickup truck slowly cruises by on the dirt trail 50 feet away. The driver, Fred Nolan, curiously surveys the scene. For twenty years he too has been waiting for the answer to the riddle of Oak Island. But Nolan is certain the answer isn't in 10–X. He drives on, knowing he's not exactly welcome on this part of the island. The feud between Nolan and Blankenship's group goes back a long way.

A half mile away from this activity a Texas contractor is examining an oddly shaped rock at the edge of a swamp. He is wondering how to get down to the two human skeletons that he is sure guard the entrances to a large vault beneath this part of the island. This chamber, he is certain, is connected to Borehole 10–X.

One hundred and twenty miles to the east, another searcher studies a strange set of symbols. These characters, part of a code he has spent eight years deciphering, tell him the location of seven traps waiting to be sprung under Oak Island. He has heard of today's planned descent into 10–X, the first time in several years that anyone has ventured below the island's crust. And he is convinced that, if anything should go wrong, he is the only person alive who may be able to rescue the Blankenships.

Far down in that eerie shaft David Blankenship slips on his safety glasses and radios that he is beginning to cut the first observation hole.

These people are but a few of the hundreds who have been lured to this island off the coast of Nova Scotia, enticed by a riddle that began 181 years earlier at a spot 180 feet southwest of Borehole 10–X.

On that summer day in 1795 a teen-age boy, Daniel McGinnis, was wandering through the densely wooded eastern end of Oak Island when he came to an area that appeared to have been worked at some previous time. It was a small clearing in which aged oak stumps were visible. But what drew his attention was a large oak tree with a thick limb about 15 feet up that had been cut off several feet away from the trunk. Below the end of this branch the ground had settled into a shallow, saucer-shaped depression.

Undoubtedly, McGinnis was as aware as anyone in the Mahone Bay area of Nova Scotia that pirates and privateers had frequently cruised these waters in the seventeenth and early eighteenth centuries and that the notorious Captain William Kidd was rumored to have buried part of his treasure somewhere on the Nova Scotian coast. With this in mind McGinnis must have quickly linked his discovery with the possibility of a buried cache beneath that oak tree. Having no digging tools with him, he returned to the mainland where he told two friends, John Smith, aged nineteen, and Anthony Vaughan, sixteen, what he had found.

The following day the three of them returned to the spot with spades and pickaxes. They set to work digging in the center of the depression and found that their shovels could easily bite into the relatively loose soil. Two feet down they encountered what was to be the first of many pieces of evidence that someone had been here before. It was a layer of carefully laid flagstones; a type of rock that was later determined to have originated at Gold River, about two miles up the coast on the mainland. The boys cleared away the earth, exposing the entire layer of stone in order to remove it. They then found that they were working in what obviously was a refilled circular shaft with a diameter of 12 or 13 feet. A section of this shaft, eventually dubbed "the Money Pit," lay beneath the sawed-off limb, which presumably had been used by the original excavators to haul up the earth.

For several days the three boys returned to the island and continued to dig. They noticed that the sides of the shaft were of tough clay and that pick marks were visible along its walls. At the 10-foot level they struck a tier of snugly fitted oak logs completely covering the pit and embedded into the clay walls. They pried the logs out and resumed digging, only to hit an identical wooden platform 10 feet later. At a depth of 30 feet, another layer of oak was encouraged. Below it, as had been the case with the upper two layers, the ground had settled about 2 feet. The logs themselves were visibly rotten on their outer surfaces, indicating they had been down there a long time.

McGinnis, Smith, and Vaughan realized at this point that the project they'd undertaken was too big to handle by themselves and that they would need to enlist outside help. So far they had found nothing more than evidence that someone long before them had gone to a lot of trouble presumably to hide something more than 30 feet underground. Treasure seemed the only likely answer to what lay below. Only years later were the three boys to learn how much deeper and more complicated the Money Pit actually was. And even then, they would go to their graves knowing only part of the island's extraordinary underground secret.

The story of the 1795 discovery and the initial attempts to (literally) get to the bottom of the mystery originated with the verbal accounts of the three discoverers, all of whom lived till about the mid 1800's. Today, the earliest published version of the story is to be found in the October 16, 1862, edition of the *Liverpool Transcript*, a long-defunct weekly newspaper that served southwestern Nova Scotia. The article was based on a letter written by Jotham B. McCully of Truro, Nova Scotia, to "a gentleman in Halifax" on June 2, 1862. Significantly, McCully was associated with Oak Island search groups in 1849 and 1861 and had interviewed both Smith and Vaughan in their later years. Another account of the discovery appears in the January 2, 1864, edition of the *Colonist*, a Halifax tri-weekly. This article was based on a lengthy letter written to the newspaper on December 20, 1863, by "a member" of the 1861 search group, possibly McCully.

Subsequent narratives of the discovery appear in Israel Longworth's "History of the County of Colchester," an unpublished work that was written in 1866, and in Mather Byles DesBrisay's *History of the County of Lunenburg*, first published in 1870. Both writers borrowed heavily from the article that had appeared in the *Colonist*. However, DesBrisay in his younger years had been well acquainted with Mary Smith, John Smith's daughter, and he presumably got some of his facts from her. The next complete account of the discovery is found in the prospectus for an Oak Island search syndicate that was formed in 1893.

In these and later accounts there are minor discrepancies in detail. But the story of the discovery as it has been presented here contains only facts that are basically common to all versions. One detail, for instance, that appears in some accounts is that McGinnis found a wooden tackle block fastened to the cut-off branch over the Money Pit. This would seem to be an apocryphal detail added later to the story, and undoubtedly based on the assumption (probably correct) that the overhanging limb had served as a support for some sort of hoisting device when the pit was originally dug. Several versions also suggest that the three boys found in the vicinity of the Money Pit red clover and other plants foreign to the local soil, and that the oak tree with the cut-off branch had strange figures cut into its trunk. And one early chronicler, Andrew L. Spedon, in his *Rambles Among the Blue-Noses*, published in 1863, even suggests that "hair and scalps" were found embedded in the log platform.

Leaving out fanciful details, early accounts agree that the Money Pit was discovered by Daniel McGinnis in 1795 and that he and his two friends excavated it to a depth of about 30 feet, striking a layer of flagstones at 2 feet and then three platforms of wood at invervals of 10 feet. At that point they temporarily abandoned their work, not a doubloon richer. But they had launched what would turn out to be the world's longest and most expensive treasure hunt.

Chapter Two

Oak Island is one of some 350 islands scattered throughout Mahone Bay on the Atlantic coast of Nova Scotia. The island, about forty miles southwest of Halifax, was so named because of its large umbrella-domed red oaks, only a few of which still stand. An early chart of the area, drawn by the British cartographer I.F.W. Des Barres in 1776, designates the bay as Mecklenburgh Bay and Oak Island as Gloucester Isle. These names, however, were never in common use and don't appear in later charts. Moreover, even prior to 1776, the name Oak Island appears in several land-transfer deeds.

The island itself is almost a mile long by less than a half mile wide at its broadest point and is roughly peanut shaped, squeezing to less than 400 yards across near its center. The narrow area is swamp and marshy ground, while the island's two ends rise to approximately 35 feet above sea level. The island's long axis runs almost east-west, with the Money Pit located near the eastern, or seaward, end. Its western edge is but 200 yards from shore and since 1965 has been connected to the mainland at Crandall Point by a causeway that was built to transport heavy digging equipment. Today much of the island is overgrown with brush and stands of evergreen, mainly spruce, though most of the eastern end is cleared and pockmarked with craters and mounds of earth,

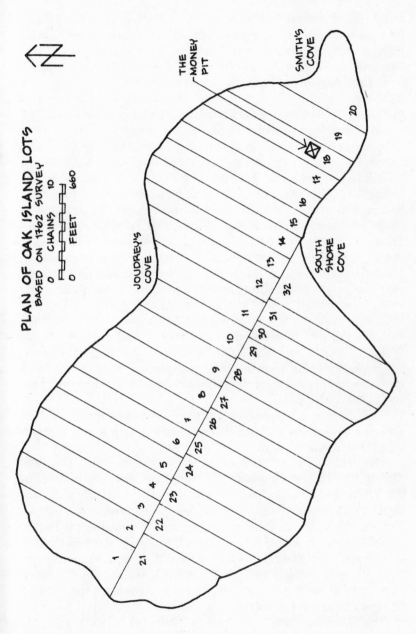

PLAN OF OAK ISLAND LOTS
BASED ON 1762 SURVEY

0   CHAINS   10

0   FEET   660

JOUDREY'S
COVE

THE
MONEY
PIT

SMITH'S
COVE

SOUTH
SHORE
COVE

testimony to almost two hundred years of digging in the Money Pit area. Geologically, the island is made up of two drumlins, oval hills of compact glacial drift that form the elevated eastern and western ends. These are composed of over 100 feet of hard clay overlying anhydrite bedrock and carboniferous limestone. A significant point is that in undisturbed areas the soil can be—and obviously was—excavated without the use of vertical shoring.

Oak Island was part of the "Shoreham Grant" made in October 1759 by Nova Scotia's then British Governor-in-Chief, Charles Lawrence, to approximately sixty-five immigrants from Britain's New England colonies. This initial grant, which established the township of Shoreham (now the town of Chester, about two and a half miles northeast of Oak Island), covered about 100,000 acres. It included several Mahone Bay islands, Oak Island among them. Prior to this the immediate area had no permanent inhabitants; the closest major settlements being at Lunenburg (founded in 1753) about ten miles down the southwest coast, and Halifax (founded in 1749) some forty miles up the coast. Over the next few years, more New England settlers arrived in the area. An October 29, 1763, report to the Governor-in-Chief gives a figure of three hundred families living in the County of Lunenburg that year, of which "Chester has about 30 families, subsisting chiefly on fishing and making lumber." Most of the balance were inhabitants of the town of Lunenburg, then the largest settlement in the county's 1,300 square miles.

According to a Lunenburg County land-grants report dealing with the allocation of island shares, most of Oak Island was granted to New England families by the name of Monro, Lynch, J. Seacombe, and Thomas Young in 1759. Most accounts of the 1795 Money Pit discovery suggest that the island was then uninhabited. While this could be true the island almost certainly was used by its grantees as a source of lumber and perhaps was even partially cultivated at its western end in the early years after the founding of Chester. In addition, Oak Island, like several others that lay close to shore in Mahone Bay, may have been used to pasture cattle in its early years. (Rafting cattle out to a nearby island to fatten them over the summer was a practice that eliminated the need for the stock fences that were necessary on the mainland).

The island was first surveyed in 1762 by Charles Morris, the province's Surveyor-General. At that time it was designated as Is-

land No. 28 in the official land records, and its 140 acres were broken up into 32 rectangular lots of about 4 acres apiece, with lots 1
to 20 running down the north side and lots 21 to 32 along the
south side of the island. A rough trail or path ran approximately
through the center of the island from west to east. This may have
been cut by either the survey party or one of the original grantees;
or perhaps, as some were later to speculate, it had something to do
with the unknown designers of the Money Pit.

The earliest existing deed pertaining to Oak Island records the
sale of Lot No. 19 by Edward Smith of Chester to Timothy Linch
(sic), also of Chester, for the sum of 5 pounds sterling on March 8,
1768. This lot lies almost at the eastern tip of the island and is
bounded on the west by Lot No. 18, the site of the Money Pit.
Whether Edward Smith was the original grantee of that part of the
island or whether he had purchased it sometime after 1759 is unclear. In any case, he may well have been the eponym of Smith's
Cove, a name that was later applied to both the small inlet at the
east end of the island and to the broader cove on the island's south
side. In fact, in some later copies of the Morris survey the whole
island is referred to as "Smith's Island," but this name didn't per-
sist for long. Also, the island's east-end inlet has been variously
referred to as Smuggler's Cove and Pirate's Cove, though today
the name Smith's Cove is the one most commonly used, as is the
term South Shore for the cove on that side of the island. (For the
sake of clarity the contemporary names will be used in all references to those coves). Edward Smith was apparently unrelated to
the John Smith who helped discover the Money Pit, as the latter,
according to DesBrisay, was born in Boston on August 20, 1775,
and immigrated to the Chester area sometime just prior to 1790.

Meanwhile, Anthony Vaughan, Sr., whose son was to be one of
the Money Pit discoverers, had arrived from Massachusetts in
1772 and began farming a 200-acre holding in what is today the
community of Western Shore, directly opposite Oak Island on the
mainland. Descendants of the Vaughan family still own that land.
The origin and parentage of the initial discoverer, Daniel McGinnis, isn't known for certain. The only clue we have is from Des-
Brisay, who says that among the early settlers in the Chester area
were "John McMullen and Daniel McInnis" (a family name that
was later changed to McGinnis and was also variously spelled
MacInnes and MacInnis).

From the evidence available it would seem that the families of the three discoverers—McGinnis, Smith, and Vaughan—had all emigrated from New England between 1770 and 1790 and that the three boys stumbled across Oak Island's mystery sometime in 1795. The actual date was probably prior to June 26, 1795, because on that day John Smith purchased Oak Island Lot No. 18, the site of the Money Pit. An extant deed shows that it was sold to him by Casper Wollenhaupt of the town of Lunenburg for the sum of 7 pounds, 10 shillings. That summer Smith, who had married several years earlier, settled with his family on Oak Island where he was to live on top of an enigma for the next sixty-two years.

Chapter Three

Following their discovery and excavation of the Money Pit down to 30 feet, Smith, McGinnis, and Vaughan finally told their mainland neighbors what they were up to and tried to enlist their help to continue the project. They were unsuccessful—partially because the hard-working farmers and fishermen of the area hadn't the time for the task, but mostly because of local superstition surrounding Oak Island. In the years preceding the discovery, inhabitants of Chester, a few miles across the bay, had reported seeing "strange lights" burning at night on the island. Some speculated that the island was being used as an occasional base by murderous pirates, while others hinted at supernatural forces of evil lurking on the island. According to one story—perhaps legend, perhaps fact—two Chester fishermen several years earlier had rowed out to investigate the nocturnal lights. The men were never seen again. Even today there are people in the area who regard Oak Island with superstitious dread, a feeling that has been supported by the additional evidence of the complexity of the underground workings as well as by the island's refusal to yield its whole secret.

Nevertheless, John Smith appears to have been convinced that the island had been selected by someone at some earlier time for burying treasure. So he built his house and began farming the eastern end of the island with the intention of eventually solving the mystery that lay beneath his property. Over the next few years he acquired several more lots on the island's eastern end, while his fellow discoverer, Daniel McGinnis, took up farming on the southwestern corner of the island. They seem to have left the Money Pit untouched for several years, though some early chroniclers reported that in the course of their wandering about the island the two young men found further evidence that the place had been visited many years before. This included a copper coin dated 1713, a bosun's whistle, and an iron ring-bolt found imbedded in a rock at Smith's Cove.

Accounts differ as to how many years elapsed before Smith, McGinnis, and Vaughan (who was living on the mainland) were able to interest anyone in their project. The *Colonist* and Des-Brisay versions say it was fifteen years after the discovery, while J. B. McCully's article in the *Liverpool Transcript* of 1862 gives the figure of seven years, or 1802. This latter date is probably correct, as it corresponds with the version handed down through the Vaughan family as well as an account written in 1867 by James McNutt, who was involved in later search groups and had interviewed some of the earlier searchers.

Accordingly, in 1802 Simeon Lynds of Onslow, at the head of the Bay of Fundy in Nova Scotia, was in the Chester area on business when he met Anthony Vaughan and heard the story of the 1795 discovery. Lynds was apparently caught up by the tale, for he returned to Onslow and formed a company to provide financing and equipment to excavate the Money Pit. The following spring this group, known as the Onslow Company, arrived at Oak Island to work under the direction of Colonel Robert Archibald. There were twenty-five to thirty financiers backing the operation, many of them businessmen from Onslow and the nearby town of Truro.

The workers, including Smith, McGinnis, and Vaughan, began digging out the pit, which had partially caved in over the years. They soon were at the 30-foot level, where they found stakes that the three discoverers had driven into the ground before giving up in 1795. Continuing down, they struck oak platforms at intervals of 10 feet to a depth of 90 feet. If these platforms puzzled them, they were equally at a loss to explain layers of charcoal, putty, and a fibrous material that covered some of the wooden tiers. At the

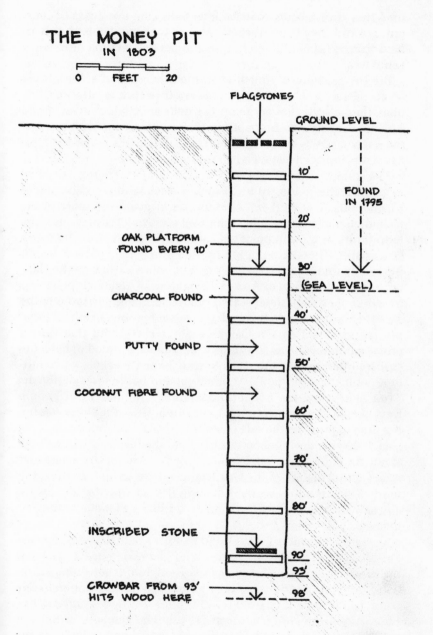

THE MONEY PIT
IN 1803

0   FEET   20

FLAGSTONES

GROUND LEVEL

10'

FOUND
IN 1795

20'

OAK PLATFORM
FOUND EVERY 10'

30'

(SEA LEVEL)

CHARCOAL FOUND

40'

PUTTY FOUND

50'

COCONUT FIBRE FOUND

60'

70'

80'

INSCRIBED STONE

90'

95'

CROWBAR FROM 93'
HITS WOOD HERE

98'

time they didn't know that the fiber was from the husks of coconut; nor did they know that there were tons more of it on this island that lies about fifteen hundred miles north of the nearest coconut tree.

But the most mystifying clue awaited the workers at the 90-foot level. Here, just before hitting another oak platform, they unearthed a large flat stone on the bottom of which was carved some sort of strange inscription. Unfortunately, as with most of the early artifacts uncovered on Oak Island, this stone has vanished, having been last seen in 1919.

The stone was described in various accounts as being 2 to 3 feet long, 15 inches wide, 10 to 12 inches thick, and weighing about 175 pounds. The workers were unable to make any sense of the etched characters, and the stone was removed and later used by John Smith as a curio piece set into the fireplace of his home on Oak Island. There it was seen by many members of later search groups, including A.O. Creighton, who was a partner in the Halifax bookbinding firm of A. & H. Creighton. In 1866, while he was treasurer of an Oak Island search syndicate, Creighton brought the stone to Halifax where it was displayed at his shop to attract prospective investors in the Oak Island project. About that time a professor of languages at a Halifax university claimed to have deciphered the code on the stone to read: "Forty feet below two million pounds are buried." (Another version has his translation as: "Ten feet below are two million pounds buried.") But people were skeptical of this enticing translation, since the stone was being used to promote the sale of stock in the Oak Island search.

In 1909 an elderly schoolteacher from the town of Mahone Bay, about six miles from Oak Island, copied down the characters and wrote a brief history of the Oak Island search. In his narrative, the unidentified teacher, without making it clear whether he personally saw the stone, gives the inscription in the diagram as the one that was found.

This teacher sent his Oak Island manuscript to Rev. A.T. Kempton of Cambridge, Massachusetts, who planned to use it in a book he was writing about Nova Scotia. Kempton never finished his book, but almost forty years later he showed the inscription to Edward Rowe Snow who used it in his book, *Mysteries and Adventures Along the Atlantic Coast* (1948). The symbols in Snow's book, which vary slightly from those in the schoolteacher's manu-

∇⍦⍉∅△⌇ ∇⠆⠆△ †⠆⌐⍉□ △□⍉

‡⠒⌐⌐⠒⍉⍉ ⊖⍉+⍉□⊙ ⋅∅⠆ ††∅⠒⠒⠆▯

THE INSCRIPTION ON THE STONE
FOUND IN THE MONEY PIT IN 1803.

script, have since been redeciphered by others to form (as will be seen later) some remarkable theories about Oak Island.

If the Mahone Bay teacher, who says he based his Oak Island account on "reliable sources, old records and old people," actually saw the inscription, it would have to have been prior to 1909, and probably even before 1890. In 1909 Captain Henry L. Bowdoin of New York, the leader of an Oak Island search syndicate, examined the stone in Halifax but said the characters were worn away. The reason was that the stone had been used by the Creighton bookbinders as a base on which to beat leather during the previous two decades.

In the early 1930's Frederick Blair of Amherst, Nova Scotia, attempted to locate the mysterious stone. Blair at that time controlled the digging rights on Oak Island. On December 19, 1933, he wrote Thomas M. Nixon, a prospective searcher, advising him that: "The last authentic word I had of this stone was from Jefferson McDonald, who told me in 1894 that some 30 years before that, he helped to take down a partition at the rear of a fireplace in which the stone was used as a back, with the cut characters at the rear. The partition was torn down for the purpose of examining and reading, if possible, the characters. He said the characters were easily discernible, but no person present could decipher them."

Fifteen months later Blair ascertained that the stone had been last seen in 1919 by Harry W. Marshall, whose father had become a partner in the Creighton firm after the death or retirement of A.O. Creighton in 1879. Marshall recalled seeing it from about 1890 till 1919 when the bookbinding business was closed and the stone was apparently discarded. In a statement to Blair on March 27, 1935, Marshall said:

"The stone was about two feet long, 15 inches wide and 10 inches thick, and weighed about 175 pounds. It had two smooth surfaces, with rough sides with traces of cement attached to them. Tradition said that it had been part of two fireplaces. The corners were not squared but somewhat rounded. The block resembled dark Swedish granite or fine grained porphyry, very hard, and with an olive tinge, and did not resemble any local stone. Tradition said that it had been found originally in the mouth of the Money Pit. While in Creighton's possession, some lad had cut his initials 'J.M.' on one corner, but apart from this there was no evidence of any inscription either cut or painted on the stone. Creighton used the stone for a beating stone and weight."

Clearly, a stone with some sort of markings on it did exist, for it is mentioned in all early accounts of the Onslow Company's operations (though a couple of versions claim it was found at a depth of 80 rather than 90 feet), and was reportedly seen by hundreds of persons in the 1800's. Some later searchers were to regard the stone and its cryptic message as the key to the entire mystery of Oak Island. Whether that's true or not, the inscription may at least have been a clue indicating how to get around the ingenious trap that lay below it.

After removing the stone and the wooden platform at 90 feet, the workers noticed that the earth was becoming soft and mushy. Yet they had encountered no vein of sand or gravel that would indicate the possibility of a natural watercourse leading into the pit. According to the account in the *Colonist*, "at 93 feet [the water seepage] increased, and they had to take out one tub of water for two of earth. Still, they had no idea that anything was wrong." With night coming on, they probed the bottom of the pit with a crowbar to see if they could strike anything below—their usual practice at the close of each day's work. And this evening, 5 feet below, "they struck a hard impenetrable substance bound by the sides of the pit. Some supposed it was wood, and others called it a chest. They then left for the night to resume operations in the morning, when they fully expected to solve the mystery."

But that next morning the diggers became the first to learn what the unknown engineer of Oak Island had in store for anyone who attempted to probe the depths of the Money Pit. The shaft, which during all those previous weeks of work had been dry, now contained about 60 feet of water. Discouraged but not defeated, they began bailing out the pit with buckets. Before long they realized their efforts were having no effect on the water level. At this point they discontinued the project for the balance of the summer because some of the workers had to return to their farms to bring in the hay. That autumn the company hired a Mr. Mosher, a mechanic from the town of Newport, Nova Scotia, to rig up a pump. It was lowered to the bottom of the pit and started up. But before the water reached the surface, the pump burst. Colonel Archibald then ordered the work halted and proposed returning with a new plan the following spring.

The next year (1804) the Onslow Company was back. They were convinced that the treasure lay just below the wooden obstruction that had been probed at 98 feet the summer before. They planned to circumvent the water and reach the treasure by sinking a shaft (No.2) 14 feet southeast of the Money Pit and tunneling through from there to the supposed cache. (For the position of this and later shafts, see the map on page 244.) This second shaft was dug to a depth of 110 feet with no water problems. "At this stage," says the *Colonist*, "they began to tunnel towards the old pit and got within two feet of it, having tunneled twelve, without encountering any hinderence. But at this time water oozed in upon them from the end of the tunnel and began to run in small streams. At length, the bank between the [Money] pit and tunnel giving away, they were obliged to effect an immediate retreat. And in less than two hours afterwards, water was standing in the new pit to the depth of 65 feet." Again, bailing was futile, and this effectively put an end to the Onslow Company's Oak Island expedition. Another forty-five years were to pass before anyone would again make a serious attempt to reach the elusive treasure.

Most of the early reports don't indicate whether the 1803–04 searchers realized what they were up against in trying to remove or circumvent the water in the Money Pit. But the workers must surely have noticed, as did others who followed them, that the water was salty and that the level in the two pits rose and fell with the surrounding tide. Thus, their bailing efforts were tantamount to recycling the ocean. But how was sea water able to penetrate the island's hard-packed clay? Without knowing it, the Onslow group had broken a primitive yet effective hydraulic seal when they removed the tightly fitted wooden platforms, particularly the one at 90 feet beneath the stone with its indecipherable message. And perhaps the designer of the Money Pit had expected and wanted them to do precisely that.

Chapter Four

After the Onslow group's failure to bring up any treasure, John Smith resumed farming on his land at the eastern end of Oak Island, and at some point he filled in the two watery shafts. Much of Oak Island was now being used by Smith and others as farm and grazing land as well as a source of timber. But the Money Pit and the frustrated attempts to reach its bottom became well known around Nova Scotia.

Not until 1849 was a new group formed to take another crack at recovering the treasure that was presumed to lie at the bottom of the Money Pit. This syndicate was known as the Truro Company, named after the hometown of most of its participants. Daniel McGinnis had died by this time, but Smith and Vaughan (both in their seventies) as well as Simeon Lynds were still around to point out the exact location of the Money Pit. The first task was to re-excavate the original shaft. This was accomplished in twelve days down to a depth of 86 feet, at which point water began entering and the workers were driven out. Once again bailing proved useless and work was temporarily suspended.

Later that summer the Truro Company returned with a hand-operated pod auger of the type then used in prospecting for coal. The previously mentioned Jotham B. McCully was the drilling engineer. A platform was set up in the Money Pit at a depth of 30 feet, just above the water level, and the 1½-inch-diameter drill pipe lowered to the bottom of the shaft. The work involved screwing a chisel-tipped auger into the earth and then removing cores of drilled material.

The drilling program, which was to yield some interesting results, was recorded separately by McCully and another member of the Truro Company, and both versions generally corroborate each other. McCully, in a letter to a friend on June 2, 1862, and later in a report to another search syndicate says:

"We bored five holes, in the first of which we lost the only valve sludger we had. . . .

"The second hole we bored struck the platform which the old [Onslow Company] diggers told us about—precisely at the depth they had told us they had struck it with a crowbar, 98 feet. After going through this platform, which was five inches thick and proved to be spruce, the auger dropped 12 inches and then went through four inches of oak; then it went through 22 inches of metal in pieces, but the auger failed to take any of it in except three links, resembling an ancient watch chain. It then went through eight inches of oak, which was thought to be the bottom of the first box and top of the next: then 22 inches of [loose] metal, the same as before; then four inches of oak and six inches of spruce; then into clay seven feet without striking anything else. In the next [third] boring the platform was struck as before at 98 feet; passing through this the auger fell about 18 inches and came in contact with, as supposed, the side of a cask. . . .On withdrawing the auger, several splinters of oak, such as might come from the side of an oak stave, and a small quantity of a brown fibrous substance, closely resembling the husk of a coconut, were brought up. The distance between the upper and lower platforms was found to be six feet."

These findings and measurements are substantiated in a letter dated September 16, 1861, to the *Nova Scotian*, a Halifax newspaper. The writer, who signs himself "the digger, Patrick," worked with the Truro Company and reports that the sound of the auger passing through loose metal, "coin, if you will," was clearly audible that day up on the drilling platform.

In the previously mentioned 1862 letter to a friend, McCully described the chain that was brought up on the drill as "three small links which had apparently been forced from an epaulette. They were gold."

This was the first piece of tangible evidence that something of value was down in the Money Pit. Unfortunately, as McCully noted, the auger couldn't pick up any of the loose metal struck at two distinct levels. The final two holes were drilled near the inside walls of the pit. These only brought up further evidence of the platforms and loose earth without striking the metal, although James McNutt in his 1867 account states that "three pieces of wire which was copper were brought up by the auger" from the fifth hole.

If the workers couldn't physically get to the pit's watery bottom, they now at least had some idea of what was below that platform at 98 feet: There appeared to be at least two large oaken chests or boxes filled with something metallic and laying one on top of the other at a depth of between 100 and 104 feet, after which there was another spruce platform spread across the pit at about the 105-foot level. Below that, in the 7 additional feet they drilled, the clay was loose, indicating that the Money Pit had originally been dug even deeper.

Shortly after these encouraging results, another Truro Company drill crew sank several more exploratory holes into the bottom of the Money Pit. The reported findings were basically the same as before. But now an element of intrigue comes into the story. John Pitbladdo, a mining engineer from Truro, was the foreman on this crew and was in charge of examining the drill-core samples that were brought to the surface. One day, John Gammell, a large shareholder in the Truro Company, happened to be on the site and saw Pitbladdo take something off the end of the drill, examine it closely, and then slip it into his pocket. Gammell, in a statement made later, says he asked Pitbladdo what he had found, but was told he would have to wait until the next Truro Company board meeting when Pitbladdo would show it to all the directors. The story is verified by George Vaughan, who in 1922 told Frederick Blair that his father David Vaughan (who was Anthony Vaughan's son) was there that day and witnessed the confrontation between Gammell and Pitbladdo after the latter had pocketed something he'd removed from the drill.

Pitbladdo never showed up at the next meeting of directors; in fact, he was never seen on the island again. But he presumably had found something that convinced him there was a treasure in the Money Pit. Nova Scotia provincial records show that on August 1, 1849, John Pitbladdo and an associate, Charles D. Archibald, who was manager of the Acadia Iron Works at Londonderry, Nova Scotia, applied to the Lieutenant General of the province for a license to dig for treasure on Oak Island. They received permission several days later, but their license was limited to "ungranted and unoccupied lands on Oak Island." The two men then made a determined but unsuccessful attempt to purchase John Smith's land.

Nothing more came of Pitbladdo's scheme to get control of the search area. Several years later Archibald moved to England and Pitbladdo was rumored to have died either in a gold mine or railway construction accident in the 1850's. However, in the second edition (1895) of DesBrisay's *History of the County of Lunenburg*, reference is made to a James Pitblado, Sr., a mining engineer from Truro, who in 1875 was superintendent of a coal-prespecting venture in Chester. This could well have been John Pitbladdo, since in most written accounts of Oak Island he was incorrectly referred to as James Pitblado. In any case, no one, other than Archibald, seems ever to have learned what was brought up from the Money Pit that summer day in 1849.

The next summer the Truro Company decided to sink another shaft (No. 3) about 10 feet northwest of the Money Pit. The intention again was to try and reach the treasure cache by lateral tunneling or, failing that, to at least use the new hole as a connecting pumping shaft to help lower the water level in the Money Pit. No water was encountered in this new shaft down to 109 feet, at which point the workers began tunneling toward the Money Pit. An account by Adams A. Tupper, one of the diggers in this operation, states that "just before reaching that point [under the Money Pit], the water burst in and the workmen fled for their lives, and in 20 minutes there was 45 feet of water in the new pit." Two pumping gins, each powered by two horses, were set up over the Money Pit and the new shaft. According to Tupper, the pumping "was carried on night and day for about a week, but all in vain, the only difference being that with the doubled appliances the water could be kept at a lower level than formerly."

It was now obvious that a huge volume of seawater was somehow entering the Money Pit at about the 100-foot level. Moreover, the flooding wasn't sporadic or accidental, since the two shafts that had been dug close to the Money Pit were in the same type of hard clay and went 100 feet deep without striking water. Only when they were connected to the Money Pit did they become flooded. And if the subterranean water channel intersecting the Money Pit was natural, then whoever originally dug the pit would have encountered it and been forced to abandon the project. Yet it was now known that wooden platforms had been laid across the pit all the way down to at least 105 feet; something that could not possibly have been done in a flooded shaft. At about this time someone noticed that at low tide in Smith's Cove, approximately 500 feet east of the Money Pit, a small stream of water was trickling from the bank; it too was salt water. So a search was made of the Smith's Cove beach and this led to an amazing discovery. The entire beach was artificial!

Almost as soon as the workers started shoveling into the sand and gravel beach between the high and low tide lines, they came across a bed of a brown fibrous material similar to that found in the Money Pit. It was coconut fiber; tons of it in a layer several inches deep and covering an area 145 feet along the shore from the high to low tide lines. Below this was another layer of 4 to 5 inches of decayed eel grass also spread uniformly across the same area. Underneath the fiber and eel grass was a tightly packed mass of beach rocks that was free of sand and gravel.

The Truro Company's next step was to build a stone and clay cofferdam in order to hold back the tides. This took several weeks. When it was completed and the area was water-free, the rocks just inside the dam were removed. Here the workers found that the clay sea bottom had been dug out and replaced with a series of five well-constructed box drains, or catch basins. They were made of lines of rock about 8 inches apart and covered with flat slabs of stone interspaced to allow water to seep in along their length. These elongated drains were situated across the width of the false beach at the low-water line and converged, like the fingers of a hand, at a common point near the shore. An account by one of the diggers describes the stones as having "been prepared with a hammer and mechanically laid to prevent caving."

The workers began dismantling the drains, starting at the cofferdam and working back toward shore. They noticed that the drain-

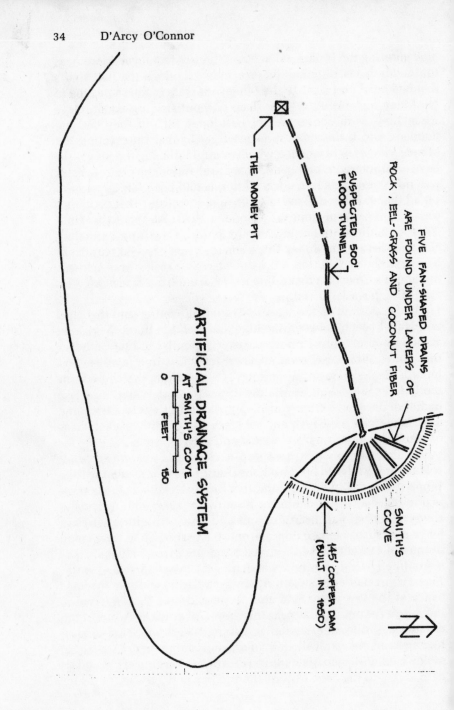

THE MONEY PIT

SUSPECTED 500'
FLOOD TUNNEL

FIVE FAN-SHAPED DRAINS
ARE FOUND UNDER LAYERS OF
ROCK, EEL-GRASS AND COCONUT FIBER

ARTIFICIAL DRAINAGE SYSTEM
AT SMITH'S COVE

0   FEET   150

SMITH'S
COVE

145' COFFER DAM
(BUILT IN 1850)

N

age system sloped downward as it approached the shore, and when they were only halfway back they were already working 5 feet below the original beach. At this point nature intervened in the form of an Atlantic gale accompanied by an unusually high tide. The cofferdam was washed away.

Rebuilding it was considered too time-consuming and expensive. A new plan was proposed. The Truro group had been able to expose only about half of the outer end of the drainage network and hadn't found the common point to which the drains apparently led. But they now had at least some indication of where the tunnel from the sea entered the island on its way to the Money Pit. Their plan therefore was to sink a shaft about 100 feet inland from Smith's Cove in the hope of intersecting and plugging the flood tunnel.

This new shaft (No.4) was dug to 75 feet before the workers realized they must have missed the water tunnel. Moving about 12 feet to the south, another shaft (No. 5) was begun. This time, at a depth of 35 feet, they came to a large boulder. As soon as they started prying it out they encountered a rush of water. Within minutes the hole was flooded to sea level. They had found the tunnel. To block the drain, they partially refilled this shaft and drove wood pilings into its bottom. They were satisfied that they had short-circuited the trap that had prevented them from finding what was in the Money Pit.

Bailing was resumed in the Money Pit. With the pumping gins working continuously the water could be lowered slightly, but it would return to sea level as soon as bailing ceased. Evidently, the tunnel from Smith's Cove hadn't been totally blocked. Or there was another possibility. According to McCully, the intersection of the flood tunnel near Smith's Cove had "slackened the flow of water in the old Money Pit, but did not stop it altogether, thereby inducing us to believe there might be another drain." McCully was beginning to comprehend the magnitude of the Oak Island workings; but he was still far from guessing the entire story.

Several writers have stated that at this point the Truro Company dug a 118-foot-deep shaft and then drove a tunnel 18 feet north to the Money Pit, thereby causing the latter's collapse. This suggestion is based on erroneous data contained in an 1893 Oak Island prospectus. From earlier documents it seems certain that the shaft in question wasn't dug until 1861 and was actually west of the Money Pit.

McCully reported that in the fall of 1850 a new shaft (No. 6) was sunk 112 feet deep and slightly to the west of the Money Pit, to which it was connected by a tunnel. This shaft, too, was quickly flooded.

This setback effectively put an end to the Truro group's work on the island. A try was made the following spring (1851) to raise additional funds to continue operations. But the syndicate's backers, no doubt discouraged by the obstacles encountered in the previous two years, weren't prepared to throw good money after bad and the company was dissolved. Yet most of its members were still certain that a great, if seemingly unattainable, treasure lay beneath the surface of Oak Island.

Despite their failure to recover the treasure, the Truro Company had learned a lot about the island that would be useful to later searchers. They had found evidence (which would later be confirmed) that someone had redesigned Smith's Cove into a gigantic feeder system capable of channeling the Atlantic Ocean at a rate of 600 gallons per minute into the Money Pit through a 500-foot-long stone-walled tunnel. The tunnel, which was 4 feet high and 2½ feet wide, sloped downhill on a 22% gradient from the shore to meet the Money Pit at a depth of 111 to 115 feet. Since the Smith's Cove catch basins were underground between the high- and low-water marks, there was some tidal effect in the Money Pit and surrounding shafts. The Truro workers observed a rise and fall of about 18 inches in the Money Pit water level, or a ratio of 1-in-4 to the normal 6-foot tidal range of Mahone Bay. Moreover, the drains in the feeder system were cleverly prevented from silting up by a mammoth sponge filter composed of eel grass and coconut fiber.

The fiber, which occasionally is still dug up under the island's offshore silt, has definitely been identified as coir, the material found between the nut and outer husk of the coconut. Botanists several times identified it as such in the 1800's. In 1916 a sample of it was submitted to the Smithsonian Institution in Washington, D.C., for analysis. The Smithsonian reported that the material "is undoubtedly from the fibrous husks surrounding a coconut" and added that "this fiber is especially resistant to the effects of sea water, and under the conditions which it was found [in Smith's Cove] might have been there for several hundred years." This has been confirmed by analysis of samples found in more recent years.

While this use as a filtering agent seems unique, coconut fiber was commonly used during the sixteenth through nineteenth centuries as "dunnage" on sailing ships. It was laid on the bottom of the cargo hold to prevent water damage and was also packed between casks and crates to prevent shifting and breakage.

To build this elaborate water trap the unknown engineer of Oak Island would have first had to erect a cofferdam around Smith's Cove. (McCully mentions that "the remains of an old dam was seen outside of the place where we found the drain and tunnel to the shore," indicating that the Truro Company's dam, even if it had held, probably wasn't built far enough out to encompass the whole drainage system.) Once the Money Pit, tunnel, drains, and rock-covered filter system were in place, the cofferdam was destroyed, thus setting the trap.

Clearly, the Money Pit with its wooden seals worked on the same principle as a thumb-capped drinking straw dipped into a jar of water. Remove the thumb and the water in the straw rises to the level in the jar. Surely, such a system would have been constructed only to hide something of great value for a considerable length of time.

Chapter Five

In the fifty-five years between the discovery of the Money Pit and the Truro syndicate's frustrated attempts to unravel the mystery there was naturally much speculation as to who designed the project and for what purpose. Everyone associated with the search assumed that no one would have dug and carefully refilled a pit more than 100 feet deep except to hide some sort of treasure; and it must be of great value considering the work that went into protecting it with a tunnel to the sea. They also assumed that the deposit was still down there. For, they argued, had the original digger returned to recover the treasure, then the Money Pit or any access shaft leading to it would not have been refilled; no more than a departing house burglar would stop to repair a lock or windowpane he'd broken on his way in.

So those early searchers were confident that a large treasure was still buried on Oak Island. And most of them were equally sure of the identity of the depositor—Captain William Kidd. From what is known today about Oak Island and the so-called pirate Kidd, the theory seems improbable. Yet there are still some who believe it.

The origin and widespread acceptance of the Kidd theory by nineteenth-century Nova Scotians probably stemmed from the area's settlers' New England background. The 1759 founders of

Chester had all heard contemporary accounts of Kidd's exploits from their parents or grandparents who had lived in Kidd's time. In the ten years prior to his execution in 1701, Kidd—who had married a wealthy New York widow and owned property in what is now the financial district of lower Manhattan—was well known for his daring seamanship as a commissioned privateer capturing French and other enemy ships for the British Crown. But in July of 1699 he was arrested in Boston on charges of murder and piracy and shipped back to England where he was hanged on May 23, 1701. Most historians who have researched Kidd's life have concluded that he was no more a pirate than the other privateers of his time, and that he was made a political scapegoat in a scandal involving high British officials and East Indian trading interests. Nevertheless, his trial and execution stigmatized him as a notorious buccaneer, and he became a legend in England and the American colonies.

As was customary, Kidd and his crew were entitled to a share in the spoils obtained under their commissions as privateers. And no doubt Kidd and his contemporaries weren't above supplementing this share by concealing part of their captured booty before arriving back at their home ports. On his return to Boston in 1699, after three years roaming the Caribbean, Indian Ocean, and China Sea, Kidd had 60 pounds of gold, 100 pounds of silver, and various other goods of value aboard his sloop *San Antonio*. Then, soon after his arrest, a party sent out by the Earl of Bellomont, Governor of New York and Massachusetts Bay, found approximately 10,000 pounds sterling worth of gold, silver, and jewels that Kidd, on his way to Boston, had buried on Gardiner's Island in New York's Long Island Sound. But many are still convinced that there had to be a lot more stashed away somewhere, and for more than two and a half centuries treasure hunters have sought the lost spoils of Captain Kidd. Legend places suspected Kidd caches in hundreds of bays and islands along the United States coast from South Carolina to Maine, as well as in the West Indies and the China Sea. Indeed, if every "authentic" Kidd map that has turned up over the centuries represented an actual treasure location, William Kidd and his crew would have spent more time digging than sailing.

Yet there is evidence that one Kidd treasure may still be awaiting its finder somewhere in the tropics. On May 12, 1701, after he had been sentenced to hang, Kidd made a desperate written appeal to the House of Commons offering to go as a prisoner aboard a government ship and lead the way to "goods and treasure to the value of one hundred thousand pounds" located somewhere in "the Indies." This was to be in exchange for a reprieve. The British government never took Kidd up on his offer and there is still some debate over whether he was bluffing. However, in the spring of 1699 Kidd had sailed from the East Indies around the Cape of Good Hope to the Caribbean aboard a captured Moorish ship, *Quedagh Merchant*, and he left this ship with some of his crew at Hispaniola and from there sailed home to New England aboard the *San Antonio*. An estimated 90,000 pounds sterling worth of looted treasure was probably aboard the *Quedagh Merchant*; and that may have been the treasure Kidd attempted to trade for his life and freedom. What happened to the wealth aboard that ship isn't known, though many believe that a good part of it is buried on some unknown island in the West Indies.

The exaggerated stories of Kidd's piratical deeds and his hoards of buried loot were carried to Nova Scotia by the early settlers. Small wonder therefore that he was given credit for the underground workings found on Oak Island. But Kidd even had an influence on the early written records of the Oak Island search. This took the form of the legend of the dying pirate.

The accounts in the *Colonist* and *Liverpool Transcript* in the 1860's, and later in the DesBrisay and Longworth essays, all begin with the statement that when the first settlers came to Chester they brought with them a widely publicized tale. Apparently, sometime in the mid-1700's an old sailor died somewhere in New England and on his deathbed confessed to those around him that he had been a member of Captain Kidd's crew. Moreover, he told his listeners that many years earlier he had assisted Kidd in burying some 2 million pounds sterling worth of treasure on an unknown and secluded island somewhere east of Boston. The sailor had reportedly kept this secret until his death for fear of being hanged as a pirate. These accounts suggest the possibility that the three 1795 Money Pit discoverers were aware of this story.

But with time the story seems to have become more elaborate, to the point where some believed that the discovery of the Money Pit was no accident. In 1939 Gilbert Hedden, who was then involved in the Oak Island search, tracked down and interviewed a certain Captain Anthony Vaughan in New York City. Captain Vaughan, who was ninety-nine at the time, said he was born on the Vaughan farm in Western Shore and was a grandson of the Anthony Vaughan who helped discover the Money Pit. He ran away to sea at the age of fifteen, taking with him a tale he had heard in the family. Hedden in a letter gives the following account of Captain Vaughan's statement:

"The Vaughans came to Nova Scotia by way of New England from Virginia. They were later followed by the McGinnises and Smiths. After having settled in the vicinity, some time in the 1790's two of the Smiths or McGinnisses, or one of each family, who were sailors, visited the [Smith or McGinnis] family after an extended voyage ending in England. While in England they had befriended an old sailor who said he was one of Kidd's crew, and in gratitude for their help and friendliness he had told them that Kidd did have a huge cache of valuable booty. He did not know exactly where it was except that it was somewhere in 'New Anglia' and that it was on an island 'covered with oaks.' This information excited the local [Smith or McGinnis] family, knowing of Oak Island, and led them to carefully explore the island with the results that we know of."

Another version appears in Andrew Spedon's *Rambles Among the Blue-Noses* (1863) in which the author introduces his account of the Oak Island search with the fabricated tale of a certain Lieutenant Lawrence, a member of Kidd's crew who jumped overboard to escape hanging just before Kidd reached Boston harbor. Lawrence is supposed to have sought refuge in a Dutch settlement in Massachusetts Bay and died a few weeks later. But on his deathbed he told his Dutch benefactors that Kidd had deposited an immense treasure on the south coast of Nova Scotia. A descendant of one of these benefactors was, according to Spedon, someone who eventually took up residence on Oak Island, presumably McGinnis or Smith.

Similar stories of this nature have cropped up over the years, all of them based on the revelations of a pirate who supposedly was once part of Kidd's crew. In one account, even Simeon Lynds of the 1803–04 Onslow group was reported to have become involved in Oak Island after coming across a map drawn by this dying crew member. This version appears in the 1909 essay written by the Mahone Bay teacher who in turn says he got it from the old people in the Chester area. The story goes that:

"Lynds became interested [in Oak Island] through a paper that was brought to light in a peculiar way. Somewhere in Virginia there lived a very old man who on his sick bed told his son, himself a man of 70, where in an old sea chest he would find a piece of paper that might reveal some buried treasure on an island somewhere up north that the old man's father had helped to bury with many others who had been compelled to work under an armed guard, under the pirate Kidd. This old man had joined Kidd's company to save his life, and after working a long time, the treasure was buried at great depth on an oak-covered island. And when the hole was nearly filled up, he and another man, fearing they would be killed when the work was done, decided they would endeavor to escape. And one very stormy night mid rain and a gale of wind, they made their way to the shore, swam to the mainland and wandered on and on. After some time his companion took sick and died. But after weeks of suffering he saw a small vessel and was taken on board and found his way down south. He drew as best he could a rough map of the island and part of the bay, and wrote out some few particulars of the burying of a lot of treasure. The grandson of this oldest man found the paper, and after his father's death endeavored to interest some local people in the matter, so as to help him look up an island such as the one marked on the old faded paper. In some way Lynds heard of this paper and from some source got an outline of the old map, and found that Oak Island compared quite well to the rough sketch on the old paper."

The likelihood of Lynds or anyone connected with the initial investigation of Oak Island having a map or other handed-down information that led them to the Money Pit seems small. Such suggestions were probably added to the Oak Island story after the accidental discovery in order to add credence to the notion that Kidd's treasure was at the bottom of the Money Pit. In *The Book of Buried Treasure* (1911), Ralph D. Paine points out that the dying-sailor story was commonly associated with hunts for pirate treasure along the United States Atlantic coast during the nineteenth century. Such stories, he notes, are "strikingly alike in that the lone survivor of the red-handed crew . . . preserved a chart showing where the treasure had been hid. Unable to return to the place, he gave the parchment to some friend or shipmate, this dramatic transfer usually happening as a death-bed ceremony."

Dying sailor myths notwithstanding, how Oak Island chroniclers could associate that particular project with William Kidd is difficult to understand. Dunbar Hinrichs of St. Petersburg, Florida, has spent much of his life researching and writing about Kidd and claims to be able to place Kidd almost daily during his years as a privateer, or from about 1676 to 1701. In an interview, Hinrichs said he has "never found a shred of evidence that William Kidd ever set foot on Oak Island in Mahone Bay or, for that matter, even knew this place existed." In addition, Kidd did not have the engineering ability to design something as elaborate as the Oak Island workings are known to be. Nevertheless (as will be seen later) the Kidd-Oak Island connection was to resurface in the 1930's under peculiar circumstances.

Kidd is not the only pirate credited with being the genius who designed the Oak Island workings. Over the years various theories have placed almost every well-known seventeenth-century buccaneer at the scene of the Money Pit's creation. These names include William Phipps (1650–94), Henry Morgan (1635–88), William Dampier (1652–1715), and Blackbeard (Edward Teach?) (?–1718). Yet, other than for Phipps, there is no record of these men ever having sailed near the coast of Acadia, as the province was known for more than one hundred years after its founding in 1604.

Phipps, born in Maine and initially a ship's carpenter, took to the sea in command of his own vessel in the 1680's. In 1686 he led an expedition to retrieve for the British Crown a sunken Spanish galleon off the coast of Hispaniola. He was successful and was knighted Sir William Phipps in 1687. As a privateer for the English he raided and looted the French settlement of Port Royal on the Bay of Fundy side of Nova Scotia in 1690. He is also reputed to have attacked other Acadian settlements on the south coast of the province. Whether he ever took the time to stash any of his plunder on Oak Island, as some have claimed, is doubtful. In 1692 he became the first Royal Governor of Massachusetts, a post he held till his death two years later.

As for Phipps' famous contemporaries, they were primarily operators in southern waters, especially the West Indies, where they preyed upon the lucrative galleons and cities of the Spanish New World empire. There seems little reason for any of them to have sailed two thousand miles north to bury their swag when there were hundreds of uninhabited islands and coastal coves to choose from in their own backyard.

Many of these pirates used Port Royal, Jamaica, as their base; a city described as "the hellhole of the Caribbean"until it slid into the sea during an earthquake on June 17, 1692, taking with it the interred bones of Sir Henry Morgan. Some people have pointed to the fortifications of Port Royal as an example of the ability of pirates to join forces in order to construct something more elaborate than a 10-foot hole in the ground in which to place a chest of doubloons. But Port Royal, unlike the Oak Island project, was built in the open (using mostly slave labor) and posed no problem of pirates having to entrust one another with secrets of hidden wealth. The buccaneers made Port Royal their communal lair, but their personal strongholds were in most cases known only to themselves. Had they not squandered their ill-gotten gains prior to their (often untimely) deaths, their secret was apt to die with them. As Blackbeard prior to his beheading in 1718 boasted: "I've buried my treasure where none but Satan and myself can find it." However, in recent years a hypothesis has been advanced to show how a group of pirates could have secretly built the Oak Island workings and yet kept from one another the exact location of their individual caches. (The basis and merits of this theory will be discussed later.)

Apart from Phipps, there were many lesser-known privateers as well as outright pirates who were active in the waters of Nova Scotia. From 1604 to 1763 control over Nova Scotia (including Cape Breton) seesawed back and forth between France and Britain. Both nations employed the services of commissioned privateers to raid Acadian settlements and shipping. Later, the Americans also used New England-based privateers to harass the British in Nova Scotia during the American Revolution of 1775 to 1783. (Similar raids were also carried out in Nova Scotia during the American-British War of 1812, though this, of course, was too late to have any bearing on the Oak Island project.)

In addition, freebooting pirates often attacked Nova Scotia and Newfoundland ports in the seventeenth century. Although the pickings in terms of coin or other such treasure were slim, these fishing communities supplied the pirates with provisions, shanghaied manpower, and additional sailing ships. So the early settlers of Nova Scotia weren't unfamiliar with piracy on their coasts. In fact, the name Mahone Bay is derived from the archaic French word *mahonne*, a low-lying sailing vessel that was popular with coastal pirates in the Mediterranean.

In the aftermath of all this larcenous activity, a number of pirate treasures have been uncovered in various parts of the province. In 1879, for example, William Moser, a farmer from Lunenburg (about ten miles from Oak Island) was digging up the floor of his barn when he encountered a cache of about two hundred French and Spanish gold coins dated in the mid to late 1700's. The barn had been built by his grandfather more than fifty years earlier, and presumably the coins had been buried long before that by unknown privateers or pirates. Similar accidental finds have been reported in other parts of the province.

But in all cases the treasures were relatively small and buried only a few feet underground. That a group of untrusting, undisciplined, hit-and-run sea thieves would take the time required for the immense amount of work that went into Oak Island is difficult to believe. Pirates were much more apt to dig a 10-foot hole in the ground from which treasure could be quickly retrieved at a later date.

If pirates weren't responsible for what has been discovered on Oak Island, who was? As the exploration of the Money Pit and adjacent workings progressed over the years, many who-did-it theories would be advanced. And these range from the plausible to the incredibly bizarre. But first, there were many more strange pieces to be found and fitted into the puzzle.

Chapter Six

It was ten years after the dissolution of the Truro Company before another syndicate was formed to resume the search. Meanwhile, the Smith property—the 24 acres (lots 15 through 20) at the island's eastern end, which included the Money Pit and Smith's Cove—was acquired by Anthony Graves. That, together with other lots he'd previously purchased, made him the island's largest landowner. His farmhouse was on the north side of the island at Joudrey's Cove. (Its foundation can still be seen.) Other than receiving a lease fee for the use of part of his land, Graves wasn't a member of the 1860's treasure-hunting groups. But (as will be seen later) there's some indication that he may have stumbled across something of value on his property prior to his death in 1888.

On April 3, 1861, the Oak Island Association was formed in Truro "for the purpose of making excavations on Oak Island in search of Hidden Treasures." Its president was Samuel Rettie and the corporate secretary was Jotham McCully, who had been with the Truro syndicate of 1849–50. Some of its other backers also had participated in the Truro group. Under its charter the Association had an issued capital of one hundred shares sold at $20 apiece, though this was added to several times in the next three years. Most of the funds were to be used for a large labor force, which was to be enticed to the island with the then-decent wage offer of $18 a month plus board and traveling expenses.

The first job was clearing out and recribbing the Money Pit, which had partially caved in over the years. The water was bailed out easily and the pit reopened to a depth of 88 feet, though no deeper, as the muddy clay below that seemed to be effectively blocking any heavy flooding from Smith's Cove. Next, a new shaft (No. 7) was dug about 25 feet east of the Money Pit with the intention of intercepting the water tunnel. But it was abandoned at 120 feet after it had obviously missed the tunnel.

The workers then began another shaft (No. 8) about 18 feet west of the Money Pit and 118 feet deep. (This is the shaft often errone-ously credited to the 1850 Truro group.) A tunnel 4 feet high by 3 feet wide was driven from its bottom to the Money Pit in the hope of striking the treasure vault.

McCully, in his letter a year later, says this tunnel "entered the old Money Pit a little below the lower platform [the one bored through at about 105 feet in 1849] where we found the soft clay spoken of in the [1849] boring. The tunnel was unwisely driven through the old [Money] pit until it nearly reached the east pipe, when the water started, apparently coming above on the east side." He then notes that three days of continuous bailing with a horse-operated pumping gin failed to reduce the water in the No. 8 shaft. Moreover, water was again seeping up through the Money Pit itself.

So a mammoth bailing operation was set up under the direction of George Mitchell, the superintendent of works. This first in-volved driving a tunnel from shaft No. 7 on the east to the Money Pit till No. 7 also began filling with water. Then, with a total of 63 men and 33 horses working in shifts, pumping gins were erected over shafts Nos. 7, 8, and the Money Pit. The bailing apparatus in each of the three holes consisted of four 70-gallon casks that were continually lowered, filled, raised and dumped. This succeeded in almost draining the pits.

McCully writes that the workers "commenced bailing on Wednesday morning, continued constantly night and day until Friday morning when the tunnel leading from the West pit [No. 8] to the Money Pit, which was 17 ft. long, 4 ft. high and 3 ft. wide, becoming choked with clay, we sent two men down to clear it out. After they had gone about half way through [the tunnel] they

heard a tremendous crash in the Money Pit and barely escaped being caught by a rush of mud which followed them into the West
pit and filled it up 7 feet [of mud] in less than three minutes. In the
meantime a stick of oak timber of considerable girth and 3½ ft. in
length was ejected with the mud."

Writing in the newspaper the *Nova Scotian* in September of
that year, "the digger, Patrick," who was at the scene of the collapse, recalled that "while the water [from the Money Pit] was
hindered by this earth [in the tunnel] from coming through [to
shaft No. 8] we took out part of the earth and wood. The wood was
stained black with age; it was cut, hewn, champered, sawn or
bored, according to the purpose for which it was needed. We also
took out part of the bottom of a keg." (According to another source
the head of a small keg painted yellow was scooped up by a worker named Publicover as he ran for safety during the collapse of the
Money Pit into the tunnel.) An account by James McNutt in 1867
also mentions that "a piece of juniper with the bark on (and) cut at
each end with an edge tool" and "a spruce slab with a mining
auger hole in it" were dug out of the mud that had gushed from
the Money Pit into the West shaft.

These diggers would obviously have been able to tell the difference between timbers used in their own tunnel cribbing and wood
that was far older. Thus, they were presented with substantial
proof that some sort of wooden construction lay more than 100
feet down in the Money Pit. And the spruce slab with the auger
hole through it may well have been part of one of the spruce platforms drilled into at the 98- and 105-foot levels in 1849. Unfortunately, carbon-dating analysis hadn't yet been invented. Many
years would pass before this technique would be applied to original wood excavated from beneath the island with interesting results.

McCully reported that when some of the mud in the connecting
tunnel between the West shaft and the Money Pit had been
cleared, the West shaft again began to flood. So the bailing was resumed and "continued until 3 o'clock P.M. of Saturday when, on
clearing the tunnel [of mud] again, another crash was heard in the
Money Pit which [we] supposed to be the upper platform [at 98
feet in the Money Pit] falling, and immediately the bottom of the
Money Pit fell to about 102 feet measuring from the level of the
ground at the top. It had been cleared out previously down [to] 88

feet. Immediately after, the cribbing [on the side walls] of the Money Pit, commencing at the bottom, fell in plank after plank until there was only about 30 feet of the upper cribbing left. On Monday the top fell in, leaving the old Money Pit a complete mass of ruins."

So on that summer weekend of 1861, the Oak Island Association had undermined and inadvertently caused the collapse of the platforms and suspected chests of treasure that the Truro Company drillers had encountered between 98 and 105 feet back in 1849. But where had they fallen to? As McCully noted, the excavated bottom of the Money Pit dropped from 88 to about 102 feet, or a total of 14 feet. This would suggest that the lower platform on which the chests rested was now down at around 119 feet. (This may have been about the level of the tunnel from the 118-foot West shaft; though not necessarily, since there is no record of whether that tunnel was horizontal or sloped upward on its way to the Money Pit.)

Much later, it was theorized that the platforms and other material had collapsed into a void 130 feet or more down in the pit. In fact there would later be strong evidence that the Money Pit had been constructed far deeper than that, and that the 1861 group had been instrumental in tripping a booby trap that lay beneath one of several treasure caches.

Samuel C. Fraser, a member of the Oak Island Association's executive committee and a participant in later search groups, outlined his theories about the collapse in an 1895 letter to A.S. Lowden, then manager of an Oak Island syndicate:

"As to the falling of the treasure, a man by the name of George Mitchell was then in charge. He finished the sinking of the 118-foot shaft [No. 8] through which the water was taken away, while the Money Pit was to be cleaned out to the treasure. I was . . . sent down to clean out the Money Pit, but before going into it I examined the 118-foot pit and tunnel which was then nearly finished. At the end of the tunnel I saw every sign of the cataclysm that was about to take place and refused to go into the Money Pit. . . . When the pit fell down I was there. . . . There went down 10,000 feet of lumber (board measure), the cribbing of the pit. Could these planks stop on their way down and turn into an 18-foot tunnel 3' by 4'? Would or could casks of treasure having 10,000 feet of lumber and hundreds of tons of earth behind them turn into a 3′ by 4′ tunnel? And if they could perform the impossible, would an 18-foot tunnel, 3′ by 4′, hold all this material?''

In his letter, Fraser theorized that the designer of the Money Pit (whom he assumed to be a pirate) ''sank the shaft at first 155 feet deep, put part of the treasure there with a branch drain [flood tunnel] into it. Then . . . he put another portion [of treasure] at 100 feet with a drain into it. Now, to dig into the Money Pit means to pull all those planks [from the 1861 collapse] out by the teeth. And to believe that they turned into that little 18-foot tunnel would require as much faith from me as that Halley's Comet went through it.'' Fraser then advised Lowden to ''sink your pumping shaft deep—deep enough to drain the Money Pit at 155 feet, and you have the treasure.''

What Fraser was getting at was that the collapse and disappearance of all that material indicated the presence of a large cavity deep in the Money Pit. In another letter to Lowden he stated that the top of the cavity would have to have been below 120 feet or so, ''because when I went into the tunnel [under the Money Pit] from the 118-foot pit, [the workers] were [digging] in disturbed earth.'' (This agrees with McCully's statement.) Fraser's theory was that whoever built the Money Pit ''must have placed strong beams across the shaft [at or below the 120-foot level] and thrown in say ten or fifteen feet of earth on these under the upper treasure.'' Much of Fraser's hypothesis would be confirmed by later exploration.

Despite the devastating collapse of the Money Pit, the Association was able to raise an additional $2,000 to continue work. That fall a cast-iron pump and steam engine were purchased in Halifax. Andrew Spedon reported that ''in the fall of 1861, at great expense, pumps were erected to be driven by steam power; but scarcely had the work been commenced when the boiler burst, causing operations to be suspended until another season.''

McCully and Spedon both fail to record the first death resulting from the Oak Island search. In an essay written in 1868, E.H. Owen of Lunenburg noted that in 1861 ''the boiler of one company burst whereby one man was scalded to death and others injured.'' The island had claimed its first victim. Others would follow.

Chapter Seven

The Association returned in the spring of 1862 and sank another hole (No. 9) 107 feet deep alongside and connected to the Money Pit. This was to serve as a pumping shaft for the steam-powered pump. The Money Pit was then cleared out and recribbed down to 103 feet, at which point the water seeping up from below exceeded the capacity of the pump.

McNutt said that while the mud was being cleared out of the Money Pit the workers came across some tools left by the 1849 Truro group at 90 feet, as well as tools belonging to the 1803 Onslow Company at 100 feet. These presumably were found in recesses in the side of the pit, since they hadn't fallen with the other material when the pit collapsed the summer before. He also reports that the last tier of the Onslow group's vertical cribbing was found intact at 90 feet, thereby proving that the wood that had been recovered after the 1861 collapse was part of the pit's original construction.

An attempt was then made to cut off the water source near Smith's Cove by sinking a shaft (No. 10) about 25 feet northeast of the No. 5 shaft, which had been excavated to 35 feet in 1850. This shaft was dug to 50 feet and tunnels were driven from various levels until the diggers were eventually flooded out.

The Oak Island Association was now broke but still determined to reach the elusive treasure.

After raising a little money, they planned another assault on the drains at Smith's Cove. Because of limited funds a proper coffer-dam couldn't be built, so work in the early spring of 1863 was limited to uncovering a section of the drains nearest the shore at low tide. Israel Longworth wrote in 1866:

"About thirty or forty feet of the drain was uncovered and removed, but as it did not tend to lower the water in the West, or pumping pit [No. 9], about thirty rods distant [from Smith's Cove], the superintendent directed that the opened drain should be filled up with packed clay, and he thought this would stop the course of the way to the Money Pit. Before the claying process commenced, the water in the Money and West pits was nearly as clear and quite as salt as that in the Bay, but while it was in progress, it became very muddy. After the drain was sufficiently packed, three or four weeks were allowed for the clay to settle and pack before the pumps were started at the West pit, when it was ascertained that the operation had been instrumental in diminishing the flow of water by one half." (However, we find from another source that this proved to be only temporary relief as the tides soon washed the clay away.)

On the theory that the No. 9 pumping shaft wasn't deep enough (at 107 feet) to efficiently drain the Money Pit, the workers selected a spot 100 feet southeast of the Money Pit where they dug a shaft (No. 11) 120 feet deep. The intakes for the pumps were placed on the bottom and a tunnel was driven from a higher level toward Smith's Cove in the hope of intersecting the water network and diverting it into the new shaft. They missed it and gave up, and instead began driving another tunnel toward the Money Pit itself.

But work was soon suspended for about three months while the Association endeavored to raise more money. On August 24, 1863, the *Nova Scotian* reported that operations had resumed and that "men and machinery are now at work pumping the water from the pits previously sunk, and it is said they are sanguine that before the lapse of one month they will strike the treasure."

The tunnel from shaft No. 11 struck the Money Pit at a depth of 108 feet, just above the water level that was being held down by pumps in various other connected shafts. The workers cribbed the area of the Money Pit between 103 and 108 feet. They then dug a circular tunnel around the outside of the pit at about 95 feet, intersecting a couple of earlier searchers' shafts in the process. It appears that one or two other lateral tunnels were dug, but their direction and depth were unrecorded. This mole labor continued sporadically into the following year, but it was generally found impossible to do any work below 110 feet in the immediate area of the Money Pit without being flooded out. And the treasure, they believed, was now below that.

Sometime in 1864 the flood tunnel was struck at about the point where it entered the east side of the Money Pit. Samuel Fraser in his letter to A.S. Lowden in 1895 recalled that: "As we entered the old place of the treasure [via a lateral tunnel at 110 feet] we cut off the mouth of the [flood] tunnel. As we opened it, the water hurled around rocks about twice the size of a man's head with many smaller, and drove the men back for protection. . . . The [flood] tunnel was found near the top of our tunnel."

They had found the man-made watercourse, but they were powerless to shut it off.

The Association was now even deeper in the red and its backers thoroughly discouraged. Moreover, the constant erosion of seawater was undermining the walls of the Money Pit and some of the workers were refusing to enter it. The shaft was inspected by mining engineers who declared it unsafe and advised that it be condemned. That was it; the Association was finished.

A new group calling itself the Oak Island Contract Company attempted to pick up where the Oak Island Association left off. At its founding meeting in Halifax on March 29, 1865, it was resolved that 1,500 pounds at 1 pound per share (a total of about $6,000) would be solicited from the general public to continue the work. H.G. Hill was president and A.O. Creighton treasurer of this company. It was about this time that the inscribed rock found at 90 feet down in the Money Pit in 1803 was removed from the Oak Island home of the late John Smith and brought to Halifax as a lure for prospective shareholders. But the company never got off the ground (only six shares were subscribed for at that initial meeting) and no work was done on the island that year.

On May 3, 1866, the Oak Island Eldorado Company was incorporated with the same officers as those of the Oak Island Contract Company. This group successfully raised $4,000 in shares of $20 apiece and obtained from Anthony Graves a lease on the eastern end of the island. According to a circular issued by the company, it proposed "to build a substantial wood and clay dam seaward [in Smith's Cove] to extend out and beyond the rock [drainage] work so as to encompass the whole within the dam, to pump out all the water within the area, and to break up the inlet from the sea; the cost of which [the directors] expect will not exceed 400 pounds." Shareholders were assured that "there cannot be any doubt but this mode of operation must succeed and will lead to the development of the hidden treasure so long sought for."

According to James McNutt who worked on the island that year, the cofferdam was 375 feet long, 12 feet high, and was situated 120 feet below the high-water mark in the cove. But like the one built in 1850, this dam was soon destroyed by Atlantic storms and abnormally high tides.

The Eldorado group then resorted to exploratory drilling to try and locate the treasure cache, which was thought to have dropped down in the collapse of the Money Pit in 1861. Three holes were drilled over a six-week period from November 26, 1866, to January 7, 1867. Significantly, the drill holes were cased inside a 3-inch-diameter metal sleeve. This was the first time casing had been used in an Oak Island drilling program, and it ensured that whatever material was brought up on the bit was something found at its original level rather than something that may have fallen into the hole from a higher position.

McNutt logged a day-to-day report on the drilling program. With the pumps holding the water at bay, the first hole was started from a platform on the bottom of the Money Pit at 108 feet. It entered near the northeast corner of the pit and was angled to the northeast. Measuring from the pit's surface, spruce wood was struck at 110 feet, then several feet of coarse gravel, soft clay, and blue mud. Water mixed with chips of wood, coconut fiber, and charcoal were brought up from 128 feet. At 132 feet there was no water but still pieces of wood and fiber. Water was struck again at about 140 feet, followed by soft clay and fine sand; then more water at about 150 feet. The next 2 or 3 feet yielded a dry reddish soil that had never been disturbed.

The second hole was drilled from a platform at 78 feet and was angled to the southeast; the third probe began at about 30 feet and slanted northeast. They were drilled to 103 feet and 160 feet respectively from the surface without striking anything of interest.

Whether the Eldorado group (which was also known as the Halifax Company) did any additional work is uncertain. (They may have dug a shaft 175 feet southeast of the Money Pit and run a series of tunnels toward the pit. But there is no original record of this work, although in the early 1940's tunnels were found that appeared to date from the 1860's.) By late 1867 the group had definitely abandoned the search and the company was dissolved.

By then the east end of Oak Island was a rabbit warren of pits and tunnels. In the seventy-two years since the Money Pit's discovery a total of 11 shafts (including the Money Pit) and hundreds of feet of tunneling had been excavated and two cofferdams built. The search at that point had cost one life and an estimated total expenditure of $50,000 (which would be well over $2 million at today's labor and material costs); and still no treasure had been brought up.

Both the mystery and the treasure appeared to be deeper than ever, and twenty-six years would pass before another serious effort would be made to solve the riddle.

Chapter Eight

For over a quarter of a century no further attempt was made to recover Oak Island's treasure. But during this period, the story, often a mixture of fact and folklore, spread to other parts of Canada and to New England, and few tourists to the Chester area missed the opportunity to take a boat out to the island and peer into the water-filled pits.

Inevitably, skepticism over the possibility that someone could or would have hidden and so elaborately protected a treasure more than 100 feet underground was often expressed. An early sample of this attitude is found in the July 1870 issue of the *New Dominion Monthly*, a Canadian magazine published in Montreal. The author J.A. Bell declared it "incredible that persons possessed of common sense could be so deluded" as to invest time and money in the Oak Island search. The quest, he predicted, "will no doubt be referred to in future times as a remarkable chapter in the voluminous records of human folly."

But treasure hunters expect and are usually inured to such derision. In 1862 Jotham McCully had observed that "the public will judge [the Oak Island searchers] by the success we meet with. Should we be successful in getting a large amount of treasure, we will be considered a very sensible lot of fellows; and if we should fail in finishing the work we will be set down as a set of phantom-following fools, fit for nothing but to be held up to public ridicule."

McCully and his contemporaries did fail; yet not before making a stronger case than ever to prove that someone had done something beneath the island. It was only a matter of time before the bug that bit them would infect someone else.

In 1893 Frederick Leander Blair, a twenty-six-year-old insurance salesman living in Boston, developed an obsession with Oak Island that was to last until his death. He was originally from Amherst, Nova Scotia, and as a boy had heard detailed accounts of Oak Island from his uncle, Isaac Blair, and from Jefferson W. McDonald, both of whom had taken part in the search during the 1860's.

Fred Blair was a conscientious researcher, and the first thing he did was amass whatever written documentation he could find relating to the work of searchers who preceeded him. He also interviewed dozens of people who had had anything to do with the island. These included Adams A. Tupper, Jefferson McDonald, Robert Creelman, James McNutt, Jotham McCully, and Samuel Fraser, all veterans of the 1849–50 or 1861–67 Oak Island campaigns. In addition, some of these men passed on to Blair information they had gotten directly from the three Money Pit discoverers, Smith, McGinnis, and Vaughan, and from Simeon Lynds, leader of the 1803–04 group. Most of the material collected by Blair survives to this day.

In the 1930's Gilbert Hedden, who headed a search group and was well acquainted with Blair, described him as "a man of very pleasing personality, extremely well preserved physically, possessing an accurate and exhaustive memory, and . . . a man of sterling character. . . . His one possible fault seems to be his undying faith in the story of Oak Island." (Hedden, incidentally, also shared that faith until his own death.)

The Oak Island Treasure Company, with A.M. Bridgman of Brockton, Massachusetts, as President, was incorporated in 1893 under the laws of the state of Maine. Most of its shareholders were Nova Scotians, though there were many from the Boston area and other parts of New England. In its original prospectus, which was written by Fred Blair and Adams Tupper, the company briefly outlined the work that had been done on the island up to that time. It then said: "It can be proven:

"1.   That a shaft about 13 feet in diameter and 100 feet deep was sunk on Oak Island in Mahone Bay, Nova Scotia, before the memory of any now living.

"2.   That this shaft was connected by an underground tunnel with the open ocean, about 365 feet distant. [It's actually about 500 feet.]

"3.   That at the bottom of this shaft were placed large wooden boxes in which were precious metals and jewels. [Presumably a reference to the loose metal struck in 1849 by drilling.]

"4.   That many attempts have been made, without success, to obtain this treasure.

"5.   That it is reasonably certain the treasure is large, because so great a trouble would never have been taken to conceal any small sum.

"6.   That it is now entirely feasible to thoroughly explore this shaft and recover the treasure still located therein."

This bold statement would be nullified by additional discoveries awaiting the new group of searchers. They would learn that Oak Island was a lot more complicated than their prospectus suggested.

The company planned to raise as much as $60,000 in shares of $5 apiece. Half of this stock was to be used to secure a three-year lease on the eastern end of the island as well as absolute right to all treasure that might be recovered. The other $30,000 worth of shares would be kept in the company's treasury, to be sold as needed to pay for labor and materials. The company expected that only 1,000 of these shares would have to be sold to complete the work. With few exceptions, those who had sunk their money into previous searches took up stock in this new venture.

Outlining its plan of action, the Oak Island Treasure Company prospectus stated:

"It is perfectly evident that the great mistake thus far has been in attempting to 'bail out' the ocean through the various pits. The present company intends to use the best modern appliances for cutting off the flow of water through the tunnel, at some point near the shore, before attempting to pump out the water. It believes, from investigations already made, that such an attempt will be completely successful; and if it is, there can be no trouble in pumping out the Money Pit as dry as when the treasure was first placed there."

The company's optimistic plan to recover the treasure was reported in several Nova Scotia and Boston newspapers. The publicity helped attract new shareholders. It also prompted a man by the name of J. Edward Wilson to write a curious letter that was printed in the *Boston Traveller* on December 26, 1893, and in the *Halifax Evening Mail* on January 3, 1894.

Wilson wrote that about six or seven years earlier he had been in New Brunswick, Canada, where he visited a relative, a man of about eighty, whom he hadn't seen in a long time. This person told Wilson that he had once seen a map showing the location of Oak Island's treasure, and that it was buried only 20 feet underground some distance away from the Money Pit. Wilson then related the story as it had been told to him by his relative:

"When a young man of about twenty years of age, and that is a long time ago, I was working in a [New Brunswick] shipyard when one day a sailor came into the yard. He was evidently from a foreign ship that had arrived to load deal [softwood timber] as the place was a great resort then for ships in the lumber trade. He was a man of about 50 years of age, large, heavy, dark, and swarthy. I entered into conversation with him. He said he was anxious to raise some money to enable him to get to Boston; that if I would advance say $20 he in return would give me a valuable secret of where there was an immense amount of money buried. It being about the time when one heard of finds that were being made of valuables that had been hidden during the French troubles and also the American war, I at once 'caught on' as the saying is. It was then arranged that he would come and sleep in my room that night, as there was a spare bed there, which he accordingly did.

"He then told me something of his history; that he had been a pirate and in later years a privateer, and that now as the latter occupation was about played out he was getting weary and wanted to get home to his native country, Spain; that if he could get to Boston he would stand a better chance of finding a ship going there. He showed a plan which he said had come into his possession, and the meaning of which he could clearly explain. It was of an island of a certain form, situated on the southwestern coast of Nova Scotia and was once the rendezvous of pirates, and that a large amount of treasure was buried there. On this island was a certain oak tree, from a branch of which hung a large ship's block that [was] used in sinking a deep shaft, the bottom of which com-

municated with the sea level by a tunnel. The shaft had been filled
up as being of no further use, as the exit for the removal of the
treasure would be through the tunnel. But for reasons unknown to
him the treasure was never put there, but buried only 20 feet from
the surface, at a certain distance from the tree, naming the distance, where it would be safer from the inquisitive intruder than if
it were at the bottom of the shaft, the most likely place to look for
it. And then it may have been the original intention of the depositor that the shaft was intended for a blind, for who would not be
deceived under such conditions.

"When the sailor had finished his story I, as you can imagine,
was worked up to a high pitch of curiosity to find out where this
wonderful island was; but on this point hinged our bargain. When
I [would have] paid him the money, he was then to give the name
and directions how to find the island, also to mark on the plan the
exact course by compass from the tree [to where] the treasure lay
buried; so that having found the island, then 'the tree with the
course and distance given, it would be an easy matter to find the
spot, when a few days digging would reveal the wonderful collection of untold wealth. Yes, of course I would agree to his offer and
the money would be forthcoming next day.

"Sleep that night to me was long delayed; it was to dream of
finding the precious coins and feasting my eyes on the glittering
gold. The next day however, when I came to look at the matter
from various points of reason, my ardour cooled somewhat. The
story seemed too good to be true. It savoured too much of the improbable; besides it was a good deal of money for me to raise at
that time. So I wavered all day, undecided what to do, until the
following day. When that day came the sailor [had] disappeared
as suddenly as he had come. I learned that he left in a vessel for
Eastport [Maine] and from there to Boston.

"When my shortlived vision of wealth had passed, I was compelled to stick to the broadaxe as the most reliable instrument to
hew out a future. But in after years I had occasion to regret my
want of decision, when I heard of parties who were digging for
treasure on Oak Island which corresponded in so many points to
that described by the pirate sailor. I have long since arrived at the
belief in his story and that it is one and the same place."

Wilson, in his letter, said he queried his relative further on the
strange encounter: "I may say that in answer to the questions put

by myself he said that the pirate did not associate Captain Kidd's name in any way whatever with the business, and furthermore, that he placed the date of the deposit at about the close of the last century, which would be long after Kidd's day. My relative also attributes considerable importance to a large rock as being an important landmark, but my memory does not serve me sufficiently to say anything about it."

Somehow, Blair didn't see Wilson's letter until a copy of it was brought to his attention in the summer of 1916. He then tried to locate Wilson but was unsuccessful. Knowing whether the story of the Spanish sailor and his chart was fact or fiction is impossible, but the suggestion that the Money Pit was a decoy to draw searchers away from the real treasure cache is one that has been seriously entertained by several twentieth-century Oak Island searchers. Also, the reference to "a large rock" serving as "an important landmark" is a clue that would have special significance many years later.

By the end of 1893 Blair and his group had organized their company and had sold enough shares to begin work on the island. They arrived there the following summer to carry out their announced plan of eliminating the water trap that had thwarted all the searchers before them. The spot selected for cutting off the flow from Smith's Cove was one that had been accidentally discovered sixteen years earlier by Sophia Sellers. She was Anthony Graves' daughter and was married to Henry Sellers; they inherited the eastern end of Oak Island from her father on his death in 1888.

One day in 1878 Sophia Sellers had been plowing with a team of oxen when the ground suddenly caved in under the animals and they dropped into a hole 6 to 8 feet in diameter and more than 10 feet deep. The oxen were extricated and the incident forgotten until many years later when Blair saw the hole and heard the story from Sellers. What interested Blair and his fellow searchers was that the hole, which they dubbed the "Cave-in Pit," was about 350 feet east of the Money Pit and directly over the suspected route of the flood tunnel from Smith's Cove.

Some had previously suggested that a 500-foot tunnel (from the Money Pit to Smith's Cove) couldn't have been built without having had at least one vertical shaft somewhere along its course. This would have provided an additional point from which earth from the tunnel could be removed; more important, it would have served as an airshaft for those digging the tunnel. Blair and his associates also suspected that the creator of the Money Pit may have installed a valve or gate somewhere in the flood tunnel, to be used to shut off the water when the depositors came back to retrieve their treasure.

So the first job was to excavate and explore the Cave-in Pit (No. 12). At a depth of 55 feet, seawater began entering it. By the next day the water was at tide level (about 15 feet from the earth's surface at that spot), and it couldn't be lowered by bailing. That project was then abandoned. But the group was still convinced that the Cave-in Pit had been part of the original work. It showed clear indications of having been hand-dug at some earlier point, and there was no record of any previous searchers having put down a shaft in that particular area.

Many years later other searchers would direct their attention to that same pit on the assumption that, if it wasn't an airshaft, it may have been designed as an access point to one or more subterranean treasure locations. They also assumed that the pit wasn't exactly in line with the watercourse, but was set off slightly to the side. For that reason, its caving in hadn't affected the flow of water to the Money Pit. Why it caved in isn't known; but perhaps an unrecorded branch tunnel dug by searchers in the 1860's had been driven under or near its base. Today the Cave-in Pit is a gaping circular crater 100 feet deep and as many feet across. And the water in it still rises and falls with the tide.

In the fall of 1894 another shaft (No. 13) was dug 30 feet east of the Money Pit and 8 feet north of the suspected line of the watercourse. Somehow, water started entering this shaft at 43 feet, probably via an underground connection to a flooded tunnel dug by previous searchers. Again the work had to be abandoned.

The Oak Island Treasure Company had gotten off to an inauspicious start. But their biggest setback would come the following summer; and it wouldn't be realized until a year after that. At this time (1895) A.S. Lowden was general manager of operations and he proposed to again "attack the Money Pit direct."

When the Oak Island Eldorado Company quit in 1867, they had refilled the top 30 feet of the Money Pit above the platform erected for their third exploratory drill probe. And either they or Anthony Graves had filled in some of the other shafts. Consequently, in the intervening quarter century, the eastern end of the island had lost many of its visible scars. Lowden's men began re-excavating the Money Pit during the summer of 1895, but they got down only 55 feet inside the old cribbing when once more water drove them out. At this point work was abandoned and wasn't resumed until the latter part of 1896.

The company's $60,000 worth of stock was still far from being totally subscribed. Shareholder dissatisfaction over the lack of progress and dissension between the Bostonian and Nova Scotian leaders of the group over how operations should be conducted led to control over the project being placed in the hands of the Nova Scotian shareholders. They formed a new board of management. This included Fred Blair (who in 1895 moved from Boston to Amherst, Nova Scotia) as treasurer and Captain John Welling as on-site manager. T. Perley Putnam and William Chappell, father of Melbourne Chappell, the Money Pit site's current owner, were also part of the new management.

The workers again turned their attention to the Money Pit. They were able to drain it with their new pumping equipment and cleared it down to 70 feet before the water again became excessive. So the old No. 4 shaft (dug to a depth of 75 feet near Smith's Cove in 1850) was cleared to 78 feet, at which point water entered it from one of the tunnels built by the Halifax group in the 1860's. But by putting a pump in this pit they found they could drain the Money Pit, which they then deepened to 97 feet.

About this time the island claimed its second victim. On March 26, 1897, Maynard Kaiser of nearby Gold River was being hoisted to the top of one of the pits when the rope slipped off the hoisting pulley and he fell to his death. One of his co-workers, Selvin Rafuse, today in his nineties and living at Martin's Point on the mainland opposite Oak Island, still recalls the accident: "I worked there when I was young. We used to hoist the earth up with horses then [and] it was when Kaiser was killed in the pits."

Following the accident, Rafuse and most of the other workers refused to go down into the pits, forcing operations to be halted for about a week. Many of them were convinced that Kaiser's death was a warning and that some ghostly guardian of the buried treasure planned to kill anyone who tried to retrieve it. If so, that "guardian" had an even more tragic warning in store for a future search expedition.

The workers were eventually persuaded back and the deepening of the Money Pit continued. Blair's notes show that on April 22, 1897, when they reached a depth of 110 feet, they came across one of the old Halifax Company tunnels entering at 108 feet and noticed that all the water flowing into the pit came through this tunnel. They explored it a short distance and came to an intersecting tunnel at the end of which was a large cribbed shaft extending up into darkness as far as they could see.

Blair says: "Water was boiling up through the bottom of this pit, and it proved to be the real Money Pit. The pit [we] had worked in all winter proved to be the old Tupper pit" (Shaft No. 3, dug in 1850 to 109 feet and situated 10 feet northwest of the actual Money Pit). Several months and a lot of money had been wasted in re-excavating the wrong pit.

Moving 10 feet to the southeast, they broke through the topsoil and soon confirmed that they were now in the original Money Pit. On June 9, 1897, digging had progressed to 111 feet in the Money Pit when the workers came upon an uncribbed tunnel 2½ feet wide on the east side of the pit. They dug down quickly, noticing that the opening was filled with smooth beach stones covered with a layer of gravel. And as they dug, water gushed through at an ever-increasing rate. They had located the flood tunnel from the sea.

Several accounts state that the tunnel was 2½ feet wide by about 4 feet high. Welling later noted that its full height couldn't be seen because of the increasing volume of water rushing into the pit.

Blair says: "It entered the pit under great pressure and finally overcame the pumps, filled the pits [Money Pit and shaft No.3] to tide level and brought operations to a standstill."

It was obvious to Blair and Welling that it would be impossible to plug the flood tunnel in the Money Pit itself; the force and volume of water rushing down from Smith's Cove was too great. Work was then temporarily halted while the company's Nova Scotia board of management met in Halifax to formulate a new plan.

Chapter Nine

In 1897 the Oak Island Treasure Company's three-year lease on the eastern end of the island expired. Shortly after it was renewed on an annual basis with Henry Sellers. But there was still one unresolved legal matter that was beginning to make the company directors nervous.

Under a British law dating back to the thirteenth century, any hidden treasure discovered in England or its colonies belonged to the Crown; and it was entirely up to the discretion of the Crown to decide what portion, if any, the finder could retain. The government normally took only a small percentage, or royalty, but it had the power to claim as much as it wanted. Anyone intending to spend time and money searching for a treasure was therefore well advised to determine beforehand how much of a cut the Crown planned to take. But in the early years of the Oak Island hunt, the government, while requiring searchers to obtain a license to dig for treasure, seemed loath to commit itself on the question of royalties.

This is illustrated in a document dated August 8, 1849, giving John Pitbladdo and Charles Archibald permission to dig on the island. The license was granted by Sir John Harvey, Lieutenant General of Nova Scotia, acting on behalf of the British Crown. The agreement stipulates that the searchers will operate by "the right of Her Majesty [Queen Victoria] to whose liberality they are willing to submit themselves for such salvage and reward as Her Majesty may graciously award them." It further states that "if any hidden treasure, monies or effects should be discovered and secured, you are hereby required to take the same into safe keeping and immediately convey every part thereof to the Receiver General of the Province of Nova Scotia at his office in Halifax."

Following the creation of the Dominion of Canada under the British North America Act of 1867, the British Crown assigned this "Treasure Trove" right to the individual provinces of Canada. The Oak Island Treasure Company, when it was formed in 1893, had obtained a Treasure Trove license from the Nova Scotia government. But this agreement also was noncommital on what portion of any discovered treasure would revert to the province. So by 1897, after having invested thousands of dollars in the search and knowing that much more would be spent, the directors of the company sought to clarify the issue.

On February 24, 1897, T. Perley Putnam, acting for the company, wrote George Murray, the premier of the province: "If you remember some time ago I called upon you in reference to the work being done and carried on by the Oak Island Treasure Co. at Oak Island, and as to the amount, if any, your government would levy or collect for any relics or treasure trove that may be obtained through our working. . . . In view of the large amount of money which has already been expended on the island in searching for treasure supposed to be hidden there, and in view of the large amount of money which we are now spending, I would humbly submit that the Crown should not collect or levy anything on the first $100,000 that we may obtain through our working, but we would be willing to pay two per cent on all realized over and above the first $100,000." In a postscript Putnam says, "as some of our people are getting quite anxious over the matter . . . I would consider it a great favor if you could look into the matter this afternoon."

Putnam and his group apparently pulled some weight with the government, for within a month the province agreed to a compromise whereby it wouldn't collect anything on the first $50,000 worth of treasure but would take 2 percent of everything thereafter. (This royalty rate has been increased several times over the years. Today, under Nova Scotia's Treasure Trove Act, passed in

1950, the province is entitled to 10 percent of anything found on Oak Island.)

Having clarified this issue with the province, the company was able to sell more shares to continue its work. After the flood tunnel's entrance into the Money Pit had been located in June of 1897, the company directors decided that the best place to stop the flow was at Smith's Cove. Their plan was to set off charges of dynamite underground near the shore. This, they hoped, would demolish the bothersome tunnel for good.

Five holes were bored in a line about 50 feet up from high-water mark at the cove. They were spaced 15 feet apart, the first at a point 30 feet south of the presumed course of the flood tunnel, and the last 30 feet north of that point. All but the third hole were bored to about 90 feet without encountering water. They were crammed with dynamite and filled with water, which served as a plug. When the dynamite was set off, the water spumed more than 100 feet into the air.

The third hole was apparently bored into the flood tunnel. At 80 feet the auger struck rocks, and seawater immediately rose to tide level. This hole was filled with a huge 160-pound charge. According to Blair, when it was detonated the water in both the Money Pit and the Cave-in Pit "boiled and foamed for a considerable time, and after the disturbance subsided, the oil in the dynamite showed on the water in both these pits."

While it seemed the third hole had hit the flood tunnel, the drillers were perplexed by the fact that the seawater this close to shore wasn't encountered until a depth of 80 feet. They concluded that the tunnel didn't simply run in a direct line from the box drains in Smith's Cove to the Money Pit, but that it first entered a sump hole that was about 75 feet deep and and just inland from shore, and that from the bottom of that hole the tunnel ran at a very slight gradient to enter the Money Pit at a depth of approximately 110 feet.

This reasoning, however, ignored two important earlier discoveries. The watercourse had apparently been struck at 35 feet by shaft No. 5 in 1850, and again at 55 feet down in the Cave-in Pit in 1894. One theory that has been suggested to explain the inconsistency is that there are perhaps two flood tunnels at different levels running between Smith's Cove and the Money Pit. But a more reasonable explanation has been offered by W.L. Johnson, a current investigator. His opinion is that the third drill hole didn't exactly penetrate the tunnel, but came very close to it. Then, while the drill was at 80 feet, the water from the tunnel suddenly burst across and into the hole at a higher level, creating the impression that it had been struck at a depth of 80 feet.

But there was a bigger puzzle to contend with. The workers assumed that the huge charge of dynamite in that third hole had effectively choked off the water supply. Yet when the pumps were subsequently run in the Money Pit, they were barely able to keep ahead of the incoming water. The blasting had had no appreciable effect on the flow from the sea. Part of the answer to this riddle would be found the following year.

While the work at the shore was being completed another crew of drillers started boring into the bottom of the southern edge of the Money Pit, which had previously been excavated to 113 feet. With the pumps holding the water level down to about the 100-foot level, a drilling platform was set up at 90 feet. Experienced drillers had been hired for the job, and overseeing operations were William Chappell, T. Perley Putnam, and Captain John Welling. A full account of the drilling program is contained in notes prepared by Blair in 1900 and in an affidavit sworn to by Chappell in October 1929.

Several holes were bored, most of them with a 2½-inch drill through a 3-inch steel casing, usually in loose and apparently disturbed ground all the way down to 171 feet. Blue clay, which Chappell said had the "characteristics of puddled clay," was encountered between 130 and 151 feet and between 160 and 171 feet. Puddled clay is a hand-worked watertight preparation of clay, sand, and water. It is similar to putty, and it may have been this material that the 1803 searchers found (and identified as putty) on some of the original wooden platforms in the Money Pit.

The first hole was bored through wood at 126 feet. Immediately below that the drill bit struck iron, which it couldn't get through. The workers extracted the drill pipe and found it crushed on one side, indicating that it had only hit the edge of whatever that iron obstruction was.

So a 1½-inch drill was put down the same hole, and it was able to slip past the obstruction at 126 feet. It then went through blue puddled clay and at about 154 feet struck what the drillers first thought was sandstone, but which was later determined to be cement. This cement was 7 inches thick, and underneath it was 5 inches of solid oak. The drill bit was replaced with an auger in order to bring up samples of this wood. Just below the wood was a 2-inch empty gap and then, according to Chappell, the auger "rested upon a substance the character of which no person would attempt to state."

The auger was twisted into his material and then carefully withdrawn. The borings were taken off the auger by Putnam who later brought them to Amherst for examination. The samples looked to him like a mixture of mud, cement, and chips of wood; but included was a tiny piece of Oak Island's puzzle.

When the auger was withdrawn, it was replaced with the drilling chisel, and this was dropped back into the hole, which was now down to about 155 feet from the surface. Here the drill seemed to be on soft metal. Chappell said it was found that this metal "could be moved slightly thereby forming a crevice or space into which the drill, when in alignment, would stick or wedge." This happened several times, and the chisel had to be continually pried loose. Driving the drill down 4 inches required two hours, after which the boring became easier. But even then the drill would go down only by continuously twisting the rods and applying heavy pressure. And the workers noticed that the material being bored would fill up the hole each time the drill was raised. Blair says they "worked five and one quarter hours getting down the two feet eight inches" of this material "and the chisel came up as sharp as [when] it went down." The drillers were certain this material was metal in small pieces; similar to that which had been struck in 1849 between 100 and 104 feet in the Money Pit. At 158 feet the drill hit the same sort of soft metal that had been found just under the wood. The chisel stuck fast in this material and couldn't be turned or driven down, so the drill was withdrawn.

The conclusion drawn by Chappell, Blair, and the others was that below the oak wood the drill had passed through four inches of metal in bars, or ingots, which were pushed aside by the chisel. Then it went through 2 feet 8 inches of small pieces of metal, or coins, that sifted back into the hole each time the drill was raised. Below this were more bars of soft metal which, from the way it felt and from the way the drill bit retained its sharp edge, was not iron.

They decided to secure this hole by putting casing below 126 feet (3-inch casing was already down to the iron obstruction) and then to bring up a sample of the metal pieces. A 1½-inch casing pipe was lowered through the 3-inch pipe and forced past the obstruction. The iron, however, deflected the pipe away from the course followed by the drill and it struck the wall of the pit instead of going down into the cement. The pipe was pulled out and the drill rods were again sent down the 3-inch casing. But they followed the hole made by the smaller pipe into the wall of the shaft. Several more attempts failed, and the passage into the cement and metal was lost.

The 3-inch casing was withdrawn and reset for a second hole into the bottom of the Money Pit. This time the drill struck wood at 122 feet. It then went through 7 feet of cement between 154 and 161 feet, and one side of the drill also encountered wood from about 154 to 158 feet. Below the cement the drill was driven through more puddled clay until it hit what appeared to be an iron plate at 171 feet.

Chappell said: "A magnet was run through this material and it loaded up with fine iron cuttings, thereby producing conclusive proof that it was iron we had been drilling on at 171 feet. No further attempt was made to go through this iron."

Among the many clues that have been discovered on Oak Island, one of the most interesting was included in the samples of bored material retrieved from that drill hole between 153 and 155 feet. Putnam had personally cleaned the end of the auger, and the samples, as he was later to swear, were never out of his possession until they were examined at the courthouse in Amherst several days later. On September 6, 1897, Dr. Andrew E. Porter, a physician then practicing in Amherst, conducted the examination in the presence of about a dozen witnesses. Most of what he saw consisted of pieces of wood and the cementlike material. But then he noticed something peculiar about what he first thought was a tiny piece of wood. It was a compact ball with a fibrous edge. He carefully untwisted it and flattened it out. After studying it under a strong magnifying glass he declared that "this is not wood and there is either paint or ink on it." He concluded it was a piece of parchment.

It was sent soon after to Pictou Academy in Pictou, Nova Scotia, and to experts in Boston. The unanimous verdict was that it was a

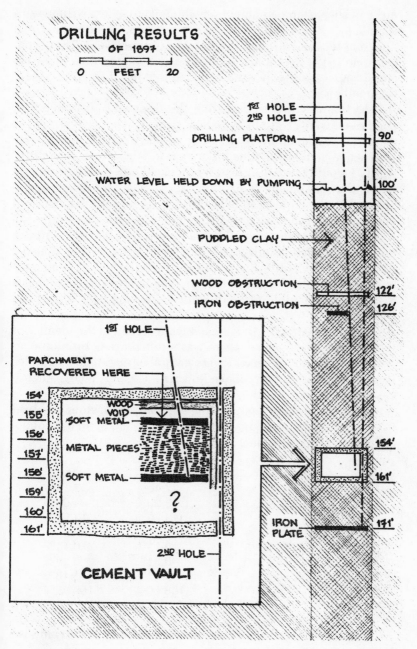

DRILLING RESULTS
OF 1897

0   FEET   20

1ST HOLE
2ND HOLE
DRILLING PLATFORM — 90'
WATER LEVEL HELD DOWN BY PUMPING — 100'
PUDDLED CLAY
WOOD OBSTRUCTION — 122'
IRON OBSTRUCTION — 126'

1ST HOLE
PARCHMENT RECOVERED HERE
154'
155'   WOOD
        VOID
        SOFT METAL
156'
157'   METAL PIECES
158'   SOFT METAL
159'
160'
161'
2ND HOLE
CEMENT VAULT

154'
161'
IRON PLATE — 171'
?

piece of sheepskin parchment on which were letters written with a quill pen in India ink. The letters appeared to be either "vi," "ui," or "wi" and seemed to form part of some word. The parchment, no larger than a five-cent piece, was kept in Blair's possession for many years. It is now owned by Mel Chappell, William Chappell's son.

The circumstances surrounding the discovery of the piece of parchment were sworn to by several persons who were present at its initial examination. Blair, in an affidavit, states that he was well acquainted with Putnam ("a man in whose honesty and integrity I would place the greatest reliance"), and that there was no doubt the parchment came from about 154 feet down in the Money Pit. Dr. Porter also later testified under oath that the sample had been handed directly to him by Putnam in the courthouse. It is also noteworthy that all those involved in the 1897 drilling program purchased additional shares following the parchment's discovery and identification. And Dr. Porter, who had had no interest in Oak Island prior to that time, became a shareholder as a result of this tangible piece of evidence having been brought to the surface.

While the examiners in Amherst were certain of the identity of the samples of oak wood, there was a difference of opinion over whether the chips of cement were natural or man-made. Samples were therefore sent to A. Boake Roberts & Co. Ltd., a large chemical analysis firm in London, England. They replied:

"We have carefully analysed the two samples of stone received from you recently and have to report that we find them to be of the following compositions:

	No. 1	No. 2
Lime (CaO)	37.40%	37.18%
Carbonate (CO¼)	33.20%	34.00%
Silica (SiO¼)	13.20%	13.92%
Iron & Alumina (Fe¼O⅜ & Al¼O⅜)	10.19%	10.13%
Moisture (at 120°C)	0.34%	0.29%
Magnesium etc.	5.67%	4.48%
	100.00%	100.00%

"These stones are very soft and both of them have the composition of cement."

Boake Roberts & Co. was then asked to give an opinion on the probable origin of the cement. They reported that "from the analysis it is impossible to state definitely, but from the appearance and nature of the samples, we are of the opinion that it is a cement which has been worked by man."

In that autumn of 1897, the directors of the Oak Island Treasure Company were more convinced than ever that a large and valuable deposit lay far down in the Money Pit. The results of their drilling program led them to believe that a cement-encased vault, perhaps 7 feet high, had been constructed. Moreover, they speculated that this chamber contained bars of a relatively soft metal such as gold or silver, wooden chests of coins and jewels, and even historical documents of some kind. Above and below the vault, they had encountered puddled clay, a material that apparently was artificial, since it hadn't been found at any depth other than in the Money Pit. Based on these findings, the company became almost a closed corporation with existing shareholders readily advancing the necessary funds to continue operations.

In early October work was begun on a new shaft (No. 14) about 45 feet south of the Money Pit. The intention was to sink it to a depth of 180 feet and then tunnel to the Money Pit at a point well below the iron obstruction encountered at 171 feet in that summer's drilling. This shaft would also serve as a pumping station to help drain the Money Pit and the latter could then be excavated down into the treasure chamber.

By December the diggers had reached a depth of 95 feet when salt water began seeping in at the 70-foot level. Overnight the shaft flooded to within roughly tide level. Work on this hole ended when a tunnel that had been dug by the 1860's searchers was found only 3 feet away. It was responsible for the heavy volume of water entering the shaft.

The workers then moved 30 feet southwest of the abandoned pit and began a new shaft (No. 15) in January of 1898. Work continued until the first of April when, at a depth of 160 feet, a large volume of salt water suddenly burst in from the southwest side of the shaft and drove the men out. Pumping attempts failed, and it was finally abandoned.

In May the workers again decided to try to plug the water entrance at Smith's Cove. In order to locate the position of the drains, they put a pump on the south shore and pumped water from the bay into shaft No.15. Their intention was to fill it above sea level and force the muddy water out through the flood tunnel and the inlet at the cove. They filled the shaft to the top and, as anticipated, the water started falling back to tide level. But the experiment yielded an unexpected and horrifying result: the muddy water was bubbling out not at Smith's Cove but at about the low water mark on the *south* side of the island about 300 feet from the Money Pit. The same thing happened the following day when red dye was poured into the pit.

The searchers now had two known flood tunnels to contend with. Moreover, the southern tunnel must have had several inlets, as the muddy water appeared at three widespread locations offshore. Presumably this had been the tunnel that had caused the sudden flooding of shaft No. 15 at a depth of 160 feet. The discovery also helped to explain why the dynamiting of Smith's Cove a year earlier hadn't checked the flooding of the Money Pit. It wasn't known at what level this second tunnel entered the Money Pit, but it was presumably lower than the 160-foot depth at which it was encountered in shaft No. 15.

The workers subsequently dumped large amounts of rock plaster and clay over and around the presumed inlets at the South Shore Cove. But Blair says this "failed to materially stop the flow of water." A proposal to build a proper cofferdam was rejected as prohibitively expensive, since the cove on that part of the island is about 1,600 feet across, considerably larger than the crescent-shaped Smith's Cove. Besides, two cofferdams built at Smith's Cove in 1850 and 1866 had been destroyed quickly by Atlantic storms.

Between June 1898 and late summer 1899 four more shafts had been dug (Nos. 16–19). These had all been started with the hope of driving them deep enough to tunnel through to the Money Pit's treasure vault about 160 feet down. No. 16 was abandoned because of the rocky nature of the soil. The other three encountered excessive flooding. Moreover, as Blair and Chappell later observed, the water problem wasn't caused only by the two known flood tunnels. It was aggravated by some of their shafts striking lateral tunnels that had been made by searchers in the 1860's. These had created an uncharted labyrinth of underground streams through the eastern end of the island. Some later searchers were to speculate that Blair and his associates had been a little hasty in assuming that all of those cribbed tunnels they encountered were the work of previous treasure hunters. Oak Island's original underground architect had possibly constructed something even more cunning than a single treasure pit with two flood tunnels feeding directly into it.

The Oak Island Treasure Company was having trouble keeping its head above water in more ways than one. The euphoria that had followed the encouraging drilling results of 1897 was beginning to wear off as some of the group's principal investors found themselves close to personal bankruptcy. T.P. Putnam, for instance, was out $20,000 on the venture, and much of this was money he had borrowed.

In early 1900 the company once more updated and reissued its prospectus in an attempt to inject much-needed capital into the treasury. This new pamphlet detailed the findings of the 1897 drilling program, but it withheld any mention of the discouraging discovery of the second flood tunnel. Funds were raised to continue the work.

Still another shaft (No. 20) was dug, flooded, and abandoned, and in May and early June several drill holes were sunk from a platform at the surface into the bottom of the now water-filled Money Pit. But because of the twisted condition of the cribbing only the southeast corner of the pit could be reached from the top. These probes went down to between 116 and 162 feet without striking anything significant.

By now the company was financially doomed. Creditors were moving in with liens on equipment, and workers were demanding back wages. That summer saw the end of seven years' work by the Oak Island Treasure Company.

Blair and his group had been beaten, but they hadn't lost faith in the existence of the treasure. In fact, the deposit seemed more valuable than ever, because they now assumed that at least two separate caches lay in the Money Pit. The first, struck at about 100 feet by the auger in 1849, had apparently fallen to some deeper level when the pit collapsed in 1861. It was thought that the wood and iron encountered between 122 and 126 feet in the 1897 drilling program may have been part of this deposit. Those drilling results had also convinced Blair and the others that an even larger cache rested below 154 feet in the pit and that the original work went down to at least 171 feet. In addition, the discovery of a second flood tunnel—though it increased their frustration—was also seen as further proof that no ordinary treasure had been hidden in the pit.

Blair would later learn more of Oak Island's strange secrets. One of these had been stumbled on by Captain Welling near the island's south shore in 1897, and he had pointed it out to Blair and Chappell. It was a large equilateral triangle made of beach stones. None of them attempted to figure out what it meant, and forty years passed before its significance was realized.

Toward the end of 1900, Blair acquired all the shares of the Oak Island Treasure Company from the other major investors. He retained a lease on the Money Pit area as well as treasure trove rights under his own name, and proceeded to work in partnership with later search groups.

But the mystery lay dormant until 1909 when a syndicate of American businessmen came along with a new plan to recover the treasure. Included in this group was a young and adventurous New York lawyer, Franklin Delano Roosevelt.

Chapter Ten

As the investigation of Oak Island moved into the twentieth century, new theories were advanced to explain the possible origin of the mysterious underground workings. Chronologically, the earliest people who might be considered the originators of the work would be the Indians of Nova Scotia. The Paleo-Indian tribes, which date back to 8600 B.C., comprise the earliest archeologically established evidence of a primitive culture in the province. But the Oak Island project is unquestionably much more modern than the paleolithic or even early post-paleolithic period. If it had been the work of any aboriginal civilization, it would have to have been that of the Micmac Indians. They apparently immigrated overland to Nova Scotia from the northeastern United States between A.D. 700 and A.D. 1100 and were thinly spread out through various parts of the province. Their total population was estimated by early French settlers at 3,000 to 3,500 in 1610.

The Micmacs were a nomadic people who moved about the province following the seasons. Winter camps were situated inland alongside rivers and lakes, and in the spring the campsites were shifted by birchbark canoe to areas of the Nova Scotia coast where fish, clams, scallops, and sea mammals such as seals and walrus were plentiful. Some of these coastal summer camps were on the shores of Mahone Bay, and Oak Island may have been visited by the Micmacs on their fishing expeditions. But there is nothing in their culture to indicate they would have had any material or religious reason to construct the island's underground workings. In fact, anthropologists are certain the Micmacs never built anything more permanent than wigwamlike dwellings of fur and bark.

Furthermore, the Micmac legends, by which their mythical and actual history was passed down orally from generation to generation, do not even remotely suggest a Micmac connection with the Oak Island project. Nor do these now-recorded legends indicate that the Indians were witnesses to whatever was done on the island. Surely they would have verbally recorded an event as awesome as strange ships and men appearing in this part of the world that was then all theirs.

The first nonindigenous people to whom the work has sometimes been credited are the Norsemen. Now historians are certain that Christopher Columbus was not the first European to discover America. The Norsemen visited North America hundreds of years prior to 1492. (The Kensington Stone, unearthed in Minnesota in 1898, is but one example of such evidence. Its runic inscription records the arrival of a group of Norsemen there in 1362, although some people question its authenticity.)

Norse sagas contain several accounts of the Vikings sailing to and even forming small colonies in parts of what are now Newfoundland, Labrador, and Nova Scotia. They had settled Iceland in the late ninth century A.D. and the southwest coast of Greenland one hundred years later. The next logical excursion from there was to the northeastern areas of Canada. In the year 1000 Leif Ericsson landed in an area he called Wineland, which many historians now believe to have been Nova Scotia. Several years later Thorfinn Karlsefni set out from Greenland with three shiploads of colonists to settle Wineland, which he renamed Markland. They spent three winters there according to records, though the location of their colonies hasn't been determined. The sagas also refer to other Viking voyages to the North American continent.

Some have thought that Oak Island and the immediately adjacent mainland had been the site of a Norse settlement and that it may have thrived for many years before all or most of its members were wiped out by epidemics or Indians. One theory suggests that the colonists at some point realized they couldn't survive the hostile environment unless they strengthened their numbers. So those that were left spent their final months carefully hiding everything that was of value to them beneath the island; including, perhaps, runic stones bearing their mythology and a chronicle of the settlement's history. They then sailed off to Greenland or Scandinavia in hopes of eventually returning with others to resettle the area, but for some reason never did.

The problem with this hypothesis, and indeed with any pre-Columbian theory, is that wood samples that have been recovered from far below the island in recent years have been carbon dated no earlier than 1500. And obviously the depositors brought, or at least had access to, tropical coconut fiber. Therefore the Norse connection with Oak Island is most unlikely.

Apart from the Norse, the first European awareness of Nova Scotia came with the voyage of John Cabot. On June 24, 1497, Cabot planted the English flag on Cape Breton Island, now part of Nova Scotia. The next year he sailed down the province's Atlantic coast and from there he crossed over to New England. (This, incidentally, made him the first non-Nordic European to land on the American continent proper.)

Cabot was followed to the Nova Scotia area by Basque and Breton fishermen who discovered the rich Grand Banks fishing grounds and who also landed on Cape Breton Island. Two unsuccessful attempts were then made to settle this new land; the first by Baron de Lery of France in 1518, and the second by the Italian explorer Giovanni da Verrazano in 1523. (Some accounts credit Verrazano with naming the area "Arcadia," and hence its original name of Acadia; but other historians say the name was derived from a Micmac word "acadie," meaning fertile land. The British changed the name to Nova Scotia in 1710.) As a result of these early expeditions, crude coastal charts of Nova Scotia were available to seventeenth-century explorers.

The territory appears to have been forgotten until 1604 when an expedition led by Sieur du Gua DeMonts and Samuel de Champlain established a temporary French colony at La Have, about fifteen miles south of Oak Island. A year later they created a permanent settlement at Port Royal, on the Bay of Fundy, thereby giving France its first colonial foothold in the province. But in 1621 the British Crown claimed ownership of the territory by virtue of the fact that Cabot had landed there first in 1497. For the next 140 years or so, France and England hotly contested their sovereignty over this part of the New World, and the flag over Port Royal and other settlements changed several times in the wake of the English-French skirmishes. Both sides employed the Micmac Indians, who had previously been a peaceful tribe, as mercenaries in their battles. Finally, in 1763, Britain's rule over the entire province was confirmed.

This period of Nova Scotia's early colonization and the resulting French and English wars has been considered by many people as the likely era in which the Oak Island project was created. However, no evidence has been found in the colonial documents of either country that the island was ever a military installation or that it served an official purpose whatsoever.

But one popular theory is that the island was used secretively by the French as a temporary repository for royal treasury funds that were used to pay the troops and laborers involved in the construction of the great fort of Louisbourg, 240 miles northeast of Oak Island.

When France lost the War of the Spanish Succession, she was forced to sign the Treaty of Utrecht in 1713 whereby England acquired most of the French colonies in Nova Scotia and Newfoundland. France was left with only the islands of Cape Breton, Prince Edward, and St. Pierre and Miquelon. The French then spent almost thirty years and millions of dollars building a huge fortress at Louisbourg near the eastern tip of Cape Breton. This supposedly impregnable fort was completed in 1744. But a year later the British led an army of New Englanders against the French at Louisbourg, and the fort was captured after a forty-nine-day seige. It was handed back to France by the Treaty of Aix-la-Chapelle in 1748, only to be recaptured by the British in 1758. In 1760 the fortress was demolished to ensure that the French would never again occupy it.

The 50 acres of Louisbourg fortifications had been built by private contractors sent from France along with engineers and artisans. Most of the labor was supplied by the French troops garrisoned in the town that the fortress was designed to surround. Perhaps, because of the uneasy truce with England, the French government was wary of keeping the vast sums that went into building the fort in the town itself. It therefore may have sought a repository or "bank" that would be convenient to Louisbourg and yet be in an unlikely and isolated part of the province. So Oak Island might have been chosen, and the underground vault and flood tunnels constructed with professional engineers and military labor.

A related theory suggests that Oak Island wasn't a government project at all, but that some of the royal treasury funds shipped from Versailles to build the fort were siphoned off by a dishonest contractor or high-ranking French officer. With the aid of trusted cohorts, this person then designed and built the underground vault in which to hide the embezzled wealth, with the intention of later retrieving it and returning to France a rich man.

Both these theories have also been applied to the period just after 1748 when France again shipped large sums to Louisbourg in order to rebuild those parts of the fort that had been destroyed in the British attack of 1745. It has also been rumored that the equivalent of about $10 million was spirited out of Louisbourg harbor on a French ship during the second British siege of 1758 and that the money was never heard of again. But there is no valid historical record of this having happened. Three French frigates did escape the British blockade and several days later succeeded in making it up the St. Lawrence River to Quebec City (which was then still in French hands).

Similar arguments contend that an earlier French pay ship destined for Louisbourg may have foundered, by accident or design, near Oak Island. Its cargo of coin and bullion was then hidden, either for larcenous reasons or to keep it from falling into the hands of the British. But the only positive record of a richly laden French ship disappearing in that area occurred in August of 1725 when the *Chameau* went down with all hands on a rocky reef just a few miles east of Louisbourg. She had 290,000 French livres (about $750,000) in cash aboard, part of which was recovered by divers in 1965.

Another suggestion links Oak Island to the ill-fated armada of the Duc d'Anville. In June of 1746 the French Crown, mortified by the fall of Louisbourg to the English the year before, assembled at Brest a fleet of 65 ships and 3,150 troops to sail across the Atlantic and retake the fortress as well as the rest of the province. The fleet, under the command of the Duc d'Anville, was plagued with bad luck all the way to the New World. Even before reaching Nova Scotian waters, several vessels were lost to storms, and pestilence had broken out on many of the others. Then off the dreaded shoals of Sable Island (known as "the graveyard of the Atlantic") the armada ran into a violent tempest that claimed more ships and lives. On September 25 D'Anville's flagship and a few other vessels managed to make it to Chibucto Harbor (now Halifax Harbor) but most of the troops and sailors were dying of scurvy and other diseases. Two days later D'Anville himself died, reportedly of apoplexy, though it was rumored he had ended his problems with poison. The intended attack on Louisbourg was never carried out, for the armada had lost most of its ships and about 2,000 of its soldiers.

Theories have been advanced to the effect that one or more of the ships presumed lost in the storm off Sable Island may have actually escaped and sailed two hundred miles west into Mahone Bay. No record indicating whether any of the ships in the fleet were carrying specie or bullion exists, but possibly some were. Had such a ship sought refuge in Mahone Bay, Oak Island may have been used as a temporary hiding place for this treasure.

This and other theories establishing a French connection to Oak Island, as either an official or unofficial deposit, conform with the necessary ingredient of secrecy. Until Halifax was settled and made the British headquarters in 1749, the southern coast of mainland Nova Scotia was virtually uninhabited. The principal settlement until then was at Port Royal on the north side of the province, and almost all the lesser settlements were in that same area. And prior to 1750 even the Micmacs appear to have made only sporadic visits to Mahone Bay. However, had the workings been secretly executed under the direction of the French government, some account of it probably would have turned up eventually in France. And if the work was done without the knowledge of the French Crown, surely some official mention would exist that a large amount of public money was unaccounted for about that time.

But what if the project was a private French venture unrelated to Crown funds? At least two possibilities exist here: the Acadians and the Huguenots.

The sixty French families who formed Nova Scotia's first permanent settlement at Port Royal in 1605 were the province's original Acadians. For more than a hundred years they prospered, mainly by farming but also through fishing and commerce. Their villages and communities were for the most part situated along the shores of the Minas Basin and the Bay of Fundy in the nothern part of the province. As early as 1632, however, a few Acadian families had settled in the areas of La Have and Merligueche, now known as Lunenburg.

The Acadians were peaceful and did their best to remain neutral during the French-English struggle for dominance in Nova Scotia. Yet they were not immune to raids on their villages by British and New England privateers who sometimes seized their livestock, farm produce, and other possessions. When the Treaty of Utrecht ceded mainland Nova Scotia to England in 1713, the new rulers tried to force the Acadians to take an oath of allegiance to the British Crown, including the promise to bear arms against the French should France again try to assume control of the territory. The Acadians resisted for several years and then signed the oath only when a clause was inserted whereby they could remain militarily neutral in times of conflict.

The situation remained thus until 1749 when Edward Cornwallis was appointed Governor of Nova Scotia. By then there were an estimated ten thousand Acadians living in the mainland part of the province, and France had once again assumed control of Cape Breton Island and the Louisbourg fortress. Cornwallis saw himself faced with a dilemma. He felt threatened by the fact that so many French people, albeit neutrals, lived in British-held Nova Scotia. But he knew that if he forced the Acadians to leave, most of them would settle in Cape Breton, thereby greatly increasing the strength of the French in that nearby colony. So once again the Acadians were urged to take an unconditional oath of allegiance; and again they refused to relinquish their neutrality.

This uneasy state of affairs remained unresolved until 1755 when the British resorted to a heavy-handed solution. The Acadians were rounded up at gunpoint, stripped of their land and possessions, and herded aboard ships that carried them into exile. In 1755 alone some six thousand Acadians were expelled, most of them dumped off at ports along the American coast from Maine to

Georgia. Another two thousand were rounded up and similarly deported in the next couple of years. (Some Acadians later drifted down to Louisiana, hence the origin of the name "Cajuns"). Not until after the Treaty of Paris in 1763 was the edict expelling the Acadians revoked. Many of them returned to Nova Scotia.

Sometime between 1749 and 1755 a group of Acadians, suspecting their eventual fate, may have designed the Oak Island project to hide and avoid the confiscation of their money and valuables. They were certainly industrious and clever enough to have built something of that nature. There is one recorded instance of a group of eighty-six Acadians in 1755 digging a long tunnel through which they escaped from Fort Lawrence (near the Nova Scotia-New Brunswick border) where they were being held pending deportation. But the Acadians' ever having amassed the kind of wealth suggested by the elaborateness of the Oak Island workings seems doubtful. Most of them were successful, but not prosperous, farmers. Some of them did carry on trading and even smuggling businesses, which would have brought in hard currency. They sold farm produce, meat, fish, and furs to the English garrisons on the mainland and to the French at Louisbourg. (This latter market was illegal under British rule and therefore involved smuggling.) In some instances they also sold supplies to coastal pirates in the Bay of Fundy and they presumably received coins, jewels, and other plundered items in return. But nothing has been found in Acadian history that hints at the concealment of substantial wealth prior to their deportation. And no indications exist that a group of Acadians retrieved a deposit on Oak Island after they were allowed back in the province, and by that time the Mahone Bay area was becoming fairly well inhabited.

Another theory involving early settlers is more tenuous, but it contains an intriguing coincidence. While the majority of the Acadians were of Catholic stock, there was a smaller group of Nova Scotian French colonists who were Protestant. These were the Huguenots, most of whom were drawn from the French nobility and well-to-do artisan class. The Huguenots were the principal victims of the religious wars of sixteenth-century France until the Edict of Nantes in 1598 assured their equal political rights with the Catholics. But on October 18, 1685, the edict was revoked and religious persecution was resumed. Consequently, despite the fact that their emigration was prohibited by law, some fifty thousand Huguenot families fled to foreign countries. Many of them headed to various parts of the New World.

In 1928 Dunbar Hinrichs was working in Chester and met a man who had come over from France to investigate a family legend. This Frenchman (whose name Hinrichs has long since forgotten) said one of his ancestors had been among a group of wealthy Huguenots who had escaped from France aboard two ships at about the time the Edict of Nantes was revoked. With them they took a great deal of money and jewelry. According to a story passed down through this Frenchman's family, the two vessels had sailed from La Rochelle across the Atlantic to St. Domingue (now Haiti). There, under the supervision of an engineer accompanying them, they constructed a complex underground vault complete with flood tunnels to guard it. A group of them deposited their personal fortunes in different sections of this vault and then sailed off on one of the ships to the British colony of New York where they settled. (In fact, some Huguenots from La Rochelle did sail into Long Island Sound in 1688 and established the town of New Rochelle).

The second vessel headed for Nova Scotia with the rest of the Huguenots and their riches. The engineer who'd designed the Haitian works was also aboard. The ship reportedly sailed into Mahone Bay where an uninhabited island was selected on which to build a repository similar to that in St. Domingue. After storing their wealth these people then settled in the province. The Huguenots' intent, presumably, was to prevent their fortunes from being confiscated or heavily taxed in the New World. The underground "banks," according to the story, had been constructed in such a way as to allow them to be reopened via a secret passage from the surface or else by the closing of a water gate somewhere in the flood tunnels. The funds could then be withdrawn as required.

In an interview in St. Petersburg, Florida, in 1976, Hinrichs recalled that he had found the Frenchman's story interesting but that he had never put too much stock in it. In fact, he had almost forgotten about it until he saw an article (by this writer) about Oak Island that appeared in the *Wall Street Journal* in August 1975. What caught his attention was the fact that (as the article explained) an underground project similar to Oak Island may exist in Haiti, and some investigators are convinced that both were designed by the same person. The curious part is that the Haitian workings (which will be discussed later) weren't discovered until 1947, almost twenty years after Hinrichs' conversation with the mysterious Frenchman. The Frenchman had been lured to Nova Scotia by publicity surrounding the Oak Island search, and he had seen a possible connection to the family legend. But he couldn't have known about the purported Haitian workings. Who this man was or what evidence he had to support the Huguenot legend will probably never be known.

Provincial records note the arrival of several prominent Huguenot families in Nova Scotia, though no conspicuous group appears around the year 1685. One of the earliest was the La Tour family, who came in the 1620's and founded a settlement (now Port La Tour) on the province's western tip. The majority of the Huguenots didn't arrive until around the time of the expulsion of the Acadians in 1755. They, as well as thousands of Germans and New Englanders, were enticed to the province with the promise of free land, much of which had been expropriated from the Acadians. (The Huguenots, being Protestant, were considered "safe" French settlers by the British.)

Among the wealthy Huguenot settlers was Louis Payzant, whose merchant family had fled from Caen to the Channel Island of Jersey after the revocation of the Edict of Nantes. In 1753 Payzant sold two of three ships he owned, packed his family, servants, and worldly goods aboard the third, and came to Nova Scotia. He selected an island in Mahone Bay on which to make his home and start a trading business. The island, which is now called Covey Island, is five miles south of Oak Island. Payzant's business prospered and by the spring of 1756 he had a farm and well-stocked trading post. But on the night of May 8, 1756, his home was attacked by a band of Micmac Indians who killed him and several of his servants and then looted and burned his store. Payzant's pregnant wife and four children were captured by the Indians and taken almost a thousand miles by canoe to Quebec City. They were turned over to the French who held them prisoners until the fall of Quebec to the British in 1759. (The French considered anyone living in English-held Nova Scotia as British, regardless of their language.)

The story of the Payzant family is of interest because they were among the first to inhabit an island in Mahone Bay. (Ironically, the British Governor-in-Chief Charles Lawrence was trying to encourage newcomers to settle these islands by claiming that they would be "more in safety from the savages" than if they lived on the mainland. A settler living on nearby Rous Island was killed by the same party of Indians on the night of the Payzant massacre.) Payzant's having had any connection with the Oak Island deposit seems unlikely, but he must have at least visited this nearby island with its tall, magnificent oak trees. The connection is strengthened by a will dated June 22, 1768, which has a Philip Payzant of Chester bequeathing Oak Island Lot No. 6 to another resident of Chester, Robert Melvin.

The fact that Payzant's trading post existed as early as 1753 would indicate that the waters in this part of Mahone Bay were being traversed with some regularity from that time on. This seems to undermine suggestions that the Oak Island project, which would have involved a great deal of labor and a long time to complete, could have been undertaken this late in Nova Scotia's development. About this time the surrounding mainland area was also attracting its first permanent settlers. Lunenburg was founded in 1753 with the arrival of some three hundred German and Swiss immigrants; the town of Mahone Bay began a year later with the establishment of a sawmill and a blockhouse in which a small detachment of British militia was garrisoned; the township of Shoreham (later Chester) was created in 1759 with the arrival of a shipload of immigrants from New England. Early census reports show that by 1770 there were fifteen hundred persons living in Lunenburg, about three hundred in Chester, and several dozen families in smaller settlements between those two places. That any of these people could have been involved with Oak Island without their neighbors knowing of it seems highly improbable. Even less likely is the idea that outsiders could have lived and worked on the island under the noses of these settlers.

Nevertheless, one theory that has been seriously promoted by several investigators is that Oak Island was engineered and used by the British army during the War of American Independence from 1775 to 1783.

Within the first year of the war, the British might have thought that Washington's troops would be the eventual victors. In March of 1776 the British forces evacuated Boston and by mid-1778 their

New York command post was under threat of attack by land and sea. This post contained an estimated several million dollars in funds used to pay troops and purchase supplies.

Suggestions have been made that the British relocated this treasury from New York to Halifax, their nearest secure base, so as to prevent its falling into the hands of the revolutionaries. Then, fearing a possible American attack on Halifax (General Washington had actually considered it in 1775), a secret repository was built on Oak Island by professional British military engineers. The island was then used as a colonial treasury for the duration of the American Revolution. However, if such an operation had taken place, the funds stored on Oak Island must have later been recovered; had they not been, a major scandal would surely have erupted back in England.

The problem with this theory is that nothing has been found in British military records alluding to any undertaking of that nature. Moreover, any military operation like that would certainly have been observed and remarked upon by the residents of the area. Those who would date the Oak Island project this late argue that the eastern end of the island, the site of the Money Pit, is on the seaward side and therefore not visible to anyone on the mainland directly opposite the island. This, they add, would permit a clandestine project to be carried out. The flaw here is that the island's eastern end is clearly visible from many other nearby sections of the mainland north and south of the island as well as from several elevated spots in Chester itself. Also, the early settlers commonly traveled between Chester and Lunenburg by canoe or fishing boat, a route that would take them directly by the east end of Oak Island.

There have been other theories proposed in connection with the War of Independence. These range from American naval privateers using Oak Island as a base, to the island's being used as a weapons cache by New England settlers in the province who were sympathetic to their Yankee brethren and who hoped to expand the revolution to Nova Scotia. Some have even thought that a group of United Empire Loyalists (those Americans loyal to the British Crown who came to Nova Scotia by the thousands after the Revolution) may have secreted a personal treasure on the island. Again, the timing would render those explanations virtually impossible.

The common element in all of the suggestions so far outlined is that they fit into the known history of the province in the centuries prior to the discovery of the Money Pit. But as further investigation disclosed the enormity and complexity of the underground workings, new theories were advanced to explain their origin. And some of these credited the work to people and civilizations far removed from recorded Nova Scotian history.

Chapter Eleven

In the spring of 1909, Fred Blair found someone willing to pick up where the Oak Island Treasure Company had left off. Henry L. Bowdoin, a noted American adventurer and engineer, had heard about the unsuccessful attempts to recover the treasure. He was convinced that with the use of divers and heavy machinery he could conquer the water trap that had frustrated his predecessors. He stirred up public interest in his plans through a series of interviews that appeared in New York, Boston, and Nova Scotia newspapers, and in April of 1909 he formed The Old Gold Salvage and Wrecking Company. The company, with offices at 44 Broadway, New York, was potentially capitalized at $250,000 in shares of $1 apiece being offered to the public.

The company's prospectus claimed that "a $10,000,000 treasure" lay at the bottom of the Money Pit and that "with modern methods and machinery, the recovery of that treasure is easy, ridiculously easy." The estimate of the treasure's worth was apparently a conversion of pounds sterling to dollars and was based on the supposed translation ("forty feet below two million pounds are buried") of the inscribed stone found 90 feet down in the Money Pit in 1803.

The prospectus went on to say that Oak Island was just the first of several treasure hunts the company planned to undertake; the others being shipwrecks that could be salvaged by the use of "Bowdoin's Air Lock Caisson." It further boasted that: "The recovery of the [Oak Island] treasure would yield a dividend of 4,000 per cent on the entire capital stock; and as operations should begin in May or June and be completed in three or four weeks, should be available this summer."

Despite his bombastic confidence, Bowdoin was able to sell only about five thousand shares in his venture. Blair, in exchange for stock, gave the company the right to work on the island for two years. On August 18, 1909, Bowdoin and several associates sailed from New York to Halifax where they purchased some additional equipment. On August 27 they arrived by schooner on Oak Island and set up their headquarters, which they dubbed "Camp Kidd."

Among those who purchased stock in Bowdoin's company was a man destined to become Oak Island's most distinguished treasure hunter—Franklin D. Roosevelt. At that time, Roosevelt was a twenty-seven-year-old law clerk with the Wall Street firm of Carter, Ledyard and Milburn. His interest in Oak Island went back to his boyhood years spent at his mother's summer home on Campobello Island in the Bay of Fundy. (FDR's treasure-hunting career seems to have begun in 1896 when, at the age of fourteen, he and a Groton prep-school roommate sailed from Campobello to the nearby island of Grand Manan. They spent four days on the island digging for a chest supposed to have been buried by Captain Kidd. All they found was an old plank on which some hoaxer had carved "W.K.") Roosevelt had always been intrigued by the Oak Island story, which was widely known in the Bay of Fundy area. In 1909 he saw an opportunity to become associated with the search, and that summer he made several brief visits to the island. Some of his New York friends, Duncan G. Harris, Albert Gallatin, and John W. Shields, shared his interest, and they too purchased shares in the venture. (Other writers have stated that Frederick Childs, a friend of FDR's at Harvard, was also a shareholder. But this is untrue since, according to his son, Childs died of typhoid in 1907 at the age of twenty-five.)

Roosevelt's fascination with Oak Island continued long after his own involvement in recovering the treasure. His extant personal papers include correspondence relating to Oak Island dating as late as 1939, while he was in his second term as President of the United States. These letters, between FDR and his fellow 1909 searchers and later investigators, cover a thirty-year span and indicate that he maintained a great interest in the baffling mystery of Oak Island.

After setting up their campsite, Bowdoin's workers spent a short time trying to locate the flood-tunnel entrances at Smith's Cove and the south shore. They couldn't find them, so they moved their equipment up to the Money Pit, which was filled to 30 feet from the surface with seawater. Because of their limited funds, a proposed 1,000-gallon-per-minute capacity pump hadn't been brought to the island and they were unable to lower the water level in the pit.

A diver dressed in a rubber suit and metal deep-sea helmet was sent down to check on the pit's condition. He reported that it was clear down to 113 feet but that the cribbing was badly twisted and out of alignment. Bowdoin then decided to probe the pit's bottom with a drill in the hope that core samples would locate the treasure vault that had been struck in 1897. Once that was accomplished, he felt it would be an easy matter to raise additional funds to enable him to sink a watertight caisson down into the vault.

First he dropped charges of dynamite into the pit and cleared out much of the smashed timbering with a steam-powered bucket.

In October a total of twenty-eight holes were bored to between 155 and 171 feet from the surface. Bowdoin reports that from 113 to 130 feet the drill encountered coarse gravel and sand; this was followed by about 16 feet of blue clay, small stones, and sand. He adds that in several of the test holes "we struck cement six inches to 10 inches thick at depths of 146 feet to 149 feet, but no traces of boxes, treasure, or anything of that kind."

At this point Bowdoin's funds ran out and he was unable to sell more shares in the Old Gold Salvage and Wrecking Company. So the equipment was put under wraps on the island and the expedition sailed back to New York on November 4. Bowdoin, who had been overconfident and undercapitalized, would later declare that Oak Island was nothing but a hoax.

Bowdoin's about-face followed an exchange of letters between him and Blair over the next year. Bowdoin wanted a new contract to allow him to resume his search, but Blair would enter into an agreement with him only if Bowdoin could first prove he had sufficient funds to carry out the work. Bowdoin then threatened to issue a report that "would not help in getting further investments in Oak Island," and Blair testily advised him to publish and be damned.

On August 19, 1911, an article entitled "Solving the Mystery of Oak Island" appeared under Bowdoin's name in *Collier's* magazine. In it the writer concluded that: "My experience proved to me that there is not, and never was, a buried treasure on Oak Island. The Mystery is solved." The article refuted the authenticity of all the previous finds made on the island or else dismissed them as natural phenomena. Bowdoin's arguments, which distorted or omitted known facts, were answered point by point in a lengthy article by Blair that appeared in the *Amherst Daily News* of February 23, 1912. This was the first serious public controversy to develop out of the Oak Island search.

Chapter Twelve

In 1912 Fred Blair moved to Calgary, Alberta, where he started his own insurance business. Although he was now living almost three thousand miles away, his obsession with Oak Island was as fervid as ever. He still had his treasure trove license from the Nova Scotia government, and he continued to pay Sophia Sellers $100 a year to retain his lease on the eastern end of the island.

That summer saw the introduction of a new proposal to recover the treasure. Professor S.A. Williams of Soldiers Grave, Wisconsin, organized the Oak Island Salvage Company, which planned to use the Poetsch freezing process to overcome the flooding problem. The company's prospectus said the process, whereby liquid calcium chloride at 35 degrees below zero would be injected into the ground around the Money Pit, had been successfully used in certain European mines where water or quicksand ruled out normal excavation methods.

But Professor Williams had even worse luck that Bowdoin in attracting shareholders. By the end of the year, he hadn't sold enough shares to pay his passage out to Oak Island, much less purchase any equipment. The company folded and its agreement with Blair was cancelled.

Over the next ten years a few more abortive attempts were made by Americans to solve the mystery. In 1916 a group headed by

William S. Lozier, an engineer from Rochester, New York, surveyed the island and did some exploratory drilling without finding anything of consequence. Another effort was made in the summer of 1922 by Edward W. Bowne of Newark, New Jersey, who planned to sink a new shaft near the Money Pit. But after he'd been on the island two months without even beginning the shaft, his agreement with Blair was terminated.

During this period Blair was approached by many people who, like Williams, had ideas and theories but who required stock promotions to finance the actual work. Blair realized that some of these individuals were hoping to milk the public by relying on the well-known history of Oak Island to raise funds that were intended to line the promoters' pockets. He avoided these charlatans and sought out persons or groups who could finance their own ventures.

(It wasn't only the stock promoters who saw a good thing in Oak Island. In the summer of 1916 the following sign was posted on the wall of the Chester Post Office: "Permit to land on Sellers farm, Oak Island, to picnic may be purchased at 25¢ per person from this date. Parties of less than six may obtain a guide by paying $1 extra. Any boat seen to land parties above high tide mark will be treated as pirates and shot on sight. Landing must be made at North Cove stone wharf." It was soon discovered that the notice had been posted by a returned World War I soldier who was camping on the north side of the island and collecting admission from tourists coming over to see the famous Money Pit. He had no connection with Blair or any of the owners of the island.)

Blair took his search for a self-financed Oak Island partner to several United States and Canadian newspapers. On December 7, 1922, the following advertisement appeared on the front page of the New York City-based *Journal of Commerce:*

BURIED TREASURE

Speculative venture, partly proven, requires $50,000 for half interest. If successful, will produce millions within one year; otherwise possible eighty per cent loss. Satisfactory credentials, proofs partially successful efforts, will prove good sporting proposition for party financially able take chance. Full frank details at interview. 228 F, Journal of Commerce.

Blair's advertisement prompted an Oak Island article on page three of the same issue.

Although the publicity drew many inquiries, Blair didn't find his wealthy backer until 1931. And the investor, William Chappell of Sydney, Nova Scotia, was no stranger to the Oak Island mystery. Chappell had been on the drilling platform thirty-four years earlier when the samples of wood, cement, and a piece of parchment had been recovered from more than 150 feet down in the Money Pit. Since then he had remained a firm believer in the existence of a large and valuable deposit somewhere in the vicinity of the 1897 drilling probe.

In the intervening years the family's contracting and lumber business, Chappells Limited, had prospered. So Chappell decided to put the company to work on the island in another attempt to recover the treasure. He was joined in this venture by his brother Renwick, his son Mel, and his nephew Claude. Blair moved back from Calgary to personally take part in the operation. That spring he and the Chappells built a campsite on the island and lived there for the next six months.

Mel Chappell is a member of the Engineering Institute of Canada, and before the 1931 project began he consulted with several prominent mining engineers on the best type of shaft to use. The consensus was that an open-timbered pit would be the most practical and economically feasible. A Smart-Turner centrifugal pump, with a capacity of 450 gallons per minute, was purchased to continuously drain the shaft. It was powered by electricity, which was routed to the island through a submarine cable from the mainland.

The plan was to sink a new shaft (No. 21) down into the chamber that had been drilled through in 1897. The first problem the workers faced was in determining exactly where to dig. No work of any consequence had been done on the island since 1909, the year in which Bowdoin dynamited and ripped out much of the cribbing in the Money Pit. Over the years, the pit had caved in and by 1931 its location could only be estimated from memory and by the general depression of the earth in that area. (Mel Chappell remembers that the area "was irregular and depressed several feet and covered with grass and weeds.") Therefore they decided to dig a relatively large pit (known as the Chappell shaft) 12 feet wide by 14 feet long that would almost surely strike at least part of the center of the original Money Pit.

Claude Chappell, now in his eighties, recalls, "When we first went [to the island] Uncle William staked out where we should put down the pit, and eventually we started it. Blair came out to the island and said, 'You're about six feet from where you should be.' 'Well,' Uncle William said, 'we can't shift the head (of the shaft) now, but when we get down there we can look around.'"

Actually, the center of the Chappell shaft was probably slightly southwest of the original Money Pit, though its northern end encompassed part of shaft No. 20 as well as a corner of the Money Pit. Most of the digging was done through previously worked soil. Salt water was encountered, but the pit was kept dry with the large electric pump.

On their way down the workers came across tools and a lot of timber from earlier shafts. They also found an old anchor fluke at 120 feet, which, according to Mel Chappell, "was imbedded in the clay on the side (of the pit) and wasn't rusted." He adds that the anchor fluke was of an ancient design and that it may well have been an original artifact; one which today he wishes he'd retained for a metal analysis. (It was in Blair's possession and disappeared after his death in 1951.)

Neither the Money Pit nor the adjacent shaft No. 20 had ever been excavated to more than 113 feet; so the old tools found below that depth in the Chappell shaft had somehow sunk from where they'd been left.

But the question of what had happened to the metal, wood, and cement encountered between 126 and 171 feet by the drillers in 1897 remained unanswered. Apart from searchers' tools the only other thing of interest found in shaft No. 21 was large chunks of what was believed to be either granite or concrete. Blair, in a report to William Chappell late that summer, offered the following explanation:

"I am convinced that down to 150 feet at least, one end of your pit was over the edge of what once was an open chamber. Due to the collapse of supports, etc. above, this chamber has been filled with broken ground or clay, through which the water being pumped has passed. Tons and tons of clay have passed out with the water this summer, and the gravel and other solids keep settling down to solid bottom as the work progresses. The wall of this chamber, undermined possibly by the water, has broken down in the vicinity of our pit, and perhaps it is some of that [granite or concrete] wall we have taken out."

By that time Blair and William Chappell realized that they were dealing with a mess down in the depths of the Money Pit area. This had been created by several collapses and reopenings of the Money Pit, the sinking of at least ten shafts within 35 feet of the pit, and lateral tunneling at several levels all around it. Add to that the effect of billions of gallons of water flowing into and being pumped out of that same area, and the total result could only be a confused subterranean soup stirred by a succession of searchers over those past 136 years.

On October 14 the Chappell shaft was down to 163 feet, deeper than any previous diggers had ever been. At that level they drilled into the bottom and determined that the disturbed earth continued for another 12 feet before they reached what felt like solid unworked clay. They also drilled horizontally at the 130-foot level through the sides of their pit. Several of the probes hit wood, but this was thought to have been timbers that had worked their way down from earlier shafts.

In order to further explore the surrounding area, a tunnel was driven at a depth of 157 feet from the north wall of the shaft for about 9 feet. A second tunnel was dug at the same level extending out from the eastern wall and then curving to the north, with the intention of joining it to the first tunnel. But before it could be reached, the soft earth began caving in, almost burying the foreman, George Stevenson, in the process. He was extricated in time by Mel Chappell. This was one of many mishaps encountered that summer. Two other workers suffered broken ribs in pit accidents, and severe storms knocked out the pump's electrical supply several times. (In addition, that summer one Chappell employee was killed, and another lost his eye in accidents unrelated to their work on the island.)

Claude Chappell also recalls that when the shaft was down to about 155 feet, " . . . we came to a sort of shale rock and more water started coming in. It was coming in from three or four feet on one side; it wasn't just coming in from one little hole. It was a round, clearly defined tunnel." The diggers weren't sure, but this may have been the mouth of the suspected tunnel from the south shore. In any case, their pump contained the flow.

Apart from the work in the shaft, the Chappells drilled and dynamited several holes on the beach at Smith's Cove. But this failed to plug the flood tunnel. More coconut fiber was dug up on the beach and was authenticated by botanists in Halifax. In addition, Mel Chappell relocated the strange triangle of stones that his father and Blair had first seen on the south shore in 1897. The younger Chappell recalls, "We did not give it too much consideration" at the time. Its significance would be discovered in another six years.

On October 29, after six months and an expenditure of about $40,000, work was halted for the season. The Chappells wanted to resume their search the following spring. However, Sophia Sellers, who owned the eastern end of the island, died in 1931 and her twelve heirs wouldn't allow the Chappells to return without a substantial cash payment to each of them. Chappells Ltd. declined to pay, but the family was determined to come back someday and continue the work they'd started.

Gilbert Hedden, who purchased that part of the island a few years later, interviewed William Chappell at length about his 1897 and 1931 operations. In a letter to President Roosevelt on September 1, 1937, Hedden said Chappell "maintained his belief and kept to the facts of his story under rigid cross-examination and averred that he would be at the site today if I had not purchased it when I did."

William Chappell died in 1946. Today, his son Mel owns most of the island and, although in his nineties, he is actively pursuing the search. "I am convinced," he says, "that whatever father drilled into (in 1897) is of immense value. I have no doubt about it. It's still down there; nobody has ever taken it out."

In his interview with Hedden, William Chappell also disclosed something he'd never before made public: When the drill that brought up the piece of parchment was examined, he'd seen traces of yellow on it that he believed may have resulted from boring through gold. (Mel Chappell confirms the story and says his father was reluctant to make anything of it at the time because the traces had been so faint.)

For some reason, the Sellers heirs permitted another searcher on their land in the summer of 1932. This was Mary B. Steward, a wealthy New York City dowager. Under an agreement with Blair, she sent John Talbot, an engineer from Brooklyn, to the island. He spent two months drilling a hole a few feet away from the Chappell shaft. He brought up a couple of chips of wood from between 113 and 150 feet. At that lower depth his drill pipe broke, and he abandoned the project.

The next searcher was Thomas M. Nixon of Victoria, British Columbia. In September of 1933 he arranged with the Sellers heirs to dig on their property and also signed a contract with Blair, who still held the treasure trove rights. The agreement allowed Nixon to work on the island from April to November of 1934, with Blair entitled to half of any treasure found.

Nixon had described himself as an engineer with enough financial backing to solve the problem within one summer. But his funding was in fact hypothetical and was based on what he hoped to raise through the sale of stock.

As April drew closer, Blair began to have misgivings about his agreement with Nixon. If Nixon didn't have the backing he claimed and didn't carry out his intended excavation, a season's work on the island would be lost. And Blair had meanwhile been approached by several other prospects. This included Mary Steward who was thinking of again financing an expedition to the island.

When the first of April arrived, Nixon wrote Blair asking for a month's extension, but he didn't arrive on Oak Island until early June. He spent the summer boring 14 holes in the Money Pit area.

On September 28 Nixon wrote Blair:

"Drilled [hole] No. 13 and on reaching a depth of 136 feet, drilled through what appeared to be a bulkhead, composed of oak and cement mixture about 14 inches thick. On breaking through this, the tool dropped to 169 feet without touching anything; then I got mud and bits of old oak, which was in such a state of decay that you could rub same into a powder in your fingers. This continued down to 176 feet, where I struck a solid substance [which he later said 'sounded like a hollow drum']. I abandoned the hole and put another one, No. 14, down within a few feet of it and encountered the same as in No. 13, so undoubtedly that is the location of the Money Pit."

These holes presumably were somewhere north of the Chappell

shaft. The report was accompanied by Nixon's promise that he would begin his planned excavation early the following year and that he therefore expected Blair to extend the agreement for another twelve months.

Nixon's drilling results were vaguely suggestive of the cement and wood-lined chamber that had been drilled into in 1897. But Blair was skeptical of Nixon's report, and on October 30 he sent him official notice that their contract was terminated. Nixon threatened legal action to force an extension, but Blair held his ground and the matter was closed.

Apart from his annoyance over Nixon's lack of progress, Blair had another reason to sever the relationship. Waiting in the wings that autumn was Gilbert Dayton Hedden of Chatham, New Jersey, who had the money and determination to take over the project and perhaps see it to its conclusion. His was to prove one of the more significant contributions to the search for pieces of Oak Island's puzzle.

Chapter Thirteen

The sporadic exploration of Oak Island during the first third of the twentieth century added little in the way of new knowledge about how the treasure could be retrieved. However, this period did produce a few more theories on the possible origin of the deposit.

Back in 1909 some of those associated with Henry Bowdoin's expedition believed they were on the trail of the crown jewels of France. The theory is historically untenable, yet it is one that still crops up.

The jewels were supposedly taken by Louis XVI and Marie Antoinette when they fled Paris on June 20, 1791, with the revolutionary mob at their heels. They were captured at Varennes a few days later and finally executed in 1793. According to legend, the crown jewels weren't found in their possession because they had been smuggled from Varennes to the fortress of Louisbourg in Nova Scotia by either a lady-in-waiting or an engineer reputed to have been Marie Antionette's lover. From this legend the suggestion was derived that the jewels were later buried on Oak Island.

The flaw in this enchanting story is that the jewels weren't brought to Varennes. In preparing for their escape, the King and Queen sent 1,500,000 livres (about $3,750,000) in cash and the royal diamonds by special messenger to Brussels. From there they were to be sent on to a contact in Austria, where Louis and Marie had planned to seek eventual refuge. After the royal couple was captured, the money did in fact disappear. But it went into the pockets of various persons in Brussels and Austria. As for the jewels, they were eventually returned to the French government.

The historical confusion entertained by those who developed the crown jewels-Oak Island theory probably relates to the famous "Affair of the Queen's Necklace."

In 1785 Cardinal Louis de Rohan approached a reputable French jeweler and ordered a necklace consisting of 647 diamonds (totaling about 2,800 carats) to be made for Marie Antoinette. It was made and turned over to him. Months later the jeweler approached the Queen and demanded payment for the necklace. She knew nothing about it; the jeweler had been conned. Rohan was questioned, and he said he'd been given the signed order (which was a forgery of the queen's signature) by the Countess de La Motte-Valois. The countess denied it, but in the ensuing trial both she and Rohan were found guilty of fraud and thrown in jail.

The necklace, which today would be worth over $4,000,000, was never found. Accomplices in the scheme probably broke it up later and sold it off in small lots throughout Europe, though that has never been proven.

But any suggestion that it was shipped to connections in Louisbourg and then buried on Oak Island is undermined by the simple fact that by 1785 Louisbourg had long since been in British hands. Also, Oak Island's treasure, whatever it is, was unlikely to have been deposited that late in the province's development.

Other historically related theories were advanced in the 1930's linking Oak Island's secret to the vast fortunes in gold and silver ecclesiastical vessels, plate, and statues that disappeared from England and Scotland during the sixteenth-century Reformation and again in the seventeenth and eighteenth centuries. Fred Blair eventually became more partial to this theory than to his earlier belief in a pirate's cache. Writing in 1930 he stated:

"One of the most reasonable explanations of the treasure is that it is royal and church plate and valuables known to have been removed from England and hidden during the Protectorate of Cromwell (1653-1658) after the execution of Charles I (in 1649). This treasure simply vanished from the face of the earth and has never been recovered. Very probably it now lies buried on Oak Island. If so, its value will far exceed, for archeological and historical purposes, anything in the way of bullion or mere precious metal."

A similar hypothesis held that the Money Pit contained the lost treasure of St. Andrew's Cathedral in Scotland. The abbey's wealth is also thought to have included the great spoils taken by the Scots from the British after the Battle of Bannockburn in 1314. In the late 1800's and early 1900's, several searches were made beneath the ruins of the cathedral itself, and a couple of secret, underground passages were discovered and explored. No treasure vault was found, however, and it was speculated that the riches may have been taken out of Scotland and perhaps even abroad by the monks of the abbey.

Blair received several letters from people who were convinced that this legendary treasure had been transported to Nova Scotia. In February 1938 Oswald L. Holland, a Canadian then living in Britain's Channel Islands, offered to invest in the Oak Island search. He stated flatly that: "priests from the Abbey of St. Andrew's in Scotland took their gold plate and other treasures over to Oak Island in 1745 after the defeat of Prince Charlie at Bannockburn. [He presumably meant Culloden.] Nova Scotia was a wilderness then of course. Do you know I spent over three months at St. Andrew's years ago trying to find out what they had done with the stuff? Their journals were all written in old Latin and it was just fearful to make sense of it, but I got the hang of it at last. The lot that sailed away never got home, so the home lot never had a clue" as to where the treasure was taken.

Gilbert Hedden, who was then in charge of the Oak Island project, discounted this theory as "a bit fantastic" and declined Holland's offer of financial assistance.

In addition to the whodunit theories, several maps allegedly connected with Oak Island were brought to Blair's attention during this period. One persistent story had to do with a mysterious stranger by the name of Captain Allen who turned up in the fishing village of Shad Bay, about fifteen miles east of Mahone Bay, sometime around 1880. According to old-timers in the area, Allen had a southern United States accent and wore a large, white, Stetson hat. On his arrival he purchased a sloop for $1,200 from a local fisherman, hired two men to sail it, and then spent two summers cruising off the coast. He brought with him an old chart that his crewmen said was worded in Swedish or some other foreign language.

Captain Allen's practice on these cruises was to go about thirty or forty miles offshore until he reached a specific latitude and longitude, which he determined by sextant. He would then sail in toward shore on a certain compass bearing that was generally northwest. This always brought him into the mouth of St. Margaret's Bay, the next bay east of Mahone Bay. He told no one what he was up to during those two years. But just before he finally left he confided in a man by the name of Pickles from Halifax. He told him he had been looking for a particular island, the name of which he didn't know, but on which there was buried a huge treasure. He then gave Pickles the latitude and longitude of the starting point, the compass bearing to follow, and a description of the island he had been searching for.

Allen departed for parts unknown, taking his chart with him. Pickles then took up the search, using the information Allen had given him. But he too kept entering St. Margaret's Bay every time and found no island fitting the description of the one he was looking for. But one day he described the mysterious island to a local fisherman by the name of Billy Ball who told Pickles that he knew where just such an island existed. It turned out to be Redmond's Island (now known as Cochran Island) in Shad Bay. Pickles said he'd been told by Allen that the correct island would have three prominent stone piles and an old well on it. The stone piles were found, but not the well. Over the years the island was dug up in several places but no treasure was found.

Redmond's Island is about the same length and width as Oak Island, and it was later speculated that perhaps Oak Island was the one Captain Allen had actually been seeking. In 1937 Gilbert Hedden discovered three rock piles in a straight line and an old well on Oak Island. He also found ashes under one of the rock piles; something that had also been found on Redmond's Island. So he investigated the Captain Allen legend and heard several closely related versions of it from the older people on Shad Bay. Pickles had died several years earlier, and his widow, though she knew the story, had no charts or correspondence of her husband's that would verify it.

Hedden noted that Allen's reported starting point of thirty to forty miles offshore in that area could have positioned him at an exact latitude and longitude of 44° N, 63° W. From there, a precise northwest course (*i.e.,* a true bearing of 315°) would invariably bring him into St. Margaret's Bay. But had Allen's bearing been just a few degrees to the west, his course would have taken him directly into Mahone Bay and Oak Island. Hedden and others wondered if Allen had perhaps made a compass error in adjusting for magnetic variation and had therefore missed his intended target. (This speculation, of course, was based on a supposition that Allen's starting point was one that could be expressed in full degrees, rather than in degrees and minutes, and that his course was an exact northwest bearing.)

Despite the widespread belief in Captain Allen, his chart, and his mysterious search, the whole story may have been pure fabrication woven in the 1880's and retold so often that it became accepted as fact fifty years later. To believe, for instance, that Allen could have spent two years searching for a treasure island in that vicinity and not be aware of the well-known story of the earlier discoveries that had been made on nearby Oak Island is difficult. Yet, according to the story, he never bothered to land on or investigate Oak Island during that whole time. Moreover, the arrival of a chart-wielding stranger in search of buried treasure is a story that appears in the oral history of several other Nova Scotian coastal communities. For example, Clam Harbor, a village thirty miles east of Halifax, has its legend of a mysterious Spaniard who showed up many years ago with a map. He chartered a boat that he sailed alone to an uninhabited island nearby. He is said to have quietly disappeared after allegedly removing the treasure he was seeking.

Nevertheless, there are some modern Oak Island theorists who still accept the tale of Captain Allen, and so-called copies of his chart have been accidentally "discovered" from time to time. One man who has spent years investigating Oak Island from a distance has even "broken the code" contained in the map. This involves a word-number cypher in which Allen's name is conveniently stretched to Captain R. Allen P.O. (for Port Officer) in order to complete the code. (This and other related codes will be discussed later.)

Another report of an Oak Island map originated in Boston in 1930 from James H. Smith. That year he came to Nova Scotia (where he'd been born) with the intention of securing a lease and treasure trove rights on the island. When he discovered that Blair controlled the search rights, he told him that he had once seen a document that could have pertained only to Oak Island. Smith later (January 13, 1931) made the following declaration under oath:

"When I was a boy living at home in Greenfield, County of Colchester, Province of Nova Scotia, in the Dominion of Canada, I frequently heard my father John J. Smith, speak of a chart, memorandum, or paper, then in possession of his father, Amos Smith, who lived in Shaw's Cove, County of Halifax, in the said Province of Nova Scotia.

"It was said by my father, John J. Smith, that the said chart or memorandum had reference to the burial of a quantity of gold on an island in Chester Basin in the said Province of Nova Scotia, and that my grandfather, the said Amos Smith, who had been a [maritime] pilot working in and out of Halifax harbor, claimed that the longitude and latitude given in said memorandum was in the vicinity of the entrance to said Chester Basin, and that the island described in the said memorandum was Oak Island, located in the said basin.

"I heard so much talk about this chart or memorandum that as I became older I determined to see and examine it personally, and to that end I went to the home of my grandfather where I did see and examine the memorandum and did read and study its contents most carefully.

"According to the best of my recollection and belief, the said memorandum told of the burial of a quantity of gold on an island located near a definitely stated longitude and latitude, the figures of which I do not now remember. It stated that the island was about one mile in length and about one-half mile in width, was similar to a bottle in shape, two coves at the northeast end forming the bottleneck; and the island was wooded with oak trees. The memorandum then stated that on a hill between the two coves, a pit was dug to a depth of 165 feet, near a large oak tree from a limb of which they hung a block and tackle; that a vault was constructed at the bottom of the pit, and the vault was walled with granite stone eighteen inches thick, and that the inside was lined with two ply of lead one-half inch thick. The vault was filled with gold bars, each four feet long and four inches square, and it was then covered with granite slabs. Two tunnels were dug forty-five feet below sea level at low tide, leading from the pit to the shore in opposite directions, and there was placed in each tunnel an iron gate arranged so as to stop the flow of water, but these gates were left open to permit the water to flow through.

"The memorandum was inadvertently destroyed with other old papers, the property of the said Amos Smith, after his decease."

Smith's father, John J. Smith, also signed an affidavit attesting to the story and added: "The memorandum recited that it was written or prepared by a person who had assisted in the burial of the gold. It was an old paper, and at this date I am unable to remember how it came into the possession of my father, the said Amos Smith."

Subsequent investigation disclosed that there was an Amos Smith who had worked as a pilot out of St. Margaret's Bay in the 1860's. But Blair suspected that the document Amos Smith had shown his son and grandson was probably something drawn up either by him or someone else familiar with the discoveries that had been made by the early Oak Island searchers.

In December 1934 Blair heard of yet another Oak Island map. W.J. Doyle of Cabri, Saskatchewan, wrote Blair and told him that a treasure map had been given to his father some fifty years earlier and that it was later passed on to him. He said the chart had subsequently been lost in a fire in 1905 but that he still remembered every detail on it, including the secret to blocking off the water tunnels from the sea. Doyle claimed that the map had been marked Oak Island but that he hadn't any idea where the island was until he'd read about Blair's search operations in an article that appeared in *Maclean's* magazine in June 1931.

Doyle didn't explain why he had waited three and a half years to bring the map to Blair's attention. But he told him: "With the knowledge I have and if it can be applied, the water can be shut off inside of two or three weeks, or maybe a little longer; as I have never been there I cannot say, but I am satisfied I can shut off the water and take out the treasure quicker and with less expense than any other man alive."

The following summer Doyle traveled to Nova Scotia where he met Blair and disclosed the particulars of the chart. Blair wrote the following account of that meeting:

"Memorandum of remarks made by W.J. Doyle to F.L. Blair on Monday, June 3rd, 1935, at Amherst, N.S., with reference to a drawing or plan which he stated was given to his father by an old sailor named Jim Thompson, between the years 1884 and 1888.

"The plan was marked 'Oak Island' and showed three pits, one at the shore about 80 or 90 feet deep, one on the hill about 470 or 480 feet distant and 176 feet deep, the third between the two first mentioned and about 270 or 280 feet from the shore and 125 feet deep.

"There appeared to be an excavation or sort of basin along the shore for about 40 feet. The plan showed that this basin had been filled with rocks and it was marked 'rocks and cocoanut.'

"The drawing showed a sort of dome at the bottom of the shore pit, and a tunnel running downward from the bottom through the center pit and into the main pit at about 130 feet. This tunnel ran northeast and southwest, the main pit lying southwest of the shore pit.

"A gate was shown in the tunnel a few feet from the dome at bottom of shore pit. A second gate was shown in center pit so rigged as to act like a clapper, allowing the water to pass inward from the shore, but not outward. The drawing showed that this gate could be closed by the pull of a chain which extended from the gate part way up the pit. It was arranged with two hooks, an iron bar, links of chain and a ball or weight, so that when dropped by the pull of the chain, the hooks would catch under the bar of iron and keep the gate closed.

"Logs or timber were shown about six feet from the surface in this pit, and a fill above.

"A second tunnel was shown leaving the main tunnel after it passed through the center pit, and it dipped and entered the main pit at 176 feet. There were also two other inlet tunnels connecting with the main tunnel, but the one gate in center pit controlled the whole flow of water. The tunnels were marked 3' x 6'.

"The main pit showed marks of some sort, each 10 feet down to 40 or 50 feet, and a deposit of treasure at about 140 feet, or a short distance below the upper water inlet. The deposit showed a plate of iron, logs and cement in addition to the treasure, which appeared to be in three distinct layers of two feet each. There were two iron plates and as near as he could remember, the cement and perhaps all else was between the two layers of logs and iron plates.

"He was of the opinion that the work was done by forced labor. The plan was exceedingly well done.

"I gathered from Doyle's remarks, coupled with his correspondence, that the two additional tunnels or inlets above mentioned, started from the bottom of the shore pit, one from either side, and taking a circular course connected with the center pit from which there was one outlet only."

Blair suspected that Doyle was putting him on. He found it hard to believe that anyone could have remembered such exact details and measurements over a period of thirty years. Moreover, many of the facts and figures conformed with what had been written in *Maclean's* magazine in 1931. Blair therefore concluded that Doyle had combined information gleaned from that article together with an imagined floodgate to recreate a map that probably never existed.

Doyle was persistent, however, and over the next few years he continued to write Blair and others involved in the search, urging them to pay his fare out to Nova Scotia so that he could show them how to recover the treasure. He finally gave up writing in 1939, but not before informing the Oak Island treasure hunters that with his knowledge they could have found "three or four carloads of silver" and "some crown jewels" to boot.

The Captain Allen, Smith, and Doyle maps all had the common feature of no longer existing other than as legend or in the memories of their promoters. But Gilbert Hedden was soon to discover a copy of a chart bearing some remarkable similarities to Oak Island. To this day, the origin and characteristics of this controversial map have never been satisfactorily explained.

Chapter Fourteen

In 1934 Gilbert Hedden of Chatham, New Jersey, decided to fulfill an ambition he'd had for six years—to go to Nova Scotia and solve the mystery of Oak Island.

The bug had bitten him in the spring of 1928 while he was browsing through the magazine section of the Sunday *New York Times* and came across an article on the famous treasure hunt. He wasn't halfway through it before he became convinced that, given the time and the money, he could, through sound engineering principles, find out what lay at the bottom of the Money Pit. At that time he was a thirty-one-year-old Vice President and General Manager of his father's steel-fabricating business, Hedden Iron Construction Company of Hillside, New Jersey. Though not a qualified engineer, he had spent two years studying civil engineering at the Rensselaer Polytechnic Institute in Troy, New York.

In 1931 the family business was sold to Bethlehem Steel Company. Hedden became plant manager of that company's Hedden Division. Within two years he left, sold life insurance for a while, and then established a Cadillac and Oldsmobile dealership in nearby Morristown, New Jersey. He also served as mayor of Chatham from 1934 to 1938.

The sale of his father's company had left Hedden fairly well off, and in 1934 he found himself with the requisite capital and free time to pursue his Oak Island goal. That fall he traveled to Nova Scotia and met Blair, who was then terminating his unproductive alliance with Thomas Nixon. Blair was impressed with Hedden's sincerity, engineering background, and—most of all—by the fact that he was self-financed. Hedden assured Blair that he would solve the riddle within two years and that he was prepared to spend up to $100,000 to do it.

Hedden had hoped to begin work the following spring, but this schedule was upset by Blair's inability to secure the surface rights on the eastern end of the island. Blair had maintained his lease of the area for thirty years until the death of the owner, Sophia Sellers, in 1931. The property was then jointly inherited by her three grown children and nine grandchildren. None of them were living on or farming the island in 1935, but they refused to make any sort of lease arrangment with Blair or Hedden as they had done in the case of Steward and Nixon in 1932 and 1934.

The reason was simple. Although Hedden had tried to keep a low profile, the word got out in the winter of 1934–35 that "a millionaire from the States" was coming up to dig on the island. The Sellers heirs felt that their own potential Oak Island "treasure" lay in the sale of the property. So instead of leasing the Money Pit area, they offered to sell all of their island lots for $5,500. This was more than ten times the appraised value of the property. Blair declined to pay what he termed their "fancy price," and instead tried another approach.

In April 1935 he had a friend in the Nova Scotia provincial legislature introduce a bill seeking to place treasure trove licenses under the province's Mines Act. This in effect would allow someone holding such a license (as Blair did) to search for treasure on private land owned by another party. Should the license-holder be unable to reach an agreement with the owner of the land, he could apply to the Provincial Secretary for an arbitration hearing on the matter. The Secretary would have the power to allow the license-holder to proceed with the search and would also determine what compensation should be paid to the landowner.

After weeks of debate, the bill was voted down in committee (although it was eventually enacted in 1950), and Blair went back to negotiating with the Oak Island owners. But they were still interested only in selling, rather than leasing, the property. Hedden eventually gave in, and on July 26 he purchased the east end of the island for $5,000. The title was put under the name of a New Jersey lawyer, George W. Grimm, acting as Hedden's trustee.

By then it was too late in the season to begin digging, so Hedden spent the remainder of the year preparing for the following spring. A survey of the island was made by S. Edgar March; electricity was again brought to the island via an underwater cable; a wharf was built at Smith's Cove; and a house was erected several hundred feet north of the Money Pit.

Hedden was a conscientous researcher, and for over a year he had been collecting all the data he could find pertaining to Oak Island. Much of this he obtained from Blair's files and notes, but he also interviewed and corresponded with many others associated with previous search attempts. He compiled all of this information in a 31-page treatise entitled "Investigation of the Legend of Buried Treasure at Oak Island—Nova Scotia." He also collected old surveys and charts and even had aerial photographs taken of the island.

Hedden had originally intended to begin by driving a new shaft down in the Money Pit area. But after conferring with William Chappell in the spring of 1936, he decided to first drain the 1931 Chappell shaft and then explore the adjacent ground by horizontal drilling at various depths in the shaft. This way he hoped to relocate the exact position of the original Money Pit. Blair expressed disappointment over this approach, stating that "there does not appear to be anything very decisive about the work outlined; it being more along the lines of previous operations and open to failure without definite results."

But Hedden had made up his mind, and in April he hired a large drilling contract firm, Sprague & Henwood Inc., of Scranton, Pennsylvania, to carry out the work. Their engineering representative, Frederick R. Krupp, arrived a month later to take charge of operations. (He and his equipment were detained at the border for several days while Canadian customs officials pondered the rules related to an American firm digging for treasure in Canada.) Hedden also purchased a 1,000-gallon-per-minute turbine pump, the largest ever used on the island, to drain the pit. It was fed by 7,500 watts of electric power and proved more than adequate for the job.

Hedden kept a diary recording that summer's work. Some excerpts:

"I arrived on Oak Island May 27, 1936. . . . Put in turbine

pump. Ran the pump two hours and 15 minutes and lowered the water 70 feet in the shaft, which would be 100 feet below the deck head. I observed that when the water was down to [that] level, an old shaft [the Cave-in Pit] was drained also, proving there is some clear passage between [the two]. . . .

" . . . I also noticed that three other old pits are gradually becoming dried out since pumping operations [began]."

During the balance of the summer, the Chappell shaft was cleared and retimbered to its original depth of 163 feet and was then driven down to 168 feet. Some lateral probing was done at various levels, but the only discovery of any consequence was two large oak splinters found several feet to the east at a depth of 147 feet. From their state of decay and the location in which they were found, Hedden believed that "these splinters must be part of a box or of an oak platform of logs which fell to that depth in the collapse" of the Money Pit in 1861.

Hedden concluded that the original Money Pit was probably slightly to the east of the Chappell shaft. He and his crew therefore left off work in September and planned to return the following spring and begin a new shaft in that location. This hole was to be large enough to allow pneumatic drills to be brought down and used for lateral drilling. The drill rods would extend out 20 feet in all directions from the shaft at vertical intervals of 2 feet apart, beginning at the 100-foot level and working as far down as necessary to locate the treasure.

Before leaving the island that summer, Hedden uncovered more coconut fiber 6 feet under the beach at Smith's Cove. He also made two other interesting discoveries.

One Saturday in July, while he was wandering along the beach at Joudrey's Cove on the island's north side, Hedden spotted a large granite rock half buried in the sand. He dug it out and discovered lettering etched into one of its flat surfaces. It bore the Roman numeral II and below that were the letters "GIN" which seemed to form only part of a word, as the rock had obviously been broken from a larger piece. He inquired around and from one of his local workers learned that a huge flat boulder bearing several inscriptions had been seen in that location sometime in the 1920's. It had been dynamited into many pieces and the ground under it excavated for a few feet in the hope that the rock covered a treasure deposit. Nothing had been found, and several of the inscribed pieces had been carried away by curio seekers. But Hedden's interest was particularly aroused when he was told that, although much of the inscription on the boulder had apparently been carved during the nineteenth century, one part of it had contained "strange symbols" which no one at the time could account for.

Hedden set his men to work exploring that part of the shoreline. In the next couple of days two more large rock pieces were discovered, one bearing the letter "W" and the other reading "S.S. Ross 1864." Hedden assumed Ross had been a worker with one of the search groups from the 1860's. (The "GIN" on the first piece may well have been part of the name "McGinnis," as several generations of that family had lived on the island since 1795.)

But then a fourth piece, weighing several hundred pounds, was found buried a few feet below the beach. On one of its flat sides was part of an inscription which was far more weathered than the others and totally unlike them.

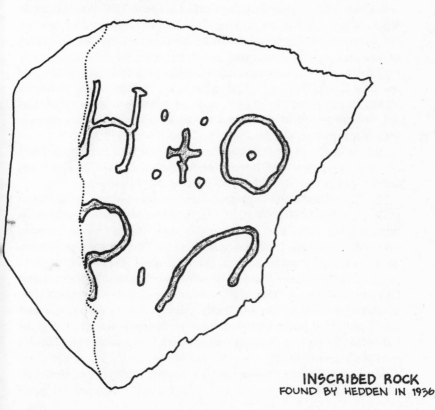

INSCRIBED ROCK
FOUND BY HEDDEN IN 1936

These pieces were rafted around the island to the dock at Smith's Cove and then hauled by a team of horses up to Hedden's cabin. No two of the four slabs, all of which had irregular and jagged edges, fit together, and Hedden realized he was missing many pieces of the original boulder. His workers continued to search, but nothing more was found.

That the symbols predated the discovery of the Money Pit seemed quite possible. And perhaps people finding it later had dug up the boulder and on a whim had added their names to it. Neither Hedden nor anyone else could make any sense of the odd characters, and that piece of rock was left lying in front of his cabin. But in the 1950's and again in the 1970's these symbols were to form part of two unusual theories about the origin of Oak Island.

Hedden's second discovery was less enigmatic, though its true nature remained unclear to him. The remnants of the second cofferdam built by searchers at Smith's Cove in 1866 were still visible at neap tides in 1936. One day Hedden noticed the ends of two large timbers protruding from the rocks inside the dam, and he had his men dig them out. His journal records:

"They were about four feet apart, roughly parallel and were buried under about four feet of sand. The timbers were about 15 inches in diameter at the butt, and were notched for a quarter of the circumference at about every four feet. In each notch was inserted a rather heavy wooden pin. Beside one of them we also found several wooden cross members about four feet long. They had the appearance of having been used as a skid at one time, though nobody at the island had ever heard of them."

Hedden at first believed he'd found an old skidway used by the builders of the 1866 cofferdam. But the fact that wooden pins rather than iron spikes had been used in the construction led him to conclude later that it was much older and that it may well have been part of the original Oak Island project. Hedden's workers dragged the timbers up on shore where they were abandoned and forgotten. Had they been able to excavate past the low-tide mark, they would have realized that what they had found was only one small part of a huge structure built by the island's unknown architects. The rest of this clue was to remain undiscovered under tons of silt until 1970.

After spending the winter with his wife, Marguerite, and their five children in New Jersey, Hedden returned to Oak Island in the spring of 1937. A large labor force was hired, and work began on a new shaft (No. 22). This pit, known as the Hedden shaft, is the only one that remains open in the Money Pit area. It was put down 3 feet to the east of the Chappell shaft (No. 21) and was built 12 feet wide by 24 feet long; large enough to accommodate the lateral drilling program that Hedden planned.

Between May and August it was excavated and strongly cribbed to 125 feet. All the way down it was evident from the disturbed condition of the soil that the workers were in an area that had long been dug up and refilled. But they weren't exactly in the Money Pit. (It was later determined with a fair degree of certainty that the center of the original Money Pit lay about 15 feet north of the north wall of the Chappell shaft and about 10 feet west of the northwest corner of the Hedden shaft.)

Hedden records that the diggers "hit a water course at 93 feet; possibly the collapsed water tunnel designed to flood the treasure tunnel." (A diagram drawn by Hedden shows this tunnel crossing his shaft near its southern end.)

On August 17, 1937, at a depth of 125 feet, work in the shaft was abruptly halted. Hedden had just seen dramatic proof of what many people believe is the key to the riddle of Oak Island. And it had nothing to do with the shaft he'd spent all summer digging.

The events leading up to this discovery actually began two months earlier when Reginald V. Harris, a Halifax lawyer who handled legal matters for both Blair and Hedden, showed the latter a map of an island in a book that had been published that year. It was *Captain Kidd and His Skeleton Island*, written by Harold T. Wilkins of London, England. Harris pointed out that the island depicted in the chart was similar in shape to Oak Island. Hedden picked it up from there.

According to Wilkins' book, the map and three others like it had been found separately hidden in false compartments of three sea chests and a desk. These items were alleged to have once been the property of William Kidd. They had been purchased in the early 1930's by Hubert Palmer, a British antique dealer and collector of pirate relics. He in turn had shown the maps to Wilkins.

The chart in which Hedden was interested bore the legend "W.K. 1669" as well as a series of measurements and compass directions. The island shown had no name; nor were there any longitude and latitude reference points. The body of water around it was simply described as "Mar Del" (sea of?).

After close scrutiny Hedden detected many points of likeness between Oak Island and the Kidd map. These included correct compass rose directions; similar shape and topographical features (Oak Island's two hills and the swamp are shown as "mountains" and a "lagoon"); and offshore soundings and reefs corresponding to those around Oak Island. He also noticed a circled dot in the general area of the Money Pit.

Hedden wrote to Wilkins, informing him of the similarities and asking for more information about the Kidd map. On July 7 Wilkins replied that his map was genuine, but that it hadn't the slightest connection with Oak Island. He said he knew the longitude and latitude of the chart in question and that it was in an eastern sea, on the other side of the world from Oak Island. Moreover, Wilkins assured Hedden that Kidd had never been in the vicinity of Nova Scotia. In a second letter (August 13) Wilkins exhorted Hedden not to "waste any time trying to identify this eastern [hemisphere] island of Kidd with Oak Island."

But Hedden was unconvinced. He felt there were too many points of agreement between Oak Island and Wilkins' map to write it all off as mere coincidence. He then turned his attention to the legend at the bottom of the Kidd map. It read:

18 W and by 7 E on Rock
30 SW 14 N Tree
7 By 8 By 4

Hedden realized that if these directions were at all applicable to Oak Island, there must have been some sort of markers that would tie in with them. He put this question to Blair, who told him about the triangle of stones that had been noticed near the south shore in 1897 and again in 1931. He also told Hedden that he'd once seen a granite boulder with a hole drilled into it somewhere north of the Money Pit.

On August 15 Hedden had his crew make a thorough search for these artifacts. The drilled rock was soon found about 50 feet north of the Money Pit. Then another one was found near the shore at Smith's Cove. In both cases the holes were obviously artificially made and were 2 inches deep by 1¼ inch in diameter.

Amos Nauss, one of Hedden's workers, was sent into the under-brush at the island's southeast end. Nauss, who now lives at Mar-riott's Cove near Chester, recalls: "Hedden gave me some idea that there was something down there at the beach that he wanted to find. So I explored around there with a hoe. I was clawing around and suddenly I hit one rock, then another and another; all in line with each other. So I decided there was something there, and I started clearing it and called Hedden over."

Nauss had found the triangle. It consisted of sixteen beach stones, each about the size of a man's head. The rocks were cov-ered with moss and other vegetation and were half buried in the ground. As the undergrowth was cleared away, the triangle could be seen to be equilateral, being 10 feet long on each side. Its south-ern base line was about 40 feet up from and roughly parallel to the beach. The triangle also had a medial line consisting of eight rocks running from the northern apex stone down through the southern side. It didn't bisect the side but crossed it at a point 4 feet from the western angle and 6 feet from the eastern angle. Be-low this base line was an arc of six stones, which gave the whole thing the appearance of a large sextant.

That evening Hedden called Charles Roper, a Halifax land sur-veyor, and asked him to come out to the island. He and his young assistant arrived the following afternoon. Roper remembers: "Hedden showed us the triangle and the drilled rocks, but he didn't tell us what we were looking for. He just told us to measure the distances and bearings between those three things."

By the next day (August 17) the surveyors established what Hedden had already suspected. The drilled rocks ran on an east-west line and were 415 feet, or almost 25 rods, apart. (One rod equals 16.5 feet.) Using the directions on the Kidd map, Hedden had Roper establish a point along that line that was 18 rods (300 feet) from the westerly drilled rock and 7 rods (115 feet) from the easterly rock. From that position, which was close to the Cave-in Pit, Roper swung his transit 45 degrees, aiming it to the south-west. A distance of 30 rods (495 feet) was chained off along that line. This brought them just below the southerly base line of the stone triangle at a point intersected by the triangle's medial line.

Roper then set up his transit on the medial line itself and sight-ed along it over the center of the triangle's apex stone. After mak-ing a quick calculation for magnetic variation, Roper announced

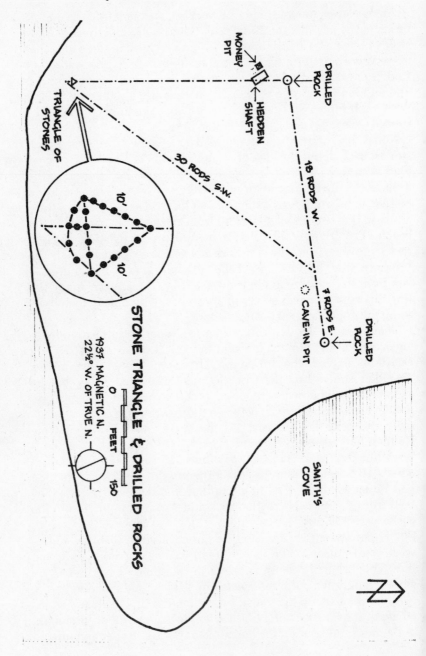

MONEY PIT

DRILLED ROCK

HIDDEN SHAFT

18 RODS W.

30 RODS S.W.

TRIANGLE OF STONES

10'

10'

CAVE-IN PIT

7 RODS E.

DRILLED ROCK

STONE TRIANGLE & DRILLED ROCKS

1937 MAGNETIC N.
22½° W. OF TRUE N.

0   FEET   150

SMITH'S COVE

N

that the line ran exactly true north; i.e., in line with the North Star. Moreover, the extension of that line passed right through Hedden's shaft and the westerly drilled rock.

These findings astounded both Roper and Hedden. Three of the directions on the Kidd map, when interpreted as rods, connected these mysterious island markers. Moreover, the fact that the line running through the triangle pointed to true north and hit the Money Pit area could not be regarded as a coincidence.

However, the direction "14 N Tree" when measured out from the triangle fell many feet short of the Money Pit. From the triangle's apex stone the actual distance to the Money Pit is 300 feet, or 18 rods. Also, nothing could be made of the last line of the legend "7 By 8 By 4." Nevertheless, Hedden had seen enough to convince him that the drilled rocks and the triangle were part of the original work that had been done on the island. And it seemed to him that the Kidd map had a definite connection to the project.

Writing to President Roosevelt on September 1, 1937, Hedden described his discovery of the map and the markers, as well as his previous research, and said these had led him to the following conclusions:

"First, that a large amount of complicated and difficult engineering was done on the site for some purpose a long time ago, probably as early as 1640.

"Second, that Kidd knew of the site and of the work and probably who did it, but was not aware of the exact location.

"Third, that the early legends of the discovery of the shaft, the tunnels, the peculiar fiber, the mysterious stone with the inscription, the objects drilled through in 1850 and 1897, are to a large extent true and can be, in a large part, substantiated today."

FDR sent Hedden a cordial reply, thanking him for the information and saying, "It vividly recalls to my mind our semi-serious, semi-pleasure efforts at Oak Island nearly thirty years ago. I can visualize the theories on which you were working. As I remember it, we also talked of sinking a new shaft on our main run out."

Hedden decided he had to meet Wilkins and see the original map owned by Hubert Palmer. He booked passage on the *Aquitania,* which was leaving New York on November 10, and wrote Palmer and Wilkins that he was coming to England.

He spent the intervening weeks at home in New Jersey poring over histories of Kidd and collecting old navigational charts of

Nova Scotia waters. His studies yielded several interesting points of evidence. He found, for example, that most sixteenth- and seventeenth-century charts referred to the Atlantic Ocean as "Mar Del Nort," and that the words Mar Del didn't appear on any sea in the eastern hemisphere. He also noticed that prior to 1675 (when the Greenwich Royal Observatory was built) longitude was shown as a meridian line measured from zero to 360 degrees east of the island of Ferro (now Hierro) in the Canary Islands. (Longitude today is measured from zero to 180 degrees east or west of Greenwich, England.) Thus, Oak Island's longitude on an ancient chart would be approximately 316° East, instead of its current longitude of 64° 18' West. Hedden therefore wondered if Wilkins, who claimed to know the latitude and longitude of his "skeleton island," was confused as to its real location.

On October 27 Wilkins wrote Hedden telling him that he'd be happy to see him but that it would be a waste of Hedden's time. He said, "When you see the actual Kidd charts, of which mine is an approximate copy, you will have realized that Oak Island and Kidd's island are not identical." This was the first time Wilkins had suggested that the chart in his book was less than authentic or exact. (Hedden should have realized that something was amiss from the fact that the legend and measurements on the map reproduced in the text of Wilkins' book differ from those shown in the book's frontispiece.)

Hedden made the trip anyway. In a letter to his lawyer, Reginald V. Harris, on December 17, he reported the outcome of his investigation:

"Wilkins is a very peculiar character, and it is difficult to describe him adequately. I would say that in appearance and manner of speech he is every bit as crazy as his book would seem to make him.

"He almost immediately admitted that the chart as shown in the Kidd book is simply a figment of his imagination, and apologised sincerely for not being able to tell me [earlier] that it was. I am sure he is getting into a bit of hot water in that regard, as he has received many letters from all over the world in which the writer professes to identify the island and offers to give its location. He admitted my claims to identity far surpassed any others he had received and agreed that his drawing was according to the evidence undoubtedly of Oak Island. When he had submitted his book to the publishers, they demanded that he include some sort of map or chart. He put the request up to Palmer who absolutely refused to permit any of the charts to be reproduced. Wilkins therefore drew the chart as shown, using symbols and marks shown on contemporary charts on file in the British Museum. The only actual marks [from the Palmer charts] were the valley and the lagoon, and he unconsciously made the general shape somewhat the same as the actual Kidd charts. The legend of the directing measurements simply came out of his mind and had no basis in fact at all. Later just before the book was published, it was necessary to make a frontispiece and, not having the first drawing in his possession at the time, Wilkins reproduced it as well as he could from memory, which accounts for the differences between the chart in the book and the one on the front and last page.

"After I had convinced him that I had actually found markers at the points designated in his imaginary directions, he was amazed and went to great lengths to convince me that he had never been in America and had never seen an outline of Oak Island. As he became more and more convinced of the truth and sincerity of my story, Wilkins, and this may be a good commentary on his character and mental capacity, began to be convinced that he was a reincarnation of Kidd or some other pirate and had been selected to disclose the secrets of this long hidden hoard to the modern world. By the time I left, he was completely certain of it."

Harris was horrified by this disclosure and told Hedden: "I have no language adequate to express my opinion of the faker Wilkins. His duplicity in advertising his book by a deliberate fraud should be exposed."

While in England, Hedden also met Palmer and saw the four original charts, which were drawn on old parchment. He noted that all were apparently of the same island; two being simple sketches and the other two bearing various landmarks, and inscriptions showing bearings and directions. These were quite different from the ones used by Wilkins and didn't tie in with the Oak Island markers. Palmer wouldn't allow Hedden to see the latitude and longitude figures on the charts, but Wilkins later gave him the figures "from memory." These placed the island somewhere in the China Sea. Palmer then offered to sell the four maps for $12,000. Hedden wisely declined.

Although Hedden wrote Wilkins off as a fraud, he still believed that Palmer's charts were at least genuine and that they may possibly have had some connection with Oak Island. Several later investigators also have sought to prove a link between those charts and Oak Island.

Following Palmer's death in 1949, the charts were inherited by his nurse-companion, Mrs. Elizabeth Dick. She sold them sometime prior to her own death in 1965, and they are now thought to be somewhere in Canada.

But apart from the fact that these maps almost certainly have no bearing on Oak Island, their very authenticity has been questioned by several experts.

In October 1969 A. Stimson, Curator of Navigation in the Department of Navigation and Astronomy at the National Maritime Museum in England, was asked about the maps by a current Oak Island theorist. Stimson replied:

"I think I should make it clear that I have no confidence in any of these charts being genuine, as they are all modeled on the chart drawn by R.L. Stevenson for his book *Treasure Island* and are part of the romantic pirate tradition.

"It seems remarkable that five chests should turn up in the 1930's, some containing treasure charts, with Kidd's name engraved upon them. It is a well-known fact that a certain Eastbourne dealer at this time could supply 'relics' to order, and it was probably he who provided Mr. Palmer with his Kidd relics."

Stimson also pointed out that the "Miss Pamela Hardy," from whom Palmer supposedly purchased one of the chests containing a Kidd map, is thought to "[be] probably a fictitous character invented by a dealer." And some of the "17th century" artifacts photographed or drawn in Wilkins' book were items that may not have existed until 1800 or later.

(This appraisal of the Kidd charts was restated by Stimson in August 1976.)

Nevertheless, there is still no satisfactory explanation for the similarities between Wilkins' map and Oak Island, especially the three measurements and directions that tied in with the drilled rocks and the triangle. Wilkins (who died in 1958) sent Hedden several rambling letters shortly after the latter's unproductive trip to England. In those letters Wilkins saw himself as an "occult" messenger of Kidd's. Alternatively, he suggested: "In some way I have had an involuntary and even subconscious backward glance at some event in the past, perhaps at an actual chart of Oak Island." While this is not entirely impossible (some people have been known to have accurate flashbacks to periods long before their time), there are other explanations.

One legend holds that in 1912 a map of Oak Island had somehow been found buried on another island in Nova Scotia and that the details of this map were disclosed to Wilkins. He then incorporated the figures onto his own map. But no factual basis has been found for this story.

Another theory is that Wilkins, who did spend most of his life tracking down and examining any treasure maps he heard of, may have at one time seen an ancient map that described but did not name Oak Island. The legend contained on it may have been unconsciously transferred from the storehouse of his mind to the Kidd chart that he invented for his book.

Then again, perhaps the whole thing was just an amazing coincidence. After all, only three out of the seven measurements and bearings tied in with the markers on the island. And even the third, "30 SW," didn't quite hit the triangle but led to a point 10 feet south of its base. (Though, interestingly enough, a line drawn from the center of the Cave-in Pit to the point where the triangle's medial line meets its base is exactly 30 rods to the southwest.)

Of course, one could also argue that Wilkins' subconscious recollection wasn't perfect; that he actually did once see a map pertaining to Oak Island but erred in mentally transcribing some of its directions. For instance, one probable error on Wilkins' part appears in the notation "Lat d.md.," written on his chart. This perhaps should have read "Lat d.ms.," which was sometimes used on seventeenth-century charts to denote degrees and minutes of latitude.

In any case, the most important result of Hedden's experience with Wilkins was the finding of the drilled rocks and triangle. These markers are significant because they were probably made and left there by the designers of the Money Pit. And the fact that the triangle points to true north seems beyond accident and suggests an advanced knowledge of navigation and/or astronomy on the part of those designers.

Ironically, the pointer line's being true north eliminates the possibility of using it to determine the year in which the deposit was made. If the line had originally been laid down on an intended magnetic north heading, the difference between that heading and true north would supply a specific declination figure. And that figure in turn would provide a probable date or dates in which the project had been created, since the difference between true and magnetic north is constantly changing. From 1550 to 1750 magnetic declination in that area moved steadily from approximately 15 degrees west of north to about 12½ degrees west of north. After 1750 it began swinging back toward the west and is currently about 22 degrees west of north. At no recorded period has magnetic declination been zero in this area, so the line must have been shot intentionally off the Pole star. And it was done with a precision duplicated by modern surveyors' instruments.

The triangle has formed the basis of several recent theories about the possible location of Oak Island's treasure. Some of these hypotheses attach great importance to the fact that the pointer line is not a median; that is, it doesn't bisect the base line into equal halves. This approximate 7 degrees difference between the bearing of the pointer line and the line that would form the median has been arbitrarily accepted by some theorists as half the magnetic declination that was applicable to the period in which the triangle was laid down. And a 14 degrees west of north declination occurred twice; once about 1620 and again around 1780.

In recent years a second triangle and several more drilled rocks have been found on the island. As will later be seen, one current group of investigators has incorporated all of these markers into a complex mathematical explanation of who did what on Oak Island.

Chapter Fifteen

Hedden's search agreement with Blair, under which each was entitled to a half share of any treasure recovered, was scheduled to expire at the end of 1937. Before leaving for England to see Wilkins, Hedden had assured Blair and Harris that he planned to renew the contract and resume work the following spring.

But on March 25, 1938, Hedden wrote Harris, informing him that he was planning to expand his New Jersey automobile dealership and that consequently "I shall have to postpone my activities on the Oak Island adventure rather indefinitely." He asked Harris "to correspond with Blair and inform him of the present condition and of the fact that I will be unable to proceed any further this summer and possibly next."

Blair was shocked at the news. In the forty-five years he'd been involved with Oak Island, he believed no one had gotten closer to the solution than had Hedden. Blair was then seventy-one, and he was desperate to see the mystery solved. In an angry letter to Harris, he said that Hedden's decision "is nothing more or less than a downright betrayal, and by a brother Mason at that." (Hedden, Blair, Harris, and several others that have been associated with Oak Island were high-ranking Masons.) But Blair and Harris weren't aware at the time that Hedden, who had already spent $51,400 on his Oak Island search, was in dire financial straits.

Hedden was being sued by the United States Internal Revenue Service for back taxes related to the sale of his father's steel-fabricating business in 1931. Years of litigation followed, and by 1942 Hedden was virtually bankrupt, having been forced by the Treasury Department to sell most of his assets to pay the taxes. The Internal Revenue Service even considered putting Hedden's Oak Island property on the block in 1940. (Hedden had owned the island's eastern end since 1935 and had purchased eight other lots in 1937.) But for jurisdictional reasons and because of the property's limited real-estate value, the government dropped this plan.

Throughout this ordeal Hedden remained hopeful that he would eventually return to Oak Island and finish the work he'd started. He visited the island briefly in the summers of 1938 and 1939 but was unable to return again until 1949. And in the following year he sold the property to another treasure hunter.

However, Hedden did not disassociate himself from the project. As owner of the Money Pit area until 1950 he had a pecuniary stake in anything that might be recovered. The normal arrangement was 40 percent to Blair (who still held the treasure trove license), 30 percent to Hedden, and the remainder to whoever was conducting the actual search.

Hedden retained his ardent interest in the mystery and continued to research and examine all the possible reasons for the construction of the underground workings. Several widely circulated magazines (including the *Saturday Evening Post* and *Popular Science*) published detailed articles on his 1935-37 operations. This publicity and the fact that he had been the owner of the Money Pit for fifteen years resulted in thousands of letters being sent to him from all over the world. Many of these were from people who had theories on how to recover the treasure or on the identity of who put it there in the first place. Hedden answered all of those writers, even the obvious eccentrics, and he built up a voluminous file of correspondence, charts, old records, photographs, and folklore concerning Oak Island.

Of the many suggestions he received concerning the origin of the project, one of the most extraordinary was that the original manuscripts of William Shakespeare, as authored by Francis Bacon, lay beneath Oak Island. This intriguing theory bears some consideration.

The Bacon-wrote-Shakespeare controversy has been alive for almost two hundred years, and approximately four hundred books, pro and con, have been written on the subject. Supporters of the Bacon theory include serious writers, critics, and statesmen— Samuel Taylor Coleridge, Benjamin Disraeli, Oliver Wendell Holmes, and Walt Whitman, to name a few. They, of course, have been vituperatively attacked by equally prominent pro-Shake-spearians.

The Baconians argue that Shakespeare (1564–1616), who left school at the age of thirteen to become a butcher's apprentice and later went on to be a two-bit stage actor, could not possibly have had the vocabulary, wit, and wisdom to write the plays and son-nets that are credited to him. Nor could he have had the legal, medical, historic, and scientific knowledge so abundantly dis-played in those works. Francis Bacon (1561–1626), on the other hand, possessed all of these assets. His books and essays show that he was a gifted writer, philosopher, linguist, lawyer, and scientist.

Bacon was appointed Solicitor-General of the British Crown in 1607 and was made Lord Chancellor and Keeper of The Great Seal ten years later. The Elizabethan court, as Bacon himself remarked, was one in which poetry and the theater were often scorned. Therefore, the custom of persons of noble rank writing under as-sumed names was established. Furthermore, these names were of-ten "borrowed" for a price from real people, such as insignificant writers or actors.

Thus, the Baconians claim that Bacon wrote all of the works at-tributed to Shakespeare and then published the folios under the latter's name. Moreover, some credit Bacon with the authorship of the works of Edmund Spenser, Christopher Marlowe, Robert Bur-ton, and several other less important writers of that era. A few Ba-conians have devoted their lives to detecting and pointing out similarities of thought, style, and actual lines in the works of all these writers, including Shakespeare. In addition, volumes have been written about Bacon's supposed use of complex word-ciphers in these pseudonymous works, whereby he "reveals" his true authorship.

One thing that Shakespeare and the other above-named authors have in common is that none of their manuscripts has ever been found. What happened to those original documents after they left the printers? Why so many manuscripts written by many different people in approximately the same period have all disappeared remains a mystery. (Original manuscripts of other writers of that era are still extant in British museums.)

The Baconian answer to that question was summed up by Dr. Burrell F. Ruth in a lecture to a group of graduate students at Iowa State College on December 3, 1948:

"The person who kept these missing manuscripts, Francis Bacon, prized them very highly. And for good reason; he had written them. But there was even a better reason. Although he had published them either anonymously or under assumed names, he wanted the world some day, perhaps hundreds of years in the future, to recognize him as their author.

"Bacon envisioned a world of the future when mankind would have become good, wars a thing of the past, and scientific development brought to a height such as he describes in his *New Atlantis*. Then, to this world of superhuman beings he intended that someone should present, all at one time, the fully documented positive proof that one single man—himself—had been responsible almost single-handedly for that English renaissance of literature and philosophy we call the Golden Age of Elizabethan Literature. The proof was to have been a great collection of well-preserved manuscripts, just as they had been returned to him by the printer, together with the explanation as to just why he had concealed his abilities under pseudonyms and the names of people either absent from England, dead or near death's door."

Bacon does make several references to the fact that he would be known for who he really was only long after his death. In his will, for example, he states: "For my name and memory, I leave it to men's charitable speeches, and to foreign nations, and to the next ages." (The reference to "foreign nations" is regarded by some Baconians as a clue that the manuscripts weren't hidden anywhere in England.) Following Bacon's death, his chaplain, William Rawley, also hinted that Bacon's true greatness would be revealed at some future time.

Bacon's scientific tracts often dealt with the preservation of books, manuscripts, and other items of value, either by encasement, freezing, or by immersion in mercury. In his book of natural history, *Sylva Sylvarum*, Bacon writes of ". . . bodies put into quick-silver. But then they must be thin; as a leafe, or a peece of Paper, or Parchment." He cites many other examples of storing parchment in mercury. In *Sylva Sylvarum* Bacon also describes the procedure for constructing "artificial springs" using stone, sand, and ferns; a system similar to that found at Smith's Cove.

Baconians are convinced that somewhere there is a secret repository containing all of the missing Elizabethan-period manuscripts. In 1911 Dr. Orville Ward Owen, a prominent American Baconian from Detroit, headed an expedition to the mouth of the Wye River near Gloucester, England, in search of that literary cache. Owen had spent years deciphering codes he claimed to have found in Bacon's works, and it was these that led him to the Wye River. After following certain directions indicated in the codes, Owen and his group sank a caisson into the riverbed and excavated through the silt. They uncovered a room-sized vault made of stone and cement. It was empty, but Owen identified certain markings cut into the walls as having been put there by Bacon.

Owen, who died in 1924, concluded that Bacon had intended to hide the priceless documents in that vault but that he had later changed his mind and sought a more distant and secure location.

In 1920 Burrell Ruth, then a student at Michigan State University, met Dr. Owen and soon became an avid Baconian. Years later, while he was a professor of chemical engineering at Iowa State, in Ames, Iowa, Ruth read about Oak Island and Gilbert Hedden's search in the October 14, 1939, issue of the *Saturday Evening Post*. From the complexity of the engineering work and the fact that a piece of parchment had been brought up from the Money Pit, Ruth concluded that here was the repository Baconians had spent years searching for.

He immediately wrote Hedden a thirty-page letter outlining his belief that below Oak Island was a vault containing the original manuscripts of works credited to Shakespeare and others, and that they were immersed in tons of mercury to protect them against the ravages of time. Hedden's initial reaction was that the idea was interesting, but incredible. Nevertheless, he was curious about a couple of things mentioned in Ruth's letter. In his reply he stated:

"Your prediction that the Money Pit contains mercury is one of the most amazing coincidences I have ever encountered. You can be certain that before sinking nearly a hundred thousand [dollars] in this venture I explored it from every angle. One of these angles was the folklore, superstitions and legends that have surrounded the Pit since 1800. One of the most widespread and persistent of these legends, and one for which I was never able to find the least basis, was the curious belief that the Money Pit contained mercury. I never gave it any serious thought—it seemed too fantastic. But one point in favor of your theory is that there does exist an old dump on the island in which are the remains of thousands of broken pottery flasks. That this dump is very old is supported by the fact that we found nearby an old coin and ivory boatswain's whistle which experts tell us date back to the Elizabethan period."

Ruth's theory was that Bacon, prior to his death in 1626, left instructions with his closest aides describing how and possibly where to conceal his "Shakespearian" and other original manuscripts. Then, perhaps years later, this group chartered a ship on which they loaded cases of paper and parchment. They sailed first to Spain, where they purchased thousands of flasks of mercury, and then to the Canary Islands or the West Indies for coconut fiber. From there they sailed to Nova Scotia and selected Oak Island on which to make their deposit. A vault of oak timber and cement was constructed and placed deep in the Money Pit, cofferdams were erected at Smith's Cove and the South Shore Cove, and tunnels were driven from those points to the Money Pit. The chests of manuscripts were then placed in the vault and covered with liquid mercury. The vault was sealed, the Money Pit refilled, and the cofferdams destroyed to activate the flood trap.

Ruth surmised that the labor had been supplied by the ship's crew who were paid well for their silence. In any case, they would have had no need to know what was in the boxes they deposited in the vault, or exactly where they were in the New World.

There are a couple historical factors that lend some circumstantial support to Ruth's amazing hypothesis.

Bacon and his friends were certainly familiar with that part of the New World. Although there's no evidence that Bacon ever visited the area himself, in 1610 he was among a group of patentees granted colonial lands in Newfoundland by James I. Also, in 1621 the king doled out baronetcies in Nova Scotia to 140 English noblemen, some of whom undoubtedly were friends of Bacon's.

William Rawley, who besides being Bacon's chaplain was also his secretary and most trusted friend, may have organized the transfer of the manuscripts to Nova Scotia. He lived till about

1660 and held all of Bacon's original manuscripts, many of which he sent to the printer long after Bacon's death.

Another possible conspirator was Thomas Bushell, who as a young man assisted Bacon in his scientific experiments. He later became a mining engineer for the English Crown, and was known to be especially adept at recovering ore from flooded Cornish mines.

The Baconian connection to Oak Island might at least explain one part of the island's mystery. Many researchers have felt that whoever made the deposit didn't intend to retrieve it. Surely, so the argument goes, it could have been concealed quite safely for a few years at a more reasonable depth and without the added work of the flood tunnels. This water trap, as hundreds of searchers have found, has made recovery next to impossible. Yet the depositors weren't trying to get rid of whatever the treasure is; otherwise they'd have simply dumped it into the ocean. So it seems they wanted it to be found eventually. Bacon, being a scientist, could foresee the day when modern technology could uncover the cache. In effect, a time capsule had been buried under Oak Island.

Hedden and Dr. Ruth continued to correspond and the former gradually became more impressed with the merits of the Baconian theory. But as a result of his strange experience with the alleged Kidd map in 1937, Hedden still believed that Kidd at least knew something about the Oak Island project. Ruth accepted that Kidd may well have been told about it by a ship's crew member involved in the project and that perhaps he had drawn up a map based on what he'd heard. But he probably didn't know the exact location of the island or the nature of the deposit.

In the early 1940's Hedden also corresponded with and interviewed Orville Owen's daughter, Mrs. Gladys Stewart of Rochester, New York. She had carried on her father's work after his death, and she too became convinced that Oak Island was the site of the Baconian cache.

In the summer of 1952, Thomas P. Leary, a lawyer from Omaha, Nebraska, visited Oak Island while vacationing in Nova Scotia. He was fascinated by the history of the search and, before returning home, he stopped off in New York, where he met Hedden. Leary recalls that he asked Hedden for his views on the origin of the underground workings. Among other possibilities, Hedden mentioned the Baconian theory.

This fired Leary's imagination, and he was soon researching Bacon's life and corresponding with Ruth. He also attempted to establish a link between Bacon and the characters etched on the granite rock that Hedden had found in 1936, as well as the triangle that pointed to the Money Pit.

In a letter to Ruth on August 18, 1952, Leary noted that the "H" symbol on the rock was thought to be derived from Solomon's pillars; the cross was an ancient mark of enlightenment; the circle with the dot in its center was the alchemists' symbol for gold and was derived from its ancient representation of the sun, or light; the triangle was the alchemists' sign for water, and had been used by the Greek biographer Plutarch to represent the Plain of Truth. Bacon would certainly have been familiar with all of these symbols and their origins.

Leary and Ruth saw several interpretations that could be drawn from these symbols, such as the triangle directly pointing toward the "truth" or "knowledge" that lay beneath the Money Pit. But nothing could be established that would conclusively identify Bacon as the designer of the project. (In 1953 Leary wrote, hand-set, and printed one hundred copies of a 36-page booklet entitled "The Oak Island Enigma." In it he gave a short history of the Oak Island search and then offered his arguments for the possible Baconian connection.)

Before his death in 1954, Ruth sent all of the particulars of the Oak Island story to the Francis Bacon Society in England. The Society considered sponsoring its own exploration of Oak Island, but for various reasons this was never carried out.

Hedden, in his later years, accepted the Baconian theory as one of the more probable explanations for the Oak Island mystery. He hinted as much in a letter to Robert Gay, another Nova Scotia treasure hunter, on May 14, 1967. In it Hedden says: "I date the original work as about 1630 and I am convinced that the engineer who made the original layout had no intention of making a recovery in his lifetime, but intended to leave it for future generations."

Hedden's wife, Marguerite, confirms that "Gilbert was willing to believe [the Bacon manuscripts] might well have been in the pit; he knew it had to be something precious because of the engineering job that was done there."

In September of 1974 Gilbert Hedden died without having

learned the answer to the mystery he'd lived with for over forty years. But his discoveries on the island and his patient research were significant contributions left for other investigators to re-examine and apply to their own particular Oak Island quests and theories.

Chapter Sixteen

The next person to take over operations was Erwin H. Hamilton, a professor of mechanical engineering at New York University. He had gotten in touch with Blair back in 1935 but was informed that Hedden owned the Money Pit area and had exclusive rights to the search under Blair's treasure trove license.

When Hedden was forced to drop out in the spring of 1938, Hamilton offered to take over his project. Hedden readily agreed and suggested a three-way split on any treasure recovered. Blair, who under all his previous arrangements had been entitled to a one-half share, balked at this proposal and argued that Hamilton's cut should be taken out of Hedden's half. After a couple of months of negotiations, a compromise was reached whereby Hedden and Hamilton were each entitled to 30 percent and Blair would get the remaining 40 percent.

Hamilton spent the next five summers and $58,000 carrying out a two-pronged investigation of Oak Island. The first involved deepening and drilling into the sides of the Hedden shaft, and the second consisted of locating, recribbing, and charting the maze of unrecorded tunnels that had been dug by searchers in the 1860's.

Hamilton contracted with Sprague & Henwood to continue the drilling program they'd started under Hedden. In the summer of 1938 a total of 58 holes were bored horizontally from various levels in the Hedden shaft (No. 22). Several of the probes from 119 feet encountered decayed oak just north of the Chappell shaft (No. 21). They concluded that the wood was from the cribbing put down in the Money Pit by searchers in the mid-1800's. If so, this confirmed the location of the original pit.

The following summer Hamilton employed eleven men (at a wage of 40 cents an hour) to retimber the Chappell shaft, which had settled and was twisted out of alignment. To further investigate the assumed center of the Money Pit, Hamilton drove a tunnel through the northeast corner of the Hedden shaft at a point 117 feet down. This 4-foot by 5½-foot tunnel ran westward for 21 feet and was then turned 90 degrees toward the north side of the Chappell shaft. After another 10 feet of digging, it was abandoned. The workers found nothing, other than the fact that much of the tunnel ran through previously worked soil.

Over the next couple summers, Hamilton's work included deepening a 6 by 6-foot portion of the west side of the Hedden shaft, which was 125 feet deep. This section went down to 168 feet, or the same depth as the Chappell pit. At the 157-foot level the diggers encountered and explored the semicircular tunnel that Chappell had run from his shaft in 1931.

Further drilling was done from the bottom of the lower section of the Hedden shaft. These probes struck a large quantity of gravel and other rocks 190 feet down in the area between the two shafts. Hamilton noted that these rocks were foreign to the soil at this depth and that only limestone and anhydrite should have been encountered.

The Chappell shaft was then deepened to 176 feet, at which level the clay ended and a thick layer of limestone was found. From there drill probes went down to below 200 feet, passing through bedrock. In a couple of instances chips of oak were brought up from below bedrock, the first time any evidence of previous work had been found that far down. And the work, as recent drilling has shown, was definitely original.

During these operations the large electric pump (which Hamilton had purchased from Hedden) was constantly running and was able to contain the large flow of seawater. In a letter to President Roosevelt on November 4, 1938, Hamilton stated that "our measurements this past summer showed approximately 800 gallons per minute" entering the Hedden shaft. (If Hamilton wasn't exaggerating, this would have been about a 50 percent greater flow than other searchers had encountered.)

Amos Nauss, who worked for both Hedden and Hamilton, recalls that: "When we were down there, there was always salt water coming in. But we couldn't find where it was coming from. We never saw the flood tunnels. But some of it was coming in from somewhere further down from where we were at 176 feet" in the Chappell shaft.

Nauss says that Hamilton conducted a dye test, similar to the one in 1898, in an attempt to trace the source of the flooding. As he remembers it, the dye was put into both shafts "and it came out on the southeast side of the island, about 100 yards out from high tide. We took my boat out to it and we could see the dye coming up from the bottom of the sea. So we knew there was a connection there with a waterway going through to the Money Pit area."

This indicated that at least one of the inlets to the flooding system was well offshore, even at low tide, and was under about 15 feet of water. But Hamilton rightly concluded that this had not always been the case. Studies done earlier by Hedden and more recently by professional geologists have established that almost all of Oak Island's erosion has taken place on the south shore. The rate is estimated to be about 2 inches a year. Thus, some 50 feet of shoreline has been eaten away in the past three hundred years. Moreover, the sea level in that part of Nova Scotia has risen about 3 feet during that same period.

Therefore, the geological conditions that existed when the island's workings were built were different from today's. How much different would depend on how old the project is.

Hamilton made another interesting discovery with respect to the flooding. When the Chappell shaft was deepened, a small watercourse was struck at 176 feet. Samples of this water were analyzed and found to have a slightly greater specific gravity than the seawater at Smith's Cove. Hamilton had apparently found a small underground stream carrying a mixture of fresh and salt water. This, however, didn't mean that the Money Pit's flood trap was a natural phenomenon, since samples taken from seepage higher up in both pits were analyzed as having the same salinity at the surrounding bay.

Concurrent with his work in the Money Pit area, Hamilton also located and traced a network of tunnels beneath the island that had been dug by the Halifax searchers of the 1860's. It was basically a large triangular system running from the Money Pit to shaft No. 4 near Smith's Cove, southwest around the Cave-in Pit to shaft No. 11, and then back to the Money Pit. The cribbed tunnels were about 100 feet deep near the Money Pit and 80 feet deep near Smith's Cove. He also located an old filled-in shaft (No. 10) near Smith's Cove and found three short tunnels leading from it at depths of between 35 and 45 feet. He dug a shaft (No. 23) from the third tunnel to a depth of 63 feet from the surface.

Hamilton's explorations ended in 1942 when, because of the war, he found it next to impossible to obtain labor. The following summer the shafts at the Money Pit and Smith's Cove were decked over and the equipment was transported to the mainland.

Hamilton then went into a boat-building business with Amos Nauss at Marriott's Cove, and lived there until his death in 1969. According to Nauss, Hamilton remained convinced that a treasure had been buried somewhere under Oak Island, his favorite theory being that it consisted of gold from a French pay ship destined for Louisbourg.

Like Hedden, Hamilton kept President Roosevelt informed on the progress he was making on the island. And FDR appeared to be genuinely interested in those reports. On August 31, 1938, for example, Roosevelt wrote Hamilton:

"Your note came while I was on my cruise in the Pacific. I wish much I could have gone up the Coast this summer and visited Oak Island and seen the work you are doing — for I shall always be interested in that romantic spot. I hope that you will let me know how you have been getting on with modern methods — ours were, I fear, somewhat antiquated when we were there more than a quarter of a century ago."

The following August the President made tentative plans to visit the island while aboard a United States Navy cruiser that had stopped briefly at Halifax. However, according to a letter to his friend Duncan Harris (August 24, 1939), news of the imminent outbreak of war in Europe "made it impossible."

(Hamilton had been eagerly looking forward to this visit and had even built a sedan chair to carry FDR from the Smith's Cove dock to the digging site.)

The President wasn't the only head of state aware of Oak Island. Hedden, knowing that King George VI was scheduled to visit Canada and later confer with Roosevelt in June of 1939, had previously written His Majesty and filled him in on the history of the search. Hedden was thanked for this information by the King's Royal Secretary. (Hedden's idea, apparently, was to make sure King George wouldn't be at a loss for words should Roosevelt suddenly switch the conversation from the deteriorating European situation to Oak Island.)

Hedden also corresponded with lesser luminaries such as Vincent Astor and Admiral Richard Byrd, both of whom were fascinated by the story of Oak Island and had considered taking part in the project.

In 1940 an approach was also made by the actor Errol Flynn to take over the search. Flynn had previously financed two unsuccessful treasure hunts in Alaska and the Caribbean, and he became interested in Oak Island after reading about Hedden's work. However, his enthusiasm waned when he learned that the search rights were already controlled by Hamilton.

After Hamilton gave up in 1942, a long period followed in which little effort was made to solve the mystery, one reason being that would-be searchers found it difficult to obtain an agreement that was satisfactory to both Hedden and Blair.

In 1944 Blair's treasure trove license expired, but he was easily able to renew it with the Nova Scotia government for a further five years. That same year Hedden transferred his Oak Island property to his own name (the title had been in the name of his attorney, George Grimm) and began searching for someone who was willing to replace Hamilton on the site.

One prospect was Anthony Belfiglio, an engineer from Toronto who said he had backers willing to put $50,000 into the search. During his negotiations with Hedden in 1945–46 he offered to buy the land in the immediate Money Pit area for $15,000. But Hedden informed him that he would either have to purchase all of his Oak Island lots for $25,000, or else lease the property on an annual basis. The negotiations soon broke down.

In May of 1946 Oak Island's briefest search attempt ever was made by Nathan Lindenbaum, a twenty-six-year-old G.I. from New York. He arrived unannounced with a pick and shovel and an "Oak Island treasure map" that he'd purchased for $125 at a New York City radio-station auction. After scooping up a few shovelfuls of earth, he terminated his treasure-hunting career and headed back home.

Hedden was approached later that year by Edward Reichert, a Broadway stage singer who wanted to lease the east end of the island and conduct a search. He claimed to have no less than $150,000 in financial support from unnamed backers. Hedden tentatively agreed, and Reichert went to Nova Scotia the following May to meet with Blair and look over the island.

Reichert's plan was to use large steam shovels that would excavate a hole 80 feet in diameter and 200 or more feet deep in the Money Pit area. While in Halifax he made arrangements to rent the required digging equipment at a cost of $4,500 a month. He estimated that the project would take him no more than ten months to complete and that his approach would meet with "absolute success."

But that summer, after he'd stirred up considerable newspaper interest in his proposed venture, Reichert vanished. Hedden spent several months trying to contact him and finally wrote him off as "just another crackpot."

Reichert surfaced a year later in Milwaukee. He wrote Blair, explaining that his original backers had changed their minds, but that he now had another group willing to finance his scheme.

By then, however, Hedden had found a new candidate, Colonel H.A. Gardner, a retired army officer from Arlington, Virginia. Gardner had visited the island briefly in the summer of 1947 and that September went to see Hedden with a unique proposal for locating the treasure. It involved using a portable radar scanner, which had been developed during the war. His plan was to take it into the various shafts and tunnels under the island and use it to locate any original tunnels or chambers that might lie nearby. Hedden was impressed with the idea and was willing to lease the property to Gardner and claim only 10 percent of any treasure that might be found.

But when Gardner learned that Blair controlled the treasure trove license he began to lose interest. The reason was that, ever since the end of the Hamilton expedition, Blair had been insisting on receiving a 50-percent share of potential treasure. This was a sore point with Hedden, who felt that Blair's demand had been part of the reason why earlier applicants were unable to retain the support of their prospective backers. As Hedden put it: "The present status seems to be a stalemate situation. I own the property rights and Blair owns the treasure trove rights. Neither can proceed without the other, and Blair sticks to his 50% [demand] thereby scaring away all ventures of any kind."

Hedden and Gardner continued to negotiate, leaving Blair out of the picture. Eventually a solution of sorts was reached. Hedden decided to sell his Oak Island property to Gardner for a small down payment with the balance to be paid over several years. Gardner then planned to go to the island and do some exploratory work with his radar equipment. He believed that if he located anything of interest, he'd be in a better position to reach an equitable agreement with Blair.

He made the trip in July of 1948, but after several weeks of tests he found that the equipment wasn't working properly. He returned to Arlington with the intention of adjusting it and trying again the following summer.

Blair was furious when he learned that someone was conducting a search without his knowledge or permission. He got in touch with Gardner and was surprised to find out that he had purchased Hedden's land on Oak Island. Hedden had kept the transaction quiet, assuming that Gardner wanted it that way.

But the situation never came to a head, because Gardner died the following January and his widow canceled the purchase agreement. Hedden was again the owner of the Money Pit. However, within a few months he was approached by another prospective buyer, John Whitney Lewis of New York.

Lewis was a sixty-year-old mining and petroleum engineer who was then working as a consultant to several oil companies operating in Latin America. In January of 1950 he happened to see a reference to Oak Island in the letters column of *Newsweek* magazine, and it sparked his interest.

The letter was from J.E. Fraser, the son of Samuel Fraser who had been associated with the search in the mid-1800's. Fraser had written the magazine (which had run an article about the island a few weeks earlier) to say that he had figured out that the pirate Blackbeard (Edward Teach?) had buried his gold on Oak Island between 1716 and 1718. Moreover, he stated that the treasure lay in a 6 by 6½-foot vault 160 feet down in the Money Pit. (He seems to have based this on his knowledge of the 1897 drilling results.)

Lewis wrote Fraser, seeking further information about the island, and asked whom he should contact with respect to joining the search. In his letter, Lewis said: "I am a mining engineer and am, to a certain extent, familiar with the geophysical methods used in both mining and petroleum exploration. I have always felt that the exact positions of the passages which connect the sea with the shaft could be determined by these methods. If this could be done, the blocking of the passages and the dry mining of the shaft and other excavations would not be too complicated or expensive."

Lewis also informed Fraser that he was a member of the Explorers Club in New York and that he might be able to interest members of that group in backing an Oak Island expedition.

Fraser put Lewis in touch with Hedden and on May 12, 1950, Lewis purchased Hedden's Oak Island lots for $6,000. He then flew up to Nova Scotia to prepare for his planned assault on the island, unaware that Blair had little intention of allowing him to proceed.

When Lewis bought the property Hedden informed him, quite correctly, that Blair's treasure trove license had expired on June 30, 1949, and that as far as he knew, it hadn't been renewed. Hedden suggested that Lewis apply for his own license, thereby avoiding the difficulties inherent in one person's holding the license and another's owning the land.

But on May 27, 1950, Lewis was advised by Blair's attorney, R.V. Harris, that Blair "has an agreement with the Government for a period of five years, under which he may search for treasure on Oak Island." Blair, according to Lewis, stated the same thing to him on June 30. Harris and Blair were stretching things a bit, for Blair had only applied for, not received, a new license. This was granted to him on July 14, 1950, for a period of five years.

Blair had meanwhile contracted with Mel Chappell of Sydney, Nova Scotia, to take over the search operations. Chappell, as a result of his own work on the island in 1931 and his father's findings in 1897, was determined to locate that elusive treasure. But he couldn't begin work until the Blair-Lewis conflict was resolved; Blair wouldn't allow Lewis to dig, and Lewis wouldn't allow Blair or his representatives to trespass on his property.

Lewis' fate was sealed by the enactment that year of a new treasure trove Act by the Nova Scotia legislature. It had been influenced in part by the lobbying of Chappell and Blair.

Under this Act, holders of treasure trove licenses could apply for "special" licenses to be used in cases where the licensee was unable to secure permission to search on another person's property. The special license granted its holder the right of trespass, providing the owner of the land was paid for any damages to his property. This in effect gave treasure hunters the same rights that mineral prospectors had under the province's Mines Act.

In October 1950 Blair applied for a special license. His application was immediately opposed by Lewis in hearings before the Provincial Secretary. Lewis argued that "misrepresentations" by Blair and Harris had caused him to delay in applying for a normal treasure trove license until September 29, 1950. He claimed that the replacement value of the two 170-foot deep shafts (Nos. 21, 22) on Oak Island would be "at least $160,000" and that "granting Mr. Blair's application, like granting a poaching license, would be the first departure of its kind from common law and accepted conceptions of private rights in the history of the Province and probably in that of the British Empire."

But the appeal was denied, and Blair was granted a special license. Lewis was left with no recourse but to sell the Oak Island property; and he found a ready buyer in Mel Chappell.

On November 27, 1950, the east end of Oak Island and eight other lots (a total of about 56 acres) passed into Chappell's hands.

As Chappell remembers it: "Lewis said to me, 'Look Mel, you might as well buy the darn island from me because I'll never get a chance to work on it now, and I can't stop Blair from going on.' Well, I said, 'If you don't want too much for it, I might consider it.' He said, 'I'll give it to you for just what it cost me.' Which I think he did." Chappell says the price he paid is "a military secret." But if Lewis was dealing off the top of the deck, it presumably was around $6,000.

Four months later, Frederick Blair died at the age of eighty-three. He had been closely associated with the Oak Island search for almost sixty years. But for him it always had been more than just a treasure hunt. It had been an obsession with a riddle whose answer he had once said would be "equaled only by the discovery of King Tutankhamen's tomb."

Blair believed that money, or rather the lack of it, remained the only obstacle between the mystery and its solution. Writing to a prospective searcher in August 1947, he had said:

"Scientific engineering and modern equipment will do the work if properly financed. Previous failures, and there have been many, were due to lack of knowledge of conditions. In other words, they knew nothing of the original work, and in addition they lacked engineering skill and were short on the financial end. Today it is the financial backing we need, not a method of recovery. The latter will come with the former."

Blair's treasure trove license was taken over by Mel Chappell. For the first time both the license and the land were held by the same person. At this point the Oak Island search entered its current phase, with Chappell calling the shots on who could dig for the treasure.

Chapter Seventeen

The shroud of mystery surrounding Oak Island has always extended beyond the frustrating question of the origin of the underground workings. There are many local Nova Scotians who are certain that supernatural forces are at work on the island and that perhaps it is these, not the flood tunnels, that are the true guardians of the treasure. This belief even preceded the discovery of the Money Pit in 1795, which is part of the reason it took the discoverers seven years to find anyone willing to join them in their search.

This sense of foreboding has much to do with the superstitious nature of many Nova Scotians, particularly among the older people. But it is also enforced by certain myths and reported phenomena associated with the island.

One legend that has been around for more than a hundred years is that of the "dog with the fiery eyes." According to some, this creature with its blood-red eyes that glow like hot coals is nothing less than Satan's own watchdog. Others contend that it is the ghost of a ship's mascot left behind by the original depositors. Hannah Dauphinee, who lived on the island in the early 1930's, claimed to have seen it several times lurking around Smith's Cove. Another woman, a relative of Anthony Graves, once was startled by a dog "as big as a colt," which "disappeared into a wall" of solid stone on the north side of the island.

Harris Joudrey, a spry octogenarian who today lives at Martin's Point on the mainland, spent the first ten years of his life on Oak Island. He saw the dog in the summer of 1900 when he was nine years old.

Joudrey recalls that he and a couple of his friends were walking past the Money Pit one evening and " . . . there was a dog sitting at the sill of a door to the boilerhouse. He watched us till we were out of sight. It was a pretty big dog with some black and white on him, and we knew there was no such a dog on the island. He was never seen before and we never saw it again after that. We were scared, I'll tell you."

A variation of the dog as the Money Pit's guardian is a long-standing belief that the spirits of the depositors occasionally appear in the form of crows or blackbirds to check on the progress of the search. But this belief isn't limited to Oak Island, as instances of these birds of omen are commonly found in Nova Scotia folklore. The origin of this superstition dates back to both the French Acadians and the Celtic settlers of the province.

A contemporary investigator of Oak Island is said to have pointed to a particular blackbird sitting on a tree branch on the island and stated, "It comes here every day around this time to watch what we're doing." His listener says he at first thought the person was fooling, " . . . but then I realized he was dead serious."

Another Oak Island specter, this time in the form of an ancient man, was seen in the 1850's by William Graves, a son of Anthony Graves. At the time, William was in his twenties and was dying of consumption. On his deathbed he is reported to have stated: "I am a dying man, and I would not tell a lie about it. I was out in my boat one evening spearing lobster on the north side of the island when I saw the figure of a man sitting beside twin trees [on the shore]. He had long white whiskers. He called to me saying, 'Come here and I will give you all the gold you can carry.' But I was so frightened that I rowed for home as fast as I could."

Other people claim to have heard unexplainable noises on the island, particularly at night. Thomas Nixon, who camped there during his search in the summer of 1934, was sitting in his tent with one of his workers one night when they heard a crash from the direction of the Money Pit. It sounded like planks being dropped, and they suspected someone might be stealing their lumber.

Nixon said the two of them left the tent and circled around to opposite sides of the Money Pit. "Our idea was to hem in whoever was there. We each got to our places and waited but there was nothing to see. But suddenly, right there between the drill and the forge, came the sound as if a man was dropping planks. We heard it again five times altogether than night."

Several weeks later they heard the same thing and again they investigated. But as before, the source of the sound could not be found; nothing existed that could be making it.

Mildred Restall, who lived on the island with her family from 1959 to 1965, acknowledges that the place did become eerie at times. She says: "I was darn scared to go out of the cabin when it was dark. It was always spooky there at night, and when the fellows [her husband and two sons] left me at night to pull up the boat or something, I'd start to chew my fingernails if they weren't back in five minutes."

Mrs. Restall says many of the local mainland people could never understand how she and her family could live alone on the island. One man, Ronald Rafuse, " . . . used to tell us about the strange lights he'd see on the island [from the mainland] when it was foggy. He used to say, 'I wouldn't spend a night on this island for all the treasure that's down there.' And he'd come out a couple of days after there'd been a heavy fog and ask, 'Did you see the lights the other night?' Then he'd describe them to us."

Several people, including a current searcher, Fred Nolan, say they have occasionally heard strange rumblings beneath the island. The Restalls sometimes heard such sounds, though in one particular case they found an explanation. Mrs. Restall recalls, "We were sitting in the cabin one night and heard this 'whumph' noise outside and everything shook. We went outside and found that part of an old [Halifax] tunnel had caved in and left a large depression in the ground."

The mystical oddities in Oak Island's history haven't been limited to reports of strange sights and sounds. There are several instances, for example, of persons having dreams that supposedly would lead them to the treasure.

Amos Nauss of Marriott's Cove remembers one such incident: "The first time I had ever been to Oak Island was when I was 14 years old [in 1911]. The people I was working for at the time, Scottish people, had a house down here. Colonel Miller was the name. They had an old woman who was their cook, and she was a superstitious sort. She had a dream that she knew where the money was buried. But the funny part was that she was never on the island. Yet she drew a map with a pencil showing where we were to land on the island, and the map showed we'd walk up and come to a fence after about 120 feet or something like that, and there'd be a gate in the fence. And we were to go through the gate where there'd be a bunch of scattered trees. Then we were to go down, come back towards the water and there would be two mounds of earth about six feet apart.

"Well, Ernest Miller, Mrs. Miller, her sister, and the old woman and I all went over there, and everything was where she said it would be. It was the same as if she had been there the day before she drew the map. I never got over to this day how she knew all that. She never left the house, and I knew and the Millers knew she was never over on the island.

"Well, I was appointed to dig. It was one of those terrible hot days in July with lots of blackflies. I got down about three and a half or four feet, and I was sweating. But I wasn't supposed to talk. None of us could talk, according to the instructions from the old woman. But I forgot about that and I finally said, 'Look, time for one of you to get down here and shovel.' Well, the old woman got mad when I talked. She said, 'Let's go home, let's go home; it's no use now.' She figured the spell was broken by my talking."

The necessity of maintaining absolute silence while digging up a pirate's treasure is a common superstition. Pirates are traditionally thought to have decapitated or buried alive one of their comrades and left his ghost to protect the treasure. However, the ghost's malevolent power could be released only if someone in the search party broke the requisite silence. The spoken word was also believed to cause the treasure cache to sink farther into the ground and out of reach of the searchers.

Oak Island's folklore contains two suggestions for appeasing the wrath of the guardian ghost: Throw either a live baby or a black person into the Money Pit and the treasure will be found. There's no evidence that these grisly solutions were ever adopted, but they do crop up in local stories.

One concerns the Boogyman of Lunenburg, and is recorded in an 1868 historical essay by E. H. Owen of that town. Owen writes:

"A few years ago while a company was at work on Oak Island, a man was seen wandering about Lunenburg. People said he was on the lookout for a baby to throw down the hole. Someone had dreamt that if a baby were put down the hole alive the treasure would be found. This man was engaged to get one and went about frightening all the little boys and girls wherever he went. A gentleman who was traveling alone through the woods some few miles from the town of Lunenburg met a boy with a fishing rod in his hand. On asking the boy, who seemed somewhat tired, if he would not like to get into his wagon and drive into town, the little fellow gave a yell, dropped his rod and ran into the woods. He [the gentleman] could not understand then, but afterwards found that the boy had taken him for the baby hunter and did not care about being carried away and thrown down a deep hole."

Another tale concerns Daniel Hirtle, who worked for a search group on Oak Island during the 1890's. His daughter, Amanda Hatt, of Western Shore, remembers a strange apparition her father described when she was a young girl:

"One night he got home from working on the island, and he lay down and had a dream where he saw something coming in the sky wrapped up in a blanket with just a head showing. This thing was hanging in the sky above where the causeway to the island is now. My father was excited. He couldn't get it out of his mind; it worried him.

"In this dream he was rowing his dory and this thing came at him right straight through the air. It was a head that seemed to be wrapped up all in a blanket, and it followed him in to shore. He thought there was something to it because he had the same dream three times the same night. The head in the sky told him he should dig in the [Oak Island] swamp; that there was money there, three chests of it. It wasn't where they had been digging [in the Money Pit area] at all. But according to the dream he had to leave one man in the hole and that was supposed to be the colored man, Sam Butler [a descendant of Samuel Ball, a freed slave], who was living on the island at the time. But father said he wouldn't think of leaving a man down in a hole like that. So he never tried to dig the treasure there."

Apart from nocturnal dreams, there are several instances of persons who've had Oak Island-inspired visions.

One case occurred on a winter day in 1940. At that time Jack and Charlotte Adams and two of their children were the only inhabitants of the island, working as caretakers for Hedden and Hamilton. The incident, which involved their four-year-old daughter, Peggy, is still vividly remembered by Mrs. Adams:

"I was in the cabin making a fire on the stove and Peggy had gone out to play. After a while she came running in, and she was crying. She was scared. She said, 'Mommy there's three big men down there' at Smith's Cove. She said, 'There's one sitting on the wharf down there that looks like Luthor,' the big man in the Mandrake [the Magician] comic strip. And she said there's another one with funny looking clothes on and there's another one with a big patch on his eye. She said they were wearing pretty red jackets and had big yellow stripes down their pants.

"About that time Jack came home and I said, 'Jack, there's somebody on the island. Peggy says she's seen men coming up from the shore.' There was snow on the ground. So he went down to the shore but he saw nothing, not even any tracks. But Peggy still said she saw those men; she knew they were there.

"Now, we had never mentioned anything about pirates or the treasure to Peggy, or even that everybody thought the island was haunted long ago. And she was never a child with a big imagination. Never in her life did she say anything like that; she didn't even say anything about any dreams. So it was unusual for her to say that."

The sequel to the story occurred many years later when Mrs. Adams was in Halifax and happened to visit the Citadel Museum. "I went into this one room and it came right to my mind that this was the kind of people Peggy saw that day. It was the same clothes she described." The room she was in contained effigies of eighteenth-century British militia in their red and yellow uniforms.

Peggy, who now has her own family and lives in nearby Bridgewater, still recalls the incident. "There's truth to it; I saw what I saw," she says. "I don't know what it means, but it was the only time something like that ever happened to me."

More recently, an individual associated with the search experienced something even more frightening. He was with another person on the island when he suddenly went into a sort of trance and, according to his companion, "started rolling around and screaming." After he had been calmed down and revived, the individual described how he had just gone through the death of a Spanish monk who had had his throat cut and been entombed in a chamber far beneath the island. He is certain that the killing did take place and that the corpse is still down there.

Incidents such as these can't always be discarded as the product of an imaginative or overwrought mind, for there are many unexplainable instances of persons having the apparent ability to see backward or forward in time. In fact, second sight, or clairvoyance, is a prevalent belief in Nova Scotia, especially among the Cape Breton highlanders for whom it is a part of their Celtic heritage.

One documented example of precognition occurred in 1877 at Mull River, in Cape Breton's Inverness County. It concerns a young man who was walking along a dirt road one night when he saw a large black object hurtling toward him. Its noise and the two streams of white light that radiated from its front terrified him, and he scurried into the brush at the side of the road. As the machine passed by him at great speed he noticed that the bright front lights had become two dim red ones at the rear. He wrote an account of his experience and told others about it. But it wasn't until about thirty years later, when he encountered his first automobile, that he realized what he had seen.

Nova Scotia's most celebrated case of a past event being recreated involves the story of the *Young Teazer*, an American privateer vessel that harassed Nova Scotia shipping and coastal communities during the War of 1812. On the morning of June 27, 1813, the schooner was sighted on the open sea and was pursued by five British warships, which chased her toward Lunenburg harbor. There the *Teazer* ran into heavy gunfire from shore batteries, and she altered her course into Mahone Bay where she hoped to use the light winds, fog, and approaching dusk to her advantage and then hide among the islands. But two of the British ships, the *La Hogue* and the *Orpheus*, spotted her as she was crossing the bay and they began closing in. The *Teazer*'s being outdistanced and captured would have been just a matter of time.

But suddenly there was a terrific explosion, and the *Teazer* went up in a ball of flame. Of her crew of thirty-six only eight survived, and most of those were seriously burned. Frederick Johnson, the *Teazer*'s first lieutenant, had purposely set fire to the ship to prevent her falling into enemy hands. But the fire had apparently gone straight to the ship's powder magazine before the crew could launch the boats or jump overboard.

This dramatic scene, which took place a couple of miles from Oak Island, was witnessed by many people along the shores of the bay. And the shock of the blast, which tore the schooner in two, was felt many miles inland.

Since that time, the *Young Teazer* has reappeared every so often in the form of a burning ghost ship slowly retracing her final voyage across Mahone Bay. The phenomenon has been observed and reported by hundreds of persons living on the shores and islands of the bay. And always the fiery schooner is seen heading east from Lunenburg and then vanishing somewhere in the middle of the bay.

One such sighting occurred around eight thirty at night in September 1967. Two young cousins, Michael Slauenwhite and Wayne Boehner, were at the Martin's River home of Michael's grandmother, Pearl Boehner, when they both noticed a fiery glow out in Mahone Bay. Their grandparents and parents also observed it. Wayne describes what they saw:

"It looked like a big ball of fire the size of a house; like it was a burning house floating on a raft. It was moving slowly toward Chester and it was coming out from between Earnest and Kaulback Islands when we first saw it. We called the rest of the family, and they all saw the same thing. We watched it for about ten minutes before it went out of sight. The next day other people around here said they'd seen it too. There was no report of a ship catching fire or anything that would explain it. It was some strange."

The boys' grandfather, Charles Boehner, told them he had also seen it once before, many years earlier, and that he had known two men who had taken a small boat out into the bay for a closer look. They never came back, and their dory was never found.

There are many others in the area who similarly describe their own sightings of this Mahone Bay equivalent of the *Flying Dutchman*. In one case, a fishing vessel out of Lunenburg happened to be in the path of the phantom ship. The fishermen claim to have heard the screams of the *Teazer*'s crew as the burning schooner approached them. When they tried to dodge it, the privateer altered course and kept coming at them. Finally, just as the fishermen were certain they were going to be engulfed in the flames, the *Teazer* vanished into thin air.

Nova Scotia's folklore is rich with examples of the unexplainable, and Oak Island is therefore an apt setting for the world's greatest treasure mystery.

Yet compared to other treasure islands, Oak Island is not an inherently forbidding place. It is not an isolated tropical isle infested with malaria, snakes, and wild animals, such as the famous Cocos Island treasure site 450 miles off the west coast of Costa Rica. On a warm summer day Oak Island, or at least the three-quarters of it that hasn't been hacked apart by searchers, is an inviting picture of thick stands of evergreens and wild apple trees, fields of raspberry and blueberry bushes, and wildlife consisting of a large variety of birds, rabbits, and even occasional deer. And all of this is surrounded by the normally calm, blue-green water of Mahone Bay.

But at night, or on those days when a thick fog rolls across the bay, or during a severe winter storm when the causeway is almost washed away and foaming breakers lash the shoreline, the island takes on a gloomy and desolate appearance. If one is alone on the island at such a time, he can be easily spooked by the fact that something weird took place at this site several centuries ago; that persons unknown lived here, perhaps for several years, while they created a covert and complex project, the nature of which has still to be fathomed; and that, as many investigators believe, the island contains not just treasure but also the bodies of workers who were killed to guarantee their silence about this secret place. Then even the most hardened realist can appreciate Oak Island's haunting aura.

Chapter Eighteen

Melbourne Russell Chappell, known simply as "M.R." to his friends, had no idea, when he acquired control of Oak Island in 1950, that he'd be chained to it for so long. He was sixty-three then, an age when most men are considering retirement. Today, almost thirty years later, he still hasn't gotten around to considering it. When he isn't putting in a full day's work at his Sydney contracting business, Island Construction Ltd., he'll often be found absorbed in his treasure-hunting avocation.

Chappell's six-foot-three frame and amazing vigor belie his age. But even more disarming is the clarity and accuracy of his memory, especially when he's discussing Oak Island. He is a walking data bank, familiar with everything that has taken place on the island from his father's time in the 1890's to the present. And what is not in his head is tucked away in his voluminous files on the history of the search dating back to 1795.

On his occasional visits to the island, he obviously carries around a cross-sectional view of the place in his mind. He'll point with his cane (his only apparent concession to old age) to a nondescript square yard of ground and tell you "That's where father brought up the piece of parchment in 1897." Then he'll point out the exact location of a long-forgotten filled-in shaft, or show you where a tunnel was dug more than a hundred years ago.

Chappell now leaves it to others, whom he designates, to do the actual search work. But this doesn't free him from the investigation. He receives an unceasing flow of letters concerning Oak Island, and over the years he has weighed and debated thousands of suggestions concerning who engineered the project or how the treasure can be recovered. The ideas pour in from all over the world; they come from scientists, school children, engineers, charlatans, historians, and madmen. And Chappell sends each and every one of them an informative reply, the result of which often locks him into a ping-pong correspondence that can continue for many years.

But he is no fool or kindly old man who answers out of mere politeness. Chappell knows there is always the chance one of his correspondents may actually have the answer, or might at least come up with a practical proposal on how to physically explore the underground workings.

Among these letters have been hundreds of requests for permission to dig up the treasure. But Chappell is obviously selective, for in the past three decades he has allowed fewer than ten individuals or consortiums to try their luck on the island. The current group he's involved with is Triton Alliance Ltd.

The first attempt was made by Chappell himself in 1950. He had heard about a miraculous gold-finding machine that, he was assured, would solve the mystery in no time at all.

The history of this device, which involved the use of photography, goes back to the summer of 1936 when Gilbert Hedden was conducting the search. Hedden was contacted by a man who claimed to possess a "Mineral Wave Ray" that had been invented by Welsford R. Parker, of Windsor, Nova Scotia.

Permission was sought to take the machine on the island in order to locate the treasure. Hedden refused, but the machine owner kept pestering him, even to the point of applying to the Nova Scotia government that November for permission to expropriate Oak Island for a "gold-mining venture." The application was denied.

But a year later Hedden's lawyer, R.V. Harris, happened to run into a legal acquaintance, who had formerly represented the machine owner. He told Harris that he had always doubted the efficacy of his client's invention until one day when he was given a demonstration of it in his office. Harris, writing to Hedden on October 21, 1937, described the experiement:

"The lawyer hid fifty two-dollar bills in a law book on one of the shelves in his law office . . . and allowed [the machine owner] to enter the room and take a photograph of the interior. [The lawyer] gave no indication where the money was deposited. He then changed the bills to the lower left-hand corner of his brief case lying on a chair, and again a second photograph was taken without any knowledge on [the owner's] part as to where the money happened to be. These photographs were taken away and developed and later copies sent to [the lawyer] with rings around the law book and the lower left hand corner of the brief case, indicating where the money had been placed. [The lawyer] was amazed at the results and was converted to a belief in the invention."

The experiment aroused Hedden's interest and he arranged for a similar test of the machine. On the owner's instructions Hedden took a dozen photographs of a bookcase in his New Jersey home. There were at least four hundred books on the shelves, and before taking each photo Hedden placed $200 in cash behind one book and a gold bracelet behind another. The locations of the bills and bracelet were randomly changed before each shot, with Hedden keeping a record of their positions. He then mailed the twelve photos off to the machine owner and waited for the results.

Months passed, and by mid-1938 the owner had sent back nothing other than excuses concerning the machine's temporary malfunction. Still, Hedden granted him the right to spend two weeks on the island that summer to test the apparatus on the site. The owner's group spent one day there and then left, explaining that "further adjustments" were necessary. At that point Hedden wrote the group and their machine off as "a complete and not very clever hoax."

Twelve years later Mel Chappell heard about the Parker Contract Company of Bellville, Ontario, which reportedly had had some success with a mineral-finding machine in the northern part of that province. One of the two principals of the company was Welsford Parker. But Chappell was unaware at the time of Hedden's prior experience.

By 1950 the "Mineral Wave Ray" was a little more sophisticated. It consisted of a black metal box about two feet long into which was crammed an assortment of wires, tubes, and batteries. A sort of camera lens protruded from one end of the box.

To operate it, Parker would put a sample of whatever material he was looking for (gold, silver, uranium, etc.) inside the box, and a photograph of the area being investigated was placed in front of the lens. Then he'd wander around the designated area with the box, waiting for it to emit a signal which would indicate a spot under which there should be more of whatever material had been placed in the machine.

Chappell decided to give it a try, and Parker arrived on the site in December 1950. Within a few days he located a spot about 150 feet north-northwest of the Money Pit and confidently stated that a large deposit of gold lay about 20 feet under the earth.

A 20-ton steam shovel was to be barged out to the island to excavate the area. But 200 yards off Smith's Cove the barge capsized, marking the first of many frustrating setbacks Chappell has faced since he acquired the island. (Fred Blair had long been inured to such adversity. When Chappell called him in Amherst and said "we seem to have had an accident with the shovel," Blair's immediate reply was, "If you tell me it sprouted wings and flew away, I'll believe you, because anything can happen on Oak Island.")

The shovel was eventually salvaged and a pit (No. 24) 30 feet across and 50 feet deep was dug in the spot indicated by Parker. Nothing was found other than the existence of an old shaft (No. 16) on the east side of the pit.

In early 1951 Parker's machine "located" four more treasure deposits in the same general area. This time Chappell brought in a drilling contractor to probe the locations down to about 60 feet. Again the results were negative.

In those few months Chappell spent $35,000 to learn what Hedden had concluded back in 1938—the gold-finder was useless. "I fell for it," Chappell concedes. "It looked possible to me at the time, but it turned out there was nothing to it."

Parker died in 1976. His partner today explains that the machine's failure was due to the simple fact that there is no treasure on Oak Island. As for the fate of the gadget, he says it was "sold down the river" many years ago "because we were afraid of it. We discovered that we held the future of the world with that machine. It was too big for us so we got rid of it." He declines to elaborate on that cryptic remark.

There is another man who claims he "had the only invention that could have unraveled the mystery" of Oak Island. He wrote Chappell several times in the early 1970's seeking to use the device on the island. Chappell, wiser by twenty years and his experience with Parker, politely declined.

This detector consisted of large metal discs that supposedly could locate copper and gold. The inventor says he would often mount the discs on the roof of his car and "pick up ore bodies at least ten miles away while driving down the highway at speeds of up to 60 miles an hour."

Alas, this wonderful machine no longer exists. Its fate is described by its inventor in a letter to this writer on August 21, 1976:

"During my inventing years I had a complete neglect of God, to work for ego and money and buried treasure; the blood of others and the loss of my soul.

"[Last] July 16 at seven in the morning I took my invention and everything pertaining to it to the town dump. I offered it up to God for His praise and glory and I was thanked through prophesy. It was not of Him, because there's no surer way of losing Him than to become rich. As I stood and watched the greatest invention go up in flames, I was proud of my offering; a supreme sort of feeling."

Another inventor in the late 1930's wrote Hedden stating that he owned a "treasure-smelling" machine that he carried in an airplane in order to detect veins of gold in the earth below. He reported that he had recently flown over Oak Island and that the delicate instrument had smashed itself to pieces when it sniffed an incredible hoard of gold in the depths of the island.

More orthodox metal detectors often have been employed on the island. Their usefulness, however, is rather limited in the case of this particular search. They are normally capable of finding either small traces of metal a few feet down, or else large mineral ore anomalies that may be far underground.

In addition, many attempts have been made to locate the island's flooding system, underground chambers, and even the treasure itself by the use of divining rods.

The art of divining or dowsing goes back thousands of years, and is even referred to in the Book of Genesis. It commonly requires the use of some sort of wand or rod, with the hazel twig giving way to metal rods in more recent times. It has been used to locate underground water, minerals, buried treasure, and even, according to some claims, buried bodies and escaped convicts.

Dowsing, because of the many instances of its proven success (particularly in locating water) cannot be dismissed as superstitious nonsense. But no satisfactory scientific explanation has yet been found. It is a gift that only some people have, and the bending or jerking of the rod in their hands may be an involuntary muscle spasm induced by psychogenic forces. Whatever the cause, some particularly gifted dowsers have been employed by mining companies and oil and gas explorers, often as a supplement to normal geologic and seismic testing. Dowsing was also used in Vietnam to locate Viet Cong underground bunkers and tunnels.

On Oak Island, Hedden occasionally amused himself by dowsing the subterranean water-filled tunnels with a supple twig from an apple or peach tree. The twig, held firmly in his hand, would invariably bend downward each time he crossed a tunnel, the position of which he would verify from his records.

Dan Blankenship, a current explorer, also has dowsing abilities. He uses two welding rods held lightly between the thumb and forefinger of each hand and waits for them to be drawn together as if by magnetic attraction. Apart from getting readings over known tunnel locations, Blankenship says he has charted out an "immense" underground system of corridors and flood tunnels. "I wouldn't be surprised," he adds, "if there were a dozen separate flooding systems" feeding into the general Money Pit area.

Blankenship once showed one of his workers how to handle the rods, but didn't tell him the locations he himself had already pinpointed. In almost every case, the other man felt the rods twist in his hands over those exact same spots.

There can be no disputing the ability of certain individuals to dowse with uncanny accuracy over subterranean cavities or watercourses. But those who use the wand (often called a mineral rod) to locate metals in other than their natural state have a far less successful track record. And on Oak Island, where treasure has yet to be brought to the surface as a result of this or any other means, that record is total failure.

Yet many have tried, and have claimed to have dowsed gold, silver, copper, and just about any other mineral in various locations under the island. In the few cases where a pit has been dug on the basis of such findings and nothing has turned up, the diviner's usual defense is that the hole wasn't dug deep enough.

In 1974 a mechanic from Ontario, who'd apparently had some

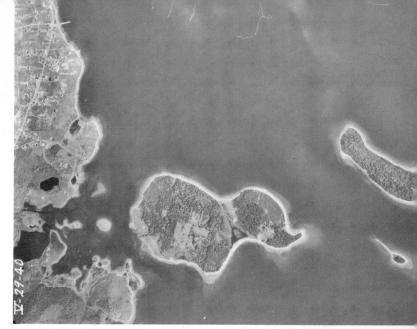

Oak Island from 5,000 feet

Oak Island from the east

The Cave-in Pit—1966

1909 Search Group. Franklin D. Roosevelt is third from right; Captain Henry Bowdoin is at left foreground.

George H. Hill, Jr.

Frederick L. Blair

Inscribed rock found by Gilbert Hedden in 1936

Thomas P. Leary

Gilbert Hedden

Drilled rock found 50 feet north of the Money Pit

M.R. Chappell, 1976

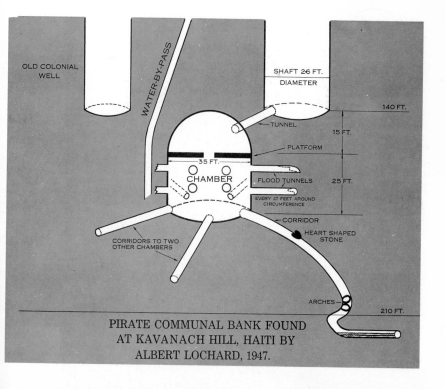

OLD COLONIAL
WELL

WATER-BY-PASS

SHAFT 26 FT.
DIAMETER

140 FT.

TUNNEL

15 FT.

PLATFORM

35 FT.

CHAMBER

FLOOD TUNNELS

25 FT.

EVERY 27 FEET AROUND
CIRCUMFERENCE

CORRIDOR

HEART SHAPED
STONE

CORRIDORS TO TWO
OTHER CHAMBERS

ARCHES

210 FT.

PIRATE COMMUNAL BANK FOUND
AT KAVANACH HILL, HAITI BY
ALBERT LOCHARD, 1947.

The Restall Family, 1964

Robert Dunfield in South Shore Trench, 1965

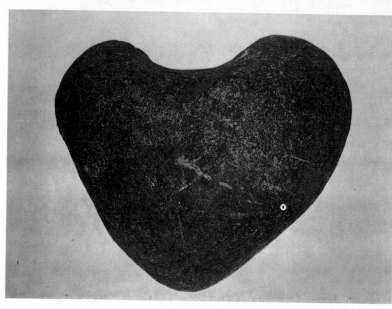

Heart-shaped stone found at Smith's Cove in 1967

Wrought-iron scissors found at Smith's Cove in 1967

Hand-wrought nail and washer found under south store in 1967

Dan Blankenship about to be lowered into borehole 10-X on September 25, 1976. His son, David, is in white t-shirt.

previous success locating ore bodies in Western Canada, was brought out to dowse Oak Island. After spending several days divining, he mapped out his findings. These consisted of fourteen granite and copper-lined chambers far below the surface of the island's eastern end. He also claimed to have located three levels of tunnels connecting these chambers. But nothing turned up in the few areas that were investigated by drilling.

Oak Island has also had its fair share of psychic investigators who go beyond the art of dowsing.

One of the most recent is a construction worker from Huntsville, Texas. In the fall of 1976 he, his wife, and several associates spent a couple of months checking out certain portions of the island. They had been led there by psychic visions the man and his wife experienced earlier that year back in Texas. He says a few friends of theirs have had similar visions pertaining to the island.

In these visions they have taken an eerie trip through tunnels and chambers far below the island's surface where they have seen part of a vast treasure and have been face to face with some of the ghosts of Oak Island.

The core of the workings seems to be a large cavern under the center part of the island, and there are several tunnels leading to it from the nearby swamp. One tunnel also appears to run southeast to the Money Pit, over 800 feet away. "I know for one thing," the man says, "there are going to be some bodies down there. In our visions there are two main exits from the cave and there's a skeleton sitting at each one of them, like guards, and each skeleton has a sword beside it."

He believes that passageways from the cave lead to "two main treasure chambers. And there will be things there that you cannot imagine. There is all kinds of religious material down there and all kinds of documents too. There'll be a blue book found down there with a cross on its cover; I'm sure of that. There'll be chalices and statues, and possibly the Holy Grail. The dates of some of this stuff will go back three thousand years; things that were kept for centuries and then stolen from many parts of the world."

One recurrent apparition he has seen is that of a monk or priest in the underground workings. "When I saw him, he had a hood on that was light tan. I saw him from the back and he had his arms spread open. My wife has seen him too, only in her case the priest was talking to a pirate down in the cave."

Through such mystical revelations he has developed a theory that the Oak Island project was built and used over a period of twenty years or more, sometime between 1550 and 1750. "I think there was a city there at one time; people living above ground and doing their work underground. I'm reasonably sure there were probably as many as 20 or 30 ships there at one time, bringing in the treasures and being refitted."

This man from Texas also believes that the project was religiously inspired; planned by some religious sect that employed pirates to convey these worldwide treasures to the secret repository. Moreover, he's certain there's a "divine reason" why the treasure was deposited on Oak Island and that "it can and will be found only if it is to benefit mankind, and not just to make a few individuals rich."

During their stay in Nova Scotia, the couple and their associates spent every day prowling around the island looking for clues to confirm their psychic findings. The man concedes, "We're considered the local crackpots of Oak Island." But he adds, "We don't care what others think. We can't expect everybody to understand the things we know."

He claims their field work uncovered "a lot of evidence" supporting their theories, including "significant" rock markers, indications that the swamp was once used as a dry dock with iron gates at either end of it, and, by dowsing, the existence of the tunnels and chambers that were revealed in their visions.

Triton Alliance, the current search group, barred him from doing any probing in the Money Pit area or on any of the other lots owned by Mel Chappell. His investigation was therefore limited to the middle portion of the island which is owned by Fred Nolan, an independent searcher. (This may have something to do with the Texan's conviction that all of Oak Island's treasure is in that central area and that the Money Pit is nothing but a decoy.) He hopes someday to interest Nolan in excavating the supposed locations of the treasure vaults.

Some psychics who have never visited the site have disclosed certain things about Oak Island that are known or at least suspected to be true.

Lavern Johnson, a searcher in the 1960's, once showed a chart of the eastern end of the island to an old woman in Western Canada who had a reputation as a clairvoyant. The woman drew a small circle with her finger on a section of the map and stated that a treasure was buried there. The circle centered exactly over the area in which Johnson, by his own calculations, is sure the treasure lies. The woman also described a small gnarled tree that she said stood in a particular spot. Her description of the tree and its location were exact. Johnson, who had approached the psychic experiment somewhat skeptically, is still baffled by the woman's findings. He notes that the details of Oak Island were obviously on his mind while he was with the woman, and wonders if perhaps her insight was the result of telepathic transference.

Oak Island has also been "read" from afar by map dowsers, those who claim to be able to locate buried items simply by concentrating on a chart or aerial photograph of the place in question.

In January 1977 a large chart of the island was "pendulum dowsed" for this writer by Eugenia Macer-Story, a Boston psychic. She used a weight suspended from a string about three inches above the surface of the map. Over certain portions of the chart the pendulum involuntarily swung in a circle. She then double-checked these areas by closing her eyes and slowly running her fingers over the map. In many of the same locations she felt a mild heat transferred from the map to her hand. These she marked as areas of "primary importance."

The chart submitted to her was an accurately scaled outline of the island, with none of the established findings such as the Money Pit included on it. She pinpointed and circled some 30 locations, half of them being described as "items of monetary value" and the others as "target areas of whatever primary importance." Most of the locations were on the island itself, though a few were up to 700 feet offshore.

Many of the onshore targets she circled happen to be sites where previous digging or drilling has brought up some sign (traces of wood or metal) of original work. However, some key locations, including the Money Pit itself, were ignored by her pendulum. Offshore, strong responses were indicated in both Smith's Cove and the South Shore Cove, where two flood tunnels are known to exist. She also received some strong readings from the swamp and Joudrey's Cove, where Nolan has found traces of early work.

Macer-Story made no attempt to guess or divine what the treasure is or who put it there, but simply limited her investigation to the response she got from the pendulum and her own psychic hunches. She is an intelligent and articulate woman who makes no pretense at understanding what this power, which she has had since childhood, is all about. All she knows from years of experience is that she has it.

"Pendulum dowsing," she says, "is a mental skill. I am not sure how or why the weight moves, but it does move independently of any physical impetus if you are doing the concentration correctly. The dowser must empty the mind of everything, including the question just being asked of the pendulum, and operate purely instinctively."

Two months later a copy of the same chart of the island was sent to another psychic, a Detroit restauranteur.

He calls himself a "geopsychic," and claims to have successfully located oil and natural gas deposits in Texas and other United States states by dowsing ordinary road maps with a pendulum. He says some of his findings were later verified by exploratory drilling.

In the case of Oak Island, he "located" eight treasure vaults, all within a radius of 100 feet from the Money Pit and varying in depth from 120 to 260 feet underground. (Some of his vaults can't possibly exist, as drilling and digging have penetrated below many of the spots he selected.)

But his "geopsychic analysis" goes much further than merely pinpointing the positions of the vaults. He says his "readings" show that four of the chambers contain gold and silver, three others are filled with gems and jewels, and the eighth contains documents and historical data. He adds that the total value of the treasure is $105,000,000.

Moreover, he has psychically determined that the Oak Island project was designed by Prussian engineers and then built and used by the Portuguese and the Spaniards over a 150-year period from 1525 to 1675. He also claims that there is a secret room in El Escorial Castle near Madrid that "contains all the records of the engineering, wealth, and history of the Oak Island project."

Naturally, the only sure way to establish the accuracy of gold-finding devices, dowsers, or psychics is to excavate (usually at great expense) the areas in which they "locate" a treasure or some other previously unestablished underground artifact. In the few instances where this has been done, the mystical prognosis has proved to be wrong. But just as there are incompetent engineers, there are undoubtedly incompetent diviners, not to mention outright frauds. Perhaps some psychics who have investigated Oak Island may yet be proven right.

Nevertheless, all the tangible proof of the island's mysterious history has so far resulted from either scientific investigation or accidental discovery. And some of the most significant finds have been made in the past two decades.

Chapter Nineteen

Following his experience with the Parker metal detector in 1950, Mel Chappell decided that he had sunk enough of his own money into the search. As Fred Blair had done before him, he decided to look for others to invest the capital while he would provide access to the island as well as the use of his treasure trove license. Any treasure found would be split equally between Chappell and those financing and carrying out the search.

In the early 1950's several Oak Island articles appeared in United States magazines (including *Life*) and Chappell was subsequently inundated with requests for permission to dig on the island. However, most were from persons who expected Chappell to put up all the money for the search in return for their "valuable" information.

One of these was a farmer from Kansas, who claimed to have inherited a map from his great-grandfather, "the only survivor of the pirate crew who buried the treasure on Oak Island." In the spring of 1954 he advised Chappell that he had the map and a four-hundred-page manuscript (written in longhand) which showed exactly what the treasure was and how to retrieve it. He said the treasure consisted of coins and 800 pounds of jewels that were buried between 1778 and 1787 "on two different islands 11 leagues apart," one of which was Oak Island. The treasure, he stated, was worth some $30,000,000. As an added bonus he also promised to give Chappell "the location of the much sought after jewels of Marie Antoinette. The man who hid her jewels was a member of the Oak Island pirate band."

In another letter the Kansan described the Oak Island burial site and his proposed method of recovery: "In my opinion it will require 120 days and at least $200,000 [to bring up the treasure]. It will be necessary to build a shaft 56 feet in diameter, properly tubed to prevent collapse. When the treasure location was first discovered [in 1795] four men could have recovered it in about 23 days had they but looked around them and followed the diagram found in the Keystone, which was very much in evidence at that time and plainly visible on the surface at a given distance from the original shaft. Now after many attempts and great expense all have proved futile and the location has been butchered and loblollied into a collapsible mess—the water still flows and will continue to do so until the system is understood and staunched. This system is composed of four 33-inch tunnels, each tunnel being 170 feet longer than its mate and each tunnel having five entrances 145 feet wide, each being covered by the sea at normal or high tide and each having a reservoir 32 by 20 by 20 feet, 90 feet below the surface."

Chappell replied that he would be happy to allow the treasure to be recovered, providing the Kansan financed the venture. The farmer, who figured that his knowledge (which seemed to be composed of facts from a recent *Saga* magazine article plus a few personal embellishments) entitled him to a free ride, quickly lost interest, and the matter was dropped.

Others who contacted Chappell had even grander visions of what their information was worth. One person flatly stated that he knew "who made the deposit, when it was made, where it came from, and how to recover it." And, "for 50% of what you recover I will give you the data and will be willing to oversee your work for $100 a day and expenses." A more blatant approach came from someone who claimed to possess "a complete inventory of what is in Oak Island." The list of goodies was offered to Chappell for a mere $5,000.

In other instances Chappell was informed that anything found on the island was not his to keep. A man from New Zealand wrote to say that he and his family were the owners of all the gold buried on Oak Island and that they had "powerful connections in England" who would see to it that the treasure was returned to them. Also, a woman from California wrote to point out that she was a direct descendant of William Kidd's and warned that she would initiate legal proceedings against Chappell as soon as anything was found on the island. Chappell heard nothing more from her after he wrote back stating (incorrectly) that Captain Kidd never had any children.

Some of the most bizarre correspondence Chappell received came during the summer of 1954 from Charles B. Thomas, a retired eighty-year-old real estate salesman who was then living at the YMCA in Great Falls, Montana.

When Thomas first read about Oak Island (in the *Saturday Evening Post*) in 1939, it was immediately clear to him what the mystery was all about. But he was forced by divine circumstances to wait fifteen years before revealing his information. He finally contacted Chappell on May 26, 1954: "My object in writing you is to inform you that I have the diagram that solves the mystery of Oak Island. Let me assure you that the treasure is not a hoard of pirate's gold, but a treasure of far greater value. I have not only the diagram, but the blueprint worked out, that shows the location of the rooms below where a sacred treasure is stored for safekeeping until the due time came for it to be recovered. And the time has come.

"It is my belief, which is based on an accurate knowledge of the divine plan of the ages, that the treasure will consist of a museum that will contain the sacred relics of the typical Kingdom of Israel, the gold and sacred things of the temple of Jerusalem, together with manuscripts and documentary evidence that will throw some light on human history and prevent a fourth world war.

"Divine providence has them stored in the Money Pit for safekeeping until this symbolic four years—1954–1958—when the statesmanship of the world has failed to end the Cold War and make peace, and it will be this treasure that will turn the tide and show the way to peace and security for all nations."

Thomas told Chappell that if he was permitted to search on the island he would solve the mystery "within one hour." He also proposed that he and Chappell share these treasures on a fifty-fifty basis, though not as owners but as "custodians" of the incredible secrets contained in the Money Pit.

In a follow-up letter Thomas explained that he had previously spent forty years solving "the mystery of the Great Pyramid of Egypt" and it was that which had led him to the solution of Oak Island. "The Master Mind that stored the treasure in the Money Pit was the agent for 'higher-ups' who knew that the time would come when someone would solve the mystery of the Great Pyramid, and that in turn would solve the mystery of Oak Island and, I might add, every other problem. I am the one, and the Money Pit puts me on the spot."

Thomas urged Chappell to waste no time in signing an agreement to allow him to search. Chappell tentatively agreed to let him try, providing Thomas could prove he had the financial ability to carry out the project and that he state exactly what it was he expected to find under the Money Pit. Thomas couldn't meet the first condition. And as for the second, he said it would "betray a sacred trust if I would divulge this secret without an agreement in order to avoid possible litigation after it is recovered."

Chappell had to wait three years before he learned the nature of the repository that Thomas knew was on the island. In the summer of 1957 Chappell was in Winnipeg on business and Thomas had previously arranged to travel up from Montana and meet him there.

In Chappell's hotel room Thomas finally disclosed his secret: Below Oak Island is an exact duplicate of the Great Pyramid of Egypt, but inverted with its apex extending hundreds of feet into the ground. It contains large chambers filled with incredible wealth and documents explaining the origins of man. The pyramid had been placed there by Divine Providence to aid and enlighten mankind, and it was destined to be located by 1958.

Chappell patiently pointed out that shafts and drill holes had been driven almost 200 feet into the soil all around the Money Pit area, and not once had any sign of a stone pyramid been encountered. But Thomas was fanatic in his insistence and it was only with a good deal of effort that Chappell was finally able to get him out of the room.

Thomas is remembered by the Great Falls YMCA staff as a kindly old eccentric who spent most of his final years writing stories and tracts about Oak Island's pyramid; a theory he clung to until his death in 1960.

Chappell has received many other equally implausible suggestions concerning who buried what under Oak Island. There are people who believe the Holy Grail will be found beneath the island, that Leonardo da Vinci designed the workings in the early sixteenth century, or that the whole thing is actually a devilish hoax engineered by Satan to instill greed in men.

But not everyone who contacts Chappell is an off-the-wall theorist. In August 1955 he was approached by George Greene, a petroleum engineer who represented a group of oilmen from Corpus Christi, Texas. They wanted to locate the treasure vault by drilling, and in September a contract was signed with Chappell. This was the first work to be done in the Money Pit area since Hamilton abandoned his search in 1942.

Greene, a burly cigar-chomping Texan replete with Stetson hat and cowboy boots, arrived the following month and set up his rented drilling equipment. Chappell showed him the approximate location of the original Money Pit as well as the drilling records from the 1897 expedition, which had brought up the piece of parchment.

Over the next three weeks Greene sank four holes with a 4-inch core drill to a depth of over 180 feet. The holes were spaced several feet apart, and in all of them he struck wood (most likely earlier searchers' cribbing) at various levels down to 111 feet. After going through some limestone at about 140 feet, Green said, "below that there is nothing but cavity; the drills just dropped right through." The cavity was approximately 40 feet deep, after which the drill entered bedrock. Greene pumped 100,000 gallons of water into the void, but it ran out. He never discovered where it went.

Greene left the island at the end of October stating: "We found enough information below the surface to know that something went on, and next May or June I'll be back to finish the job" with heavier equipment. But the following year he was tied up with a large oil-drilling contract in Louisiana, and his agreement with Chappell expired.

Greene, incidentally, believed that any treasure under Oak Island was probably put there by the Spanish during their conquest of Central and South America in the sixteenth century. It's a theory that (as will later be seen) holds possibilities.

Chappell continued to look for someone to resume the search. He had been disappointed in Greene's drilling program because Greene had angled his boreholes rather than driving them down vertically into the spot that Chappell had outlined.

The next application came in 1957 from William and Victor Harman, two brothers from northern Ontario who had previously been involved in gold-prospecting ventures. Their personal funds were limited, but they were in the process of organizing the Oak Island Exploration Co. Ltd. through which they proposed to issue one million shares at 25 cents apiece.

A one-year agreement was signed with Chappell, and in May 1958 the brothers arrived on the island with drilling equipment and a professional driller. Like Greene, they believed the treasure consisted of a Spanish deposit, and they predicted they'd bring up as much as $200,000,000 in gold by the end of the summer.

They spent a couple of months drilling in the vicinity of the Money Pit, with their deepest hole going down past bedrock to 212 feet. In late June the Harmans reported that they had brought up samples of oak and spruce, coconut fiber, and ship's caulking (probably puddled clay) from depths of 150 feet and more. They confidently stated that the treasure "is there for the taking and we're going to take it."

But at this point their money ran out, and the Ontario Securities Commission refused to allow them to launch a public stock company unless they could first secure a guaranteed five-year lease on the island.

Chappell was not about to tie up the property with a group that had no assurance of being able to sell enough shares to raise the required working capital. So the Harman brothers joined the long list of those who had been forced to give up because of insufficient finances.

However, Chappell was soon to find himself involved with interrelated search groups that would provide some of the most significant developments in the long history of Oak Island. It was the beginning of an era in which the search would continue almost uninterrupted to the present day.

Chapter Twenty

Bob and Mildred Restall met in England in 1931 while she was an aspiring seventeen-year-old ballerina and he was a daredevil motorcyclist from Toronto on tour with a circus. Within a year they were married. But they became partners in more ways than one. Bob had found someone with the nerve and coordination to help him create a spectacular new routine known as the Globe of Death.

For the next two decades they toured circuses and carnivals throughout Europe and North America, thrilling audiences with an act that became legendary. It involved whipping around on high-powered motorcycles at speeds of up to 65 miles an hour inside a 20-foot diameter steel mesh sphere.

"It was a precision act with timing down to a split second," explains Mildred, a frail and attractive woman who is now in her sixties and still retains her Yorkshire accent. "I'd be riding around the globe horizontally while Bob was looping over the top. We did have a few accidents, of course. I broke my jaw once doing it in Germany and Bob had his arm broken. But it was a good act, and we did pretty well with it."

In the early 1950's the couple settled in Hamilton, Ontario. They had three young children to rear and were tired of continually being on the road. Although they still occasionally spun around the Globe of Death (their last ride was in 1956), Bob also worked at various jobs in steel mills and contracting. Their life at last seemed to be settling into a mundane middle-class pattern, which was not regretted by Mildred.

But a chance visit to Nova Scotia in the fall of 1955 would eventually change all that. It was then that Bob first visited Oak Island, though he had read about it many years earlier. He met George Greene on the island and received a firsthand account of the problems presented by the baffling mystery. "After that," says Mildred, "it was all he could talk about."

Bob soon contacted Chappell and waited for an opportunity to take a turn at matching wits against the unknown designer of the booby-trapped treasure chamber. That chance came in 1959. Meanwhile, he had been busy reading everything he could find pertaining to the island's history. In 1958 R.V. Harris, Hedden's former lawyer, had published *The Oak Island Mystery*, a book that gave Restall a good idea of the frustrations he could expect in his search. Restall also scouted around among his friends in Hamilton, lining up prospective backing for the venture.

A contract was signed with Chappell and in October 1959 Restall, then fifty-three, and his eighteen-year-old son, Bobbie, set up camp on the island. The following summer they were joined by Mildred and their youngest child, nine-year-old Ricky. (Their daughter, Lee, was then married and living in Oakville, Ontario.)

The Restalls were something of a Swiss Family Robinson. For more than five years they lived and worked on the otherwise uninhabited island, their only link to the mainland being a 16-foot outboard motor boat.

Life there was spartan and often lonely. Home consisted of two 16-by-16-foot one-room shacks, one for Bob and Mildred, the other for the boys. There was no indoor plumbing, running water, telephone, or even (for the first three years) electricity—things that they had always taken for granted. Warmth was provided by space heaters, which often proved inadequate during the severe winter storms, and cooking was done on a small propane stove.

"Primitive is the only way to describe it," says Mildred, for whom the isolated conditions were the hardest. Bob and Bobbie worked enthusiastically from dawn to dusk, certain that every shovelful of earth was bringing them that much closer to the treasure. But for Ricky the island was one big playground all his own, especially during the long hot summer days when he'd fish, swim, and explore the fields and woods with Carnie, a Belgian sheep dog who never left his side.

Mildred maintained the house under these difficult conditions and helped Ricky with his correspondence schooling. But she never really had her heart in the treasure-hunting aspect of their life. "That was my husband's and Bobbie's dream," she explains. "They believed it, so I went along with it. I wanted so much for them to find it. But I was never that sure there was any treasure there."

What Mildred missed most was living in a city or town with other people she knew; having women friends; being able to talk about anything other than Oak Island and "the search." Always the search. In the summers, of course, there were tourists to talk to. But then they too were primarily interested in the search.

Yet in many ways the family was probably closer than they would have been back in Hamilton. Like castaways on a desert isle, they depended a great deal on one another emotionally, materially, and socially. Evenings were usually spent together in the main cabin, the four of them reading, playing chess, or discussing the future. Naturally, the conversation often turned to how they'd spend their wealth once the Money Pit coughed up what it owed them. Bob talked about yachts; Bobbie about racing cars; Mildred about long vacations in warm places where there were a lot of people.

Bob put the treasure's value at $30,000,000. He based this on the legend ("Forty feet below two million pounds are buried") supposedly deciphered from the inscribed stone that had been found in the Money Pit in 1803. He then converted pounds to dollars on an estimated rate for the early 1700's when, in his opinion, the treasure had been buried.

Restall believed the island may have been used as a long-term repository by English privateers during their raids on Spanish ships and settlements in the seventeenth century. He thought, for instance, that part of the loot from the city of Panama may have found its way eventually to the island after the city was sacked by Henry Morgan in 1671.

Mildred, on the other hand, believes that any treasure on Oak Island was probably removed before the Money Pit was discovered in 1795. And her favorite theory is that the deposit was designed by a group of Acadians prior to their expulsion from the province in 1755.

Restall spent most of the first couple of years exploring the artificial drainage system at Smith's Cove. He had come to the island with only his life's savings of $8,500; hardly enough to purchase or rent heavy digging machinery. So it was basically a tedious pick-and-shovel operation. The old cofferdam (built in 1866) was still visible at low tide, and Restall and his son concentrated their search between the dam and the shoreline, a distance of about 70 feet. They dug some 65 holes, 2 to 6 feet deep, and uncovered sections of the five finger drains that had first been noticed in 1850. They also found layers of eel grass and coconut fiber anywhere from 8 to 24 inches thick under parts of the false beach.

In his 1961 progress report, Restall said, "We now have a complete picture of the beach work, and it is incredible." He described it as being 243 feet across near the cofferdam, and composed of "paving stones" overlayed with the eel grass, fiber, sand, and rocks. Much of it had previously been ripped up and destroyed by the 1850 searchers. Although Restall noticed that the drains all converged toward one point near the shore, he wasn't able to find the main channel. Either the drains were no longer connected to it, or else it was far deeper than he was able to dig by hand.

While digging one of these holes, Restall uncovered a small stone slab with "1704" carved into it. He was certain it had something to do with the original work, though others believe the inscription had been made by a prankster or someone in a previous search group.

Through a few of his Ontario friends, Restall was able to raise $11,000 to continue work. In 1961 he purchased the large pump that both Hedden and Hamilton had used on the island and set it up over the Hedden shaft. He explored and recribbed parts of both that shaft and the Chappell shaft and did some short tunneling work between the 100- and 120-foot level. He also examined some of the Halifax tunnel system of the 1860's, much of which was still in good condition.

By 1964 Restall had again turned his attention to the flood system at Smith's Cove. He poured cement into several of the exposed sections of the drain, but the water continued to flow into the Hedden shaft. Then he began digging his own shaft (No. 26) on the beach at Smith's Cove on a line with the Cave-in Pit and the

Money Pit. (No. 25 will be discussed later.) He was determined to locate and block the main feeder line from the cove to the treasure vault. This hole was abandoned at a depth of 24 feet and a new shaft (No. 27) was started about 30 feet northward on the beach.

All of this time, Restall was worried about losing his hold on the island. His contract with Chappell was on an annual basis, and this made financing difficult, for it was always possible that Chappel at the end of any given year might decide to allow a new searcher to take over the site. In order to resolve the uncertainty, Restall tried in late 1964 to raise money to purchase the island. But Chappell wanted $100,000 for it, and the proposal eventually fell through.

Still, Restall occasionally was able to sell shares in his venture and to continue working on a limited scale. One of his backers was Karl Graeser, a Long Island marina operator. Another was Robert Dunfield, a Los Angeles geologist who joined the search in July 1965. Both were on the island the day Bob Restall's six-year treasure hunt ended.

That was on Tuesday, August 17, 1965, a humid, leaden day when the air hung oppressively heavy. Bob and his son had been working since six that morning down in the Hedden shaft. At 2 P.M. Bob came up to remind Mildred that he was going into town later and that he'd be at the cabin around three to wash up and change his clothes. At about a quarter to three he walked down to Smith's Cove to check on shaft No. 27. It was 27 feet deep, and a pump was keeping the water down to about 4 feet from the bottom.

No one is quite sure what happened next. Restall was either descending the shaft or else peering into it when suddenly he was lying in the black stagnant water at its bottom. Bobbie saw that something was wrong. He yelled for help and then went scampering down the ladderway after his father. Seconds later Karl Graeser, thirty-eight, arrived on the scene and saw both Restalls lying unconscious in the pit. He quickly climbed down to rescue them. Behind him was sixteen-year-old Cyrill Hiltz, one of Restall's workers from nearby Martin's Point. Both he and Graeser toppled from the ladder before they had reached the bottom. Another worker, Andy DeMont, seventeen, met the same fate.

By this time several tourists and a group of youngsters who were camping on the island had heard the calls for help and rushed to the pit. With them was Edward White, a vacationing fireman from Buffalo, New York. White's training led him to realize that there was some sort of deadly gas in the shaft, and he quickly tied a rope around his waist and had others lower him down. He lashed another line to the unconscious DeMont and then desperately groped around in the murky water looking for a sign of the others. But he could feel nothing, and now he too was on the verge of passing out. He and DeMont were hauled out and given artificial respiration.

The bodies of Bob and Bobbie Restall, Karl Graeser, and Cyril Hiltz were eventually fished up from the bottom of the death pit. The Oak Island search, in its 170th year, had claimed four more victims.

Debate continues over what killed them. The autopsies found all four to have died by drowning. Yet no one is certain of the nature of the gas that had caused them to plummet into the water. Some believe it was marsh gas (methane) that had seeped into the pit. But methane is colorless and ordorless, and many of those at the scene said the gas had a definite stink to it. The other possibility is that carbon monoxide fumes from the pump's gasoline engine on the surface had somehow accumulated in the depths of the shaft.

Following the tragedy Mildred and Ricky moved to the village of Western Shore, only a mile from the island that had been their home those many years. Mildred still lives there, working in an administrative capacity at a Chester medical center. "It all seems so hard to believe," she says, "and one of the sad ironies is that Bob thought he was close, really close, to finding the treasure."

The aftermath of the accident is still a sore point with Mrs. Restall. She states that within days, "before my husband and son were even buried," she was being urged to go to Halifax to work out a legal transfer of the search rights to Bob Dunfield, who took over Restall's operations. "Everybody was in such a hurry to keep the search going," she recalls. "And what good has it done them? Not a damn bit."

Dunfield, who had first heard about Oak Island as a young boy in Denver, saw it as a problem that could be solved by heavy digging equipment. In the fall of 1965 the thirty-nine-year-old geologist brought in several wealthy backers from California to help him finance the project. Also in his group was Daniel Blankenship, a Miami contractor who was to become Oak Island's most dedicated current searcher. Mrs. Restall was also given a small interest in the venture.

Dunfield's first move was to barge two bulldozers out to the island. They were used to clear away about 12 feet of overburden in the entire Money Pit area, exposing cribwork from several filled-in pits. One of these, 15 feet north of the Chappell shaft and 10 feet west of the north end of the Hedden shaft, appeared to be the original Money Pit.

The bulldozers were also used to push hundreds of tons of earth and clay over the beach at Smith's Cove in an effort to permanently block the flooding system. This totally muddied the water in the cove, but when Dunfield pumped out the Hedden shaft, he found that the water entering it was clear. He was therefore confident that he had blocked the eastern tunnel. But obviously at least one other flood tunnel, probably from the south shore, was still operational.

Dunfield's next plan was to bring in even heavier machinery. He leased a 70-ton crane with a 90-foot boom from which was suspended a large bucket capable of digging a hole 200 feet deep and 100 feet across. But there was no possibility of getting this behemoth out to the island on a barge.

On October 17, 1965, Oak Island ceased to be an island. That day bulldozers completed a 600-foot causeway linking the island's western end to the mainland. Dunfield was now ready for his major assault.

The crane was first put to work on the south shore to find and block the second flood tunnel. A trench about 15 feet deep and 80 feet long was dug with a dragline bucket along the beach. This produced a discovery. In one section of the trench there appeared a refilled shaft 8 feet in diameter. It had no cribbing in it and there is no record of it in any previous search attempts, so Dunfield was certain it had been excavated prior to 1795. Significantly, the shaft (No. 28) was about 25 feet directly south of the mysterious triangle of stones. The shaft was followed down to a depth of about 45 feet, which seemed to be the extent of the original digging. But its purpose was never discovered.

The south shore trench didn't intersect the flood tunnel; nor did it decrease the flow of seawater into the Hedden shaft. Rather than deepen the hole, Dunfield decided to move the crane up to the Money Pit itself.

For the next two months Dunfield was plagued with mechanical failures and heavy rains. Digging the pit quickly enough became a constant struggle, with the sides caving in and refilling the bottom portion. Each time work was halted for a day or more, as much as 20 feet of fill would slide into the hole, and it would take another couple of days just to re-excavate it. He eventually created a pit almost 140 feet deep and 100 feet across. In the course of digging it, he scooped out most of the timbers from early shafts, leaving only the Hedden shaft intact.

Dunfield later refilled the huge hole he had spent two months digging in order to gain a suitable surface from which to do some core drilling in the same spot. A series of 6-inch-diameter holes were put down to almost 190 feet. In several Dunfield found the same cavity structure that George Greene had encountered in 1955. Dunfield says it consisted of a 2-foot layer of limestone between 140 and 142 feet, then a 40-foot void that extended to about 182 feet. Below that was bedrock. Dunfield planned to use the crane to examine the cavity the following spring when the ground would be drier and less susceptible to caving.

Meanwhile, he excavated the Cave-in Pit to 108 feet, finding old timbers at 68 feet and again at 100 feet (perhaps part of the Halifax tunnels). But once again heavy rain and mechanical failures halted the work, and the pit began caving in rapidly.

In April, Dunfield returned to California to dry out his clothes and count his losses. He and his partners had spent $131,000 during their seven months of investigation. He still hoped to reopen the Money Pit, but before proceeding any further he wanted to purchase the island from Chappell. The undisclosed asking price (about $100,000) was more than Dunfield could raise or wanted to pay, and he gradually lost interest.

Although his direct involvement in the search ended, Dunfield is a shareholder in Triton Alliance, the current search group. He is still sure that a complex mystery remains to be unraveled under the island.

Dunfield, who currently lives in Encino, California, and is president of a gold and silver mining company, says, "A preponderance of evidence suggests underground work done by men many years in the past" on Oak Island. In his opinion as a geologist, however, the so-called cement found underground at various times is "nothing more than limestone" forming part of the Windsor Formation in that part of Nova Scotia. As for the cavity he drilled into, Dunfield suggests it "could be a natural feature as found in limestone units throughout the world. Normally I would have considered this a natural cavity, and I doubt that this geologic concept could have been known by the depositors before burying anything of value."

But he adds, "If something is buried on Oak Island, the limestone could have been a surprise to any depositors and used to their advantage." He also notes that samples of wood and metal found in and below the cavity by Triton in recent years "are manmade and foreign to glacial deposits."

Dunfield's heavy-equipment approach to finding the treasure evoked a lot of criticism among local people in the Mahone Bay area as well as from other investigators of the mystery. Some feel he contributed more than anyone to turning the east end of the island into a scarred mess of water-filled pits and mounds of earth. But that's an aesthetic complaint voiced by locals and tourists; the more significant damage may have been archeological. A clam bucket capable of gobbling up more than 60 cubic feet of dirt in one bite can hardly be expected to discriminate between earth and underground artifacts. Dunfield did sift through material brought up from lower depths, but some persons involved with him believe the investigation was often cursory. The apparent underground damage was probably limited to previous searchers' shafts, though that may never be known for certain.

But on the surface, the stone triangle, one of the island's most interesting landmarks, disappeared as a result of the trench Dunfield dug on the south shore. The triangle, which almost every investigator including Dunfield considered original and significant, wasn't purposely destroyed, but fell into the trench as a result of erosion after Dunfield left the island. In addition, the drilled rock near Smith's Cove hasn't been found since Dunfield's time. The westerly drilled rock was at least moved before the crane began excavating the Money Pit.

Fortunately, the location of all these markers had been accurately plotted by Charles Roper in 1937 and again in the early 1960's.

The local hostility toward Dunfield may partially explain his many equipment breakdowns. Chappell states that some of the crane's broken cables had "the appearance of having been [previously) cut with a hacksaw or other tool." (Some of the coastal fishermen also objected to the causeway he'd built.)

The early 1960's saw the start of another controversy concerning Oak Island. In April 1963 Frederick G. Nolan, a surveyor from Bedford, Nova Scotia, bought seven lots (No. 5 and Nos. 9 through 14. See p. 17.) in the center part of the island along the north shore. They were purchased for about $3,000 from several descendants of the Henry Sellers family and amount to almost a quarter of the island's real estate. Mel Chappell, who had been under the impression he owned the whole island, was horrified by this development, and he still insists that he owns the property.

The dispute goes back to 1935 when Hedden (through his New Jersey lawyer, George Grimm) purchased property from Sellyn Sellers and other heirs. The deeds on file at the Registry Office in Chester state that Hedden purchased Lots 15 through 20, or the whole eastern tip of the island. No other lot numbers are mentioned. However, also on file is a survey plan dated September 9, 1935, described as "Sellyn Sellers to George W. Grimm—52 acres," which by measurement appears to include Lots 5 and 9 through 20.

Nevertheless, when the property in question was sold by Hedden to John Whitney Lewis and then by Lewis to Chappell in 1950, again only the numbers 15 through 20 were recorded on the actual deeds. (Chappell also purchased other lots unrelated to the dispute.) Eventually the courts may decide the case.

In 1971 Nolan was granted a treasure trove license on his lots and began digging for treasure, despite opposition presented in ministerial hearings by Chappell and Triton Alliance.

The ownership matter has resulted in a continuing fifteen-year feud between Nolan and Chappell, and more recently between Nolan and members of Triton Alliance. Matters got worse in 1966 when Nolan purchased Crandall's Point, where the causeway (owned by Chappell) from the island meets the mainland. Since then there have been numerous instances of Nolan and Triton personnel blocking or threatening to block each other's access to and across the island.

Nolan is in a position to prevent direct access to the causeway;

Triton is in a position to prevent Nolan from driving out to the island and (because Chappell also owns the west end of the island)
from getting to his lots; Nolan is in a position to prevent Triton
from crossing his land to get to the Money Pit. Both sides have at
times exercised these options by setting up chain barriers or other
obstructions. The current situation seems to be an uneasy truce.

The bottom line, of course, is treasure. Nolan (as will later be
discussed) is convinced that Triton is wasting its time and that
most of Oak Island's treasure lies in the swamp and other areas
covered by his lots. Chappell and Triton are equally convinced
that it will be found in the Money Pit area, though it's always possible that the underground system extends well into the center of
the island.

As Nolan puts it, "Treasure hunters who are dedicated are a
very suspicious lot, and perhaps with just cause. Who knows
what could be at stake; it could be nothing, but also it could represent a vast fortune."

Chapter Twenty-one

In the long history of the Oak Island search the two most-often-asked questions have been: Who built the project, and how can the treasure be recovered? But three other relevant questions are: Is it possible Oak Island is a natural geological phenomenon or even a man-made hoax? Or if it is real, is it a treasure cache, or could it have served some other purpose? And, if it was designed to hide something of value, is that something still there?

On the first of these points, the suggestion has been made that the original Money Pit may have been a natural sinkhole caused by an underlying fault. According to this line of reasoning, the sinkhole occurred decades or even centuries prior to the Money Pit's discovery and in the intervening years the surrounding earth slumped into it, taking with it vegetation such as dead logs. So in 1795 the three young boys found a depressed area in the ground, which, when excavated, had the appearance of a refilled shaft containing wooden platforms.

Some support for this argument was accidentally discovered in 1949 at Mader's Cove, five miles south of Oak Island on the shore of Mahone Bay. In a recent interview, Dr. G.D. Donaldson recalls that he had hired some workers to dig a well on his property, and a spot was selected where the earth was relatively soft. At about 2 feet down a layer of fieldstone was struck. Then logs of spruce and oak wood were found at irregular intervals, and some of the wood was charred.

The immediate suspicion was that another Money Pit had been discovered. Researchers from Dalhousie University in Halifax rushed out to Mader's Cove to take part in the excavation and to examine the material. The hole was dug to 85 feet, at which point fresh water started seeping in.

Donaldson says the project was abandoned about this time because the experts concluded that the pit "was nothing more than a natural shinkhole that had occurred hundreds or even thousands of years earlier." Over those centuries the original hole, which may have been more than 100 feet deep, had been gradually refilled with washed-in earth. And at various periods the surrounding trees, some of them killed by lightning or forest fires, had fallen into the pit.

Geologically, a similar sinkhole could have occurred on Oak Island. Some people think the so-called Cave-in Pit, for example, may have been just a case. Others believe that it was an air shaft dug by the original depositors when driving their flood tunnel to Smith's Cove. Perhaps both explanations are wrong. The collapse may simply have been a delayed result of the ground under the pit being undermined by a section of the Halifax tunnels dug near that area in the 1860's.

However, any theory that seeks to explain the Money Pit as a sinkhole is untenable. For such a rationale would have to assume that the accounts of the wooden platforms being embedded into the clay walls and evenly spaced every ten feet were either gross exaggerations or outright lies. The same assumption would have to be made for the accounts of pick marks found in the walls of the pit, as well as the putty, charcoal, coconut fiber, and the inscribed rock discovered when the pit was dug to 90 feet in 1803. One would have to assume that two of the discoverers, Smith and Vaughan, as well as Lynds and others in the 1803–04 group, took part in the next search of 1849 knowing full well that the earlier "evidence" was fabricated or nonexistent. (In fact, a significant point is that from 1795 to the present day there has always been an overlapping of investors and searchers from one group to the next, each of them interviewing those who preceded them.)

Similarly, the idea has sometimes been proposed that the flood tunnels are actually natural water-bearing fissures running through the soluble anhydrite and limestone known to exist anywhere from 140 to over 200 feet down in the Money Pit area. This would be geologically possible under certain conditions. But it doesn't explain the flooding that was encountered at about 100 feet down in the Money Pit when the surrounding soil was all hard, unworked clay. Nor does it explain the drainage system that was found at Smith's Cove in 1850 and re-examined since that time.

The best guess, and one frequently advanced by geologists, is that the flooding is due to a combination of natural and man-made systems. That is, the tunnels from the sea were artificially designed, but once the seawater was channeled into the east end of the island, it may have created other watercourses through gravel fills and soluble bedrock. Moreover, the various tunnels dug by searchers over the years have undoubtedly added new branches to this underground water network above bedrock.

The ingenuity and labor of men, not nature, constructed the Money Pit, the Smith's Cove drains, and other works known to exist on the island. Considering the tools and technology available in the 1700's or earlier, modern engineers have estmated that roughly 100,000 man-hours went into the project. If, for argument's sake, the labor force consisted of twenty persons, the operation may have taken as long as two years. And the workings may eventually be found to be even larger than is so far known.

Although the authenticity of the workings themselves can be accepted, room for debate still exists on the naturalness or artificiality of some of the findings within the Money Pit.

The cement, for example, has been inspected by many geologists and laboratories over the years and there has always been a difference of opinion as to whether it was worked by man. Under certain conditions a "natural cement" can be produced underground in limestone-bearing strata. Then again, some investigators say that if the island's limestone was used by the original depositors as a source of lime (by calcining the limestone in kilns) to prepare cement, the end product would be rather crude and indistinguishable from natural cement. (The charcoal found in the Money Pit may have been used to fuel just such a kiln.)

As for the "putty" found in the original pit, this was probably the puddled clay brought up by other drillers and excavators. Because of its malleability and oiliness, it is thought by many, including a contemporary expert, to have been made from the island's blue clay and used as a sealing agent by the original workers. In 1937 Gilbert Hedden found large quantities of it while digging his shaft. He described it as "a putty-like clay" that "could be worked with the hands exactly like good putty." He noted that he used it to putty the windows of his cabin and that "it worked very well."

One thing that Oak Island cynics have never been able to explain is the discovery of tons of coconut fiber beneath the beach at Smith's Cove. It can still be found today.

There have been suggestions in the past that the material is something other than coconut fiber. In 1937 the Botanical Museum of Harvard University examined a sample and suspected that it was "manila hemp fibers" that may have come from "the partly disintegrated remains of some ship's cables or hawsers." But considering the amount of it that was found, this is most unlikely. In the early 1940's, Erwin Hamilton theorized that it was hemlock bark, which may have been thrown on the shore by either the original depositors or the 1803–04 search group after they had stripped logs that were used for their cribbing. The problem with this suggestion is that hemlock bark would deteriorate rapidly in salt water and also that the fiber was found in short pieces of 6 inches or less; hardly the way in which someone would debark a tree.

In point of fact, there should be no doubt the material is coconut fiber. As already noted, it was analyzed and declared to be such by the Smithsonian Institution in 1916 and again in 1930. This same conclusion has also recently been stated by several Canadian botanists.

There can be no explanation for its presence on the island except that it was brought by ship. One Oak Island debunker, in an article in the *Atlantic Advocate* magazine of October 1965, claimed the fiber could have drifted north from the Caribbean via the Gulf Stream and been deposited by storms on the shores of Smith's Cove. But the article fails to note that the Gulf Stream cuts to the east a good 400 miles south of Nova Scotia. More important, we are given no explanation as to why one island out of some 350 in Mahone Bay (not to mention the province's hundreds of miles of southern coastline) is the only known beneficiary of this freak of nature.

Actually, there are reports of coconut fiber having been found on the shores of Sable Island, two hundred miles east of Oak Island. This is not surprising, since Sable Island is the scene of some 250 shipwrecks and, as stated earlier, the fiber was often carried aboard as dunnage to protect cargo. But any suggestion that a similar dunnage-laden ship was long ago wrecked on Smith's Cove still doesn't explain the rest of the stone drainage system or how the coconut fiber found its way into the Money Pit.

Among the island's other mysterious features are the stone triangle and the drilled rocks. No way exists to prove that the triangle was laid out by the original depositors, but no other explanation makes much sense. The record shows that it was first seen by Blair, Welling, and William Chappell in 1897 and none of them had previously heard of its existence, though they interviewed persons who'd worked with search groups from 1850 on, and those people had similarly interviewed the searchers before them.

Since the triangle's medial line pointed toward the Money Pit, some have speculated that it may have been put there by an early search group after they abandoned their attempt, and that it was meant as a guide to relocating the Money Pit at some future date. But then why place it so far away from the pit? Why would it have to be laid out exactly on a true-north line? And why not simply plant stakes or other markers directly on or beside the pit?

Another guess is that the triangle was put down as a reference point by Charles Morris when he first surveyed the island and divided it into 32 lots in 1762. The fact that it pointed to the yet undiscovered Money Pit would then have to be considered an amazing coincidence. The parallel lot lines run approximately 30 degrees east of true north. But they evidently do so because that was the most logical way to divide the island into equal 4-acre tracts, each with its own water frontage. And Morris or any surveyor could have easily ascertained that without needing to know where true north lay.

Charles Roper, who worked with Hedden in 1937 to establish the still unexplained relationship between the Wilkins' Kidd map and the triangle, has been a surveyor most of his life. He is still sure that the triangle was laid down by whoever built the Money Pit and says that he has never heard of anything like it being used for land surveying purposes. This opinion is shared by other Nova Scotian surveyors who examined the triangle and tried to fathom its purpose.

Then there are the drilled rocks; the two that Hedden found, and others discovered since. Here again no conclusive proof exists that they were part of the original work, though most investigators believe they were. Roper and other surveyors discount the possibility that they were used by Nova Scotian surveyors as markers or as foundations for sight-line poles. Why go to the trouble of hand-drilling a hole in granite when you could get someone to hold the pole or else drive the pole into the ground?

But the rocks may have had nothing to do with surveying or measurement; and in this respect there are a couple of possible explanations.

Erwin Hamilton suggested that perhaps the rocks were drilled by earlier searchers to make sockets for whim axles. These would have been used as part of a capstan system by which dirt and water were hoisted out of the Money Pit and other shafts by either man or horse power. The explanation is plausible except that if it's true, the holes probably date back to the original depositors. Even the searchers of 1803–04 would have had a more efficient system at their disposal, such as axle sockets made of cast iron.

Another possibility is that the holes were drilled by early farmers on the island. In eighteenth-century New England rocks were sometimes split by using an auger to drill a hole into which a wooden plug was tightly inserted. Water was poured over the plug and, with luck, the plug would expand enough to crack the rock apart, usually leaving two flat surfaces. This method was used to break boulders that were too large to haul off a field or in cases where the flat surfaces were required for construction purposes, such as barn or house foundations.

This might suggest then that the drilled rocks found on Oak Island had been bored by early settlers (most of whom were New Englanders) in order to split them. But the water-dampened plug hadn't worked and the rocks were left lying where they were found, the wood by then having rotted away. Of course, here too, the builders of the Money Pit and artificial drains could have drilled the rocks for that same purpose.

In any case, the triangle and the drilled rocks are real and they cannot be dismissed as a hoax or practical joke left behind by members of earlier search groups. They are too elaborate and subtle for that. However, many of the inscribed boulders that have been found occasionally on the island may be regarded with suspicion. A common practice for some of the workers with various search groups was amusing themselves by carving their initials or even cryptic dates or names on rock surfaces.

For instance, Amos Nauss recalls that during Hedden's time there was a large flat rock on the island on which someone had carved "Capt Kidd 1671." Nauss says that at the end of the Hamilton expedition in 1943, "I took the rock over to the South Shore Cove and buried it under the bank near a tree, thinking that the next guy that came along looking for the treasure would go crazy when he found it." (Apparently, it still awaits discovery by some unsuspecting searcher.) The "1704" rock found by Restall at Smith's Cove was also probably the result of a prank.

A good example of how misleading these "clues" can be is the story of the Gaspereaux River rock. This large boulder, located near the mouth of the river, about 80 miles east of Halifax, bears a weathered inscription carved into its surface. The message includes the name "Kidd," the date "1670," the letters "JMD," and several symbols such as a jackboot, crossed flags, and a carpenter's square.

Harold Wilkins heard about it from a local treasure hunter in 1937 and mentioned it in a letter to Hedden. He in turn told R. V. Harris about it, and the latter visited the site in 1957 to photograph and sketch the rock. He also made inquiries in the area and learned from several of the local old-timers that their grandfathers had reported seeing the inscription as young boys in the mid-1800's.

Harris had always believed that William Kidd was the most likely architect of the Oak Island project, and here was the proof he needed that Kidd had indeed visited Nova Scotia. He subsequently submitted this evidence, complete with a sketch of the rock, in his book about Oak Island. Harris also did a fair amount of research trying to interpret all of the symbols on the rock. But he'd always been stumped by the meaning of the letters "JMD."

In 1969, a year after Harris' death, the apparent source of the inscription was brought to light. It had been carved around 1850 by James MacDonald (JMD) while he was a young boy living in the Gaspereaux area. MacDonald, who was later president of the Nova Scotia Historical Society and also a historian of the North British Society of Halifax, reported this fact to a friend prior to his death in 1914. But not until 1969 was the information brought to the attention of the Public Archives of Nova Scotia, where it is now on record.

In the case of Oak Island, false clues haven't been limited to pirate messages carved on stone. Several instances of workers salting a shaft with artifacts have temporarily excited their fellow searchers. Nauss, for instance, remembers that ". . . Some of those guys used to bring stuff like old chains and broad axes down into the pit where they were working and would sent it up in the buckets. They'd always make sure that guys like Hedden and Hamilton were around to see it come up. It would stir up a little commotion every time."

But such mischief occasionally served a more practical purpose. Early search operations sometimes employed as many as sixty local men to help with the digging and, when fishing was bad, this was about the only other available work to be had in that area. The treasure hunt also provided additional income for local merchants who supplied the operators with food, lumber, and digging equipment. Consequently, rumors exist that on more than one occasion a company would "accidentally" strike something of interest just about the time its backers were getting discouraged and preparing to give up the search. The new discovery would then keep operations going for a bit longer.

For example, one version of the discovery of the three links of gold chain brought up on the end of a drill from 100 feet down in the Money Pit in 1849 is that one of the men operating the auger overheard a director of the Truro Company state that, if nothing of significance was found by the end of the week, the company would be pulling out. The next day the gold links appeared on the drill bit. But in all the excitement no one noticed that the driller's watch chain was exactly three links shorter.

In other instances, earlier searchers may have had their hopes raised not by hoaxes, but by their own false assumptions. For example, during the 1849 and 1897 drilling programs the drillers felt the bit "going through metal in pieces." Since none of this material (thought to be coins) was ever brought up, we are left with only the faith these drillers had in their ability to distinguish between loose metal and gravel. Could these drillers also have been sure of the difference between the feel of a "metal plate" and an extremely hard rock? And could they have been sure that the wood they brought up with their augers was original rather than timber from an earlier search group's shaft?

Only in recent years, has any metal (nonprecious) actually been brought to the surface. Moreover, the metal and a quantity of wood have been retrieved from depths and parts of the island where no previous search work was ever done. This fact, together with scientific analysis of the samples, is more than enough proof to establish that Oak Island is by no means a natural phenomenon, hoax, or mere wishful thinking on the part of its investigators.

Ample evidence exists that the project is real and ingeniously designed. But what proof is there that it was built for the purpose of concealing treasure? So far, this question can be answered only by deductive reasoning, and a treasure cache is the most logical explanation, though other possibilities have been advanced.

Some have speculated that the workings were either underground living quarters built by a Micmac Indian band, or else a mining operation dating back to the original French colonists. But both these theories may be quickly discarded. Micmac history has been well researched by anthropologists, and there isn't the slightest indication of their having the ability or any reason to attempt such a project. And as for a mine, the island contains no minerals of value. Furthermore, a mine shaft would not have been carefully refilled and hooked up by tunnels to the sea.

In 1970 one theorist, Edward Parker of Philadelphia, suggested that the Money Pit was built as "an ancient maritime water purification system used to replenish the water casks of ships." Basically, his idea was that seawater would flow to the bottom of the Money Pit from Smith's Cove and then rise to sea level (about 30 feet from the top of the pit) through a series of filters consisting of loose metal, layers of wood, coconut fiber, and charcoal. At that point, according to his theory, the water would be potable.

Apart from the fact that desalinated water couldn't be produced that way, digging freshwater wells on the island (as the early settlers did) or else taking it from streams and rivers on the nearby mainland would be easier.

Actually, after almost two hundred years of investigation the only reasonable nontreasure theory has been that the workings comprise an ancient dry dock. This hypothesis was formulated by George Bates, a Halifax surveyor, amateur historian, and cartographer. His first involvement with Oak Island was in 1937 when, as a young apprentice to Charles Roper, he helped check the measurements between the drilled rocks and the stone triangle. Ever since, he says, "I had always asked myself, 'If it's not treasure

down there, what else could it be?' Then one day it hit me; the
first shipyard in North America, maybe a dry dock or ship repair
base.''

The historical setting Bates chose for his theory is the period
1690 to 1710, a time during which the French were in control of
Port Royal, Acadia's capital. Jacques de Brouillan was Governor
during much of that era, and he sought to disrupt the trading link
between Britain and her American colonies, particularly Massachusetts. He therefore issued an open invitation to pirates, most of
whom were then operating in the West Indies, to come to the
French stronghold of La Have, fifteen miles south of Oak Island,
and to use it as a base from which to capture booty from English
ships traveling the North Atlantic between Britain and America.
The pirates were at liberty to keep all goods seized, and they
could find a ready cash market for their swag at Port Royal. History shows that many freebooters took de Brouillan up on his offer.

Some of the pirate vessels would certainly have been damaged
during their sorties out in the shipping lanes, and the traditional
lairs where they could be repaired were all a good fifteen hundred
miles away in the West Indies. So Bates' theory is that de Brouillan used French military engineers to design and build a nearby
base—Oak Island—where the repairs could be done quickly and
in secret.

The shipyard, according to Bates, consisted of a large dry dock
made of wood and earth at Smith's Cove. Once a vessel entered it,
the seaward end of the dock would be closed and a floodgate
would be opened up to allow the water within the dock to flow
down a tunnel and into a chamber (the Money Pit). The ship was
now high and dry and could be replanked, caulked, or whatever
was needed (with a lot of coconut fiber dunnage in the hold being
removed in the process). As soon as the work was done, the seaward gate was reopened and the ship refloated.

But in order to repeat the process for the next damaged vessel,
the chamber beneath the "Money Pit" first had to be emptied.
Here Bates believes that the pit was in fact a large pumping shaft
operated by either a windlass or windmill power from the surface.
The water would be pumped up and allowed to run downhill toward the south shore. The oak platforms found every ten feet in
the Money Pit, he believes, were actually the horizontal support
structures for the pump casing.

The theory is interesting, but it contains serious flaws. First, there is nothing in recorded French or British Acadian history to suggest that such an elaborate dry dock was ever built. Second, its construction, even if technically possible, would have been most expensive and time-consuming. Surely careening would have been a simpler method. In fact, some of the best careening ground in the world exists near Port Royal in the Bay of Fundy where tides (that have as much as a 50-foot rise and fall at the head of the bay) can easily leave any ship high and dry for six hours or more. And with enough man power a vessel could be rolled a short distance on logs to put it out of reach of the next high tide.

Bates' proposal also runs contrary to the fact that what was done on Oak Island is one of the best-kept secrets known to man. And one must assume that such a project involved something that was not known to hundreds of vagabond pirates from the West Indies or to the large military force that presumably would have built it.

(Bates was not the first to suspect that Oak Island was a ship-refitting base. In the winter of 1941, while the Adams family was living alone on the island, seven heavily armed Canadian Navy intelligence officers suddenly arrived and insisted on inspecting the Hedden and Chappell shafts. They had received a tip that German U-boats were using the island for a supply and refueling station; a rumor that apparently began when a local fisherman spotted a moose swimming from the mainland to the island and mistook it for a submarine. The searchers, according to Charlotte Adams, spent several hours examining the pits, storehouses, and other parts of the island before satisfying themselves that the underground workings hadn't been converted into a submarine pen.)

Accepting the weight of evidence and logic that Oak Island was designed as a repository for something of great value, is the treasure still there? Why would someone have gone to all that trouble to bury something and yet not come back to retrieve it?

Obviously, searchers who have spent large sums and years on Oak Island have had reason to believe there was gold at the end of the rainbow. But the basic argument used to support this belief is that there is not, and apparently never was, any indication to the contary; that is, no physical evidence exists that the treasure was removed prior to the Money Pit's discovery in 1795.

Some investigators believe that access to the treasure was

through the Money Pit. Others theorize that the pit was intended to be entered via a secret tunnel from some other part of the island. Still others state that the treasure was never in the Money Pit, but in chambers at the ends of tunnels that radiated out from the pit. But whichever theory is accepted, the depositor would have had to either open the Money Pit or dig a hole somewhere else to reclaim his wealth. Had he done this, so the argument goes, why would he have refilled the pit or any other access shaft?

According to the records, all that was found in 1795 was the depression indicating the location of the Money Pit. That same year Smith and McGinnis took up farming on the island, and within a couple of decades many others had followed them. If any of the settlers on this relatively small island had seen surface evidence of another shaft, it surely would have been remarked upon, considering the interest aroused by the Money Pit.

Dan Blankenship is just one of hundreds of persons who have carefully explored the island looking for signs of an access shaft. He insists that the treasure is still there, ". . . because I haven't seen any physical evidence of anything having been taken out of the ground. And I believe that if they took anything out, they wouldn't have been careful about concealing it. Why should you cover up your tracks once you've taken something out?"

Lavern Johnson, a former searcher, agrees completely with that argument. "If the depositor had returned and retrieved his cache, he would have left the open recovery shaft and departed in haste. The remains would have been visible to early settlers and searchers, and it would have been examined and explored. There are no reports of anything like that having happened."

David Tobias, the president of Triton Alliance, is not so certain, and he puts the chances of recovering any treasure at about one in four. But then Tobias believes (as will later be seen) that the underground vault was meant to be used more than once and that it was carefully sealed up each time. Thus, some or all of the treasure may have been removed, with the repository left concealed for possible future use. However, Johnson and most other investigators don't buy this theory and maintain that the Oak Island project was planned and executed as "a one shot deal."

Another factor to consider is that the project almost certainly dates back at least one hundred years prior to the Money Pit's discovery. Suppose the depositor had returned within a few years, dug a small access pit that led to the treasure chamber or to an entrance tunnel, removed the treasure, and sailed off. The shaft could have been almost anywhere on the island and needn't have been more than 10 or 20 feet deep if the tunnel to which it led sloped upward from the Money Pit. After a hundred years of natural erosion, the access shaft could have been filled in and completely covered by the island's vegetation.

For that matter, who's to say the depositor didn't have a weird sense of humor that prompted him to refill the access shaft (a relatively quick and easy task) and leave, knowing that perhaps he might be responsible for someday totally befuddling anyone who tried to understand what had happened on Oak Island? This possibility is advanced only half-seriously; but were it true, the depositor's joke has obviously exceeded his wildest expectation.

If indeed the treasure is still there, perhaps the depositors died or were killed before they had a chance to return to the island; or maybe the cache was intended, as some theories maintain, to be a sort of time capsule.

Along with the question of whether the treasure was ever reclaimed by its owners are rumors that some or all of the booty may have been secretly found and removed since 1795. This is the opinion of many in the Mahone Bay area, though there are no facts to substantiate such stories.

Some of the locals are convinced that the three discoverers of the Money Pit found a small treasure a few feet down and that John Smith then encouraged the later search groups to dig even farther; his motive being to lease his property and sell lumber for the shafts. Others will tell you that the treasure was removed by the Halifax Company or some other nineteenth-century search party, and that they purposely kept quiet about it in order to avoid paying the compulsory royalty to the Nova Scotia government.

One long-standing local legend concerns Anthony Graves, who purchased much of the island after John Smith's death in 1857. Graves built his house at Joudrey's Cove and lived there till he died in 1888. Graves is rumored to have occasionally purchased supplies on the mainland with Spanish coins of gold or silver. In 1930 a silver Spanish coin dated 1785 was found near the foundation of his house. Another coin, a Spanish maravedi said to be dated 1598, was supposedly found in 1965 near Joudrey's Cove (though the coin's authenticity is suspect).

The Graves story would seem to be nothing more than gossip, since his own family wasn't aware of it. Graves' granddaughter, Florence Eisenhauer, told Mel Chappell in 1955 that she hadn't heard of any discovery of hidden treasure by her grandfather. But she did say that her aunt, Sophia Sellers (Graves' oldest daughter), "believed that if any treasure were buried on Oak Island, it was carried away, because she remembered a vessel coming into the cove one evening, and it disappeared or departed before morning, and there were marks in the sand on the shore like a barrel having been rolled out."

Edward Vaughan of Western Shore is another whose name often springs up in local discussions of who made off with the island's treasure. His father George (a grandson of Anthony Vaughan) is rumored to have found a chest on the island in the late 1930's. He died in 1941 and some say he left one of his two sons, Edward, an inheritance consisting of several gold ingots. Edward disappeared shortly after that, leaving his wife and children behind. He turned up somewhere in Ontario many years later and died around 1968.

If Vaughan or anybody else did find something on the island, Fred Nolan, the owner of several Oak Island lots, would not be surprised. He is certain that no less than eleven separate caches have been carted away "in the past 80 years or so." He bases that claim on his discovery in recent years of several previously dug holes, none of them more than 4 feet deep, and most of them in the island's swamp area.

Nolan says he had the first indication of a treasure's being removed one night back in 1960 when he and a team of surveyors were camped on the island's northwest side. "We heard digging going on over the southwest side between the swamp and Crandall's Point. We knew it wasn't Restall because he never worked at night, and besides he just was interested in the Money Pit area." Nolan's group went to investigate the next morning and found "four holes, all shallow and all concentrated in a 12-foot-square area. It looked like they took a treasure off by boat on the south side. They left a trail, marks of something being dragged to the shore. Also, they dropped something significant. But I can't say what it was, though it wasn't a part of the treasure."

Nolan says he "kept this a secret all these years because nobody would believe me without proof. So I've been waiting and watching; looking and trying to hear some report of somebody in this area showing wealth. But that hasn't happened yet." He cryptically adds, "Whoever it was, he's still thinking about Oak Island and he's going to come back again." Nolan believes there are "many more treasure locations" still to be discovered on the island.

Stories of people buying their groceries with Spanish coins, inheriting unaccountable wealth, or finding mysterious holes in the ground may be intriguing, but they offer no proof that any part of Oak Island's treasure has been removed. And until such evidence is forthcoming, the assumption that any treasure left behind by the depositors is still there seems reasonable.

In any case, the most enticing aspect of Oak Island is the established existence of the deep underground workings. Even if the depositors did return for their wealth, they left behind an enigma. And from an archeological and historical standpoint, the value of the solution will be more important than chests of gold and silver.

For once the flood trap is bypassed or disconnected and the island's interior examined, the searchers will be presented with a secret chapter from history that has gone unrecorded for hundreds of years and (as will be seen) may turn out to be the record of an ancient civilization.

Chapter Twenty-two

In January of 1965 Daniel Blankenship, a successful contractor with a $100,000-a-year business in Miami, Florida, picked up a copy of the *Reader's Digest*. Toward the back of the magazine he came across an article that would profoundly change his life—the story of "Oak Island's Mysterious Money Pit."

Blankenship immediately decided to spend his summer vacation on Oak Island. Then he met Restall and Dunfield and invested $21,000 in the latter's venture. By the time Dunfield quit in the spring of 1966, Dan had seen enough to be convinced that the workings were probably far more intricate than anyone had previously thought. And, he explains, "I just knew I wasn't going to let it beat me. We all have our mountains to climb and this one's mine."

Today, about thirteen years after reading the article, Dan and his wife Janie are full-time residents of the island. And Dan is still climbing that mountain. "Sometimes I regret that morning Dan saw the story in the *Digest*," says Janie. "I remember he showed it to me at breakfast and said, 'What do you think about that? I'll bet I could stop the water from getting through.' I should have torn up the article then and there."

But apart from the frustrations of the search, the Blankenships, both now in their fifties, are happy with the life they've chosen.

For the first few years Dan did a lot of commuting between Nova Scotia and Florida, spending summers in a Western Shore motel and winters at home with Janie and their three children. But as the treasure hunt became increasingly complex, they realized it was more a full-time job than an avocation. So they sold their Miami home and moved to the Mahone Bay area where they rented a house for a couple years. In the fall of 1975, Dan built a comfortable and spacious bungalow on the southwest corner of Oak Island. It has been their home ever since.

The Blankenships adjusted quickly to life on the island. Unlike the Restalls, they have the conveniences of other modern homes. And their neighbors and friends are only a short drive across the causeway. Their life, however, is centered on the island. Dan's idea of relaxing after a long day at the Money Pit is to help Janie tend a large quarter-acre garden behind their house. Both are occasional vegetarians and they are almost self-sufficient in their produce needs. What is not eaten in the summer is canned and preserved for the long winter ahead. Another of Dan's hobbies is wine making, much of it produced from the variety of berries that grow wild on the island.

In the summers their tranquility is often disrupted by hordes of tourists coming to take a look at the digging site. In 1976 Janie resourcefully made the best of the situation by setting up a snack bar near her home.

The Blankenships are a popular couple around Mahone Bay. The locals had often resented previous Americans who arrived full of brashness and conviction that they'd be able to scoop out the treasure easily. But Dan and Janie are both pleasant, low-key people with a sort of down-home folksiness. As one friend remarked, "They're more like Nova Scotians than Americans." Consequently, they have made many friends on the mainland, even if some of those people believe that Dan or any other Oak Island treasure hunter is living in a fool's paradise.

Blankenship is now Canada's most famous treasure hunter. His years of patient exploration have been featured in articles in the *Wall Street Journal, Newsweek, Esquire* magazine, and many other publications in North America and abroad. Like Mel Chappell, Dan receives a constant stream of letters from strangers offering encouragement, derision, or suggestions on how to solve the mystery. (One recent letter from a group of Australian schoolchildren was simply addressed to: "The Mayor, Oak Island, Canada." It reached Dan with no trouble at all.) But unlike Chappell, Dan doesn't personally answer his fan mail. "If I did that," he explains, "I'd be spending all day writing instead of digging."

Dan, a muscular six-footer whose tanned and leathery features reveal his many years spent working out of doors, has an unshakable conviction that each day brings him closer to the solution of an amazing mystery. "I know it must seem crazy to be at it as long as I have," he says. "But when you've seen the evidence I've seen, there's no way you can let go. No way." Because of that evidence Dan has put more man-hours into the search than anyone. The project has so far cost him about $80,000 of his own money and, in several instances, nearly his life.

Dan's son David, an energetic and affable young man in his late twenties, shares his parents' enthusiasm and confidence in the eventual successful outcome of the search. David lives close by on the mainland, and he and his father spend six days a week probing the interior of the island's eastern end. They are aided by Dan Henskee, a lanky young former science student from upstate New York. Henskee, the island's only other permanent resident, lives by himself near the Money Pit in one of the former Restall cabins.

When Dunfield's lease with Chappell expired in August 1966, Blankenship was ready and eager to take it over. But he knew that a thorough search would require far more money than he had.

He soon found a backer. David Tobias, a forty-two-year-old label manufacturer from Montreal who had previously invested some funds in Restall's work, decided in late 1966 to jump in with both feet. But being more of a shrewd businessman than a romantic treasure hunter, he set out to prove beyond doubt that the mystery was more than mere legend and coincidence. And this he knew would involve a comprehensive and expensive drilling program, complete with professional analyses of everything that was found.

Now, a dozen years later, Tobias has long had that proof and is still heavily committed to the search. "At first," he says, "I thought it was just a legend. But my involvement has been predicated on the stuff I've seen myself. So my participation is based on my own judgment and on nothing I've read" about earlier findings.

Tobias, through his business connections, was instrumental in bringing in other wealthy investors. In April 1969 Triton Alliance Ltd. was formed, with Tobias as president and Blankenship as the Oak Island field manager. (Triton was the name of a Greek demigod who was half man and half fish.)

Although Triton's specific goal is to find and bring up the island's treasure, its letters of incorporation give it the power to "promote and/or participate in activities of an historical nature and/or archeological value related to the early settlers and history of Canada or elsewhere." It also has the authority to exhibit publicly "such objects of historical interest or archeological value which the company may find or otherwise acquire."

Today there are about thirty shareholders in Triton. The minimum investment is set at $5,000, but many, including Tobias and Blankenship, have put in a lot more than that. In fact, Triton's members have so far spent about $800,000 on the search, considerably more than any previous Oak Island syndicate. (Since 1795 an estimated $2,000,000 has been poured into the aptly named Money Pit.)

Significantly, Triton's shareholders are not the sort of people to be taken in by get-rich-quick schemes. They include heads of large Canadian and United States companies, lawyers, and scientists. Men like George Jennison, a past president of the Toronto Stock Exchange; Charles Brown, a wealthy Boston land developer; Donald Webster, a Toronto financier; Bill Sobey, chairman of one of Canada's largest supermarket chains; and Bill Parkin, a Wayland, Massachusetts, designer of weapons systems for the Pentagon. Gordon Coles, Nova Scotia's Deputy Attorney-General, was also one of the founding members before he joined the government. Mel Chappell is another major shareholder and a member of Triton's six-man board of directors. These people are dedicated to solving the mystery and have no illusions about making a killing on their investment. As Tobias puts it, "It has become more of an archeological and historical puzzle than a way to get rich."

Blankenship began his investigation by studying the island's history and obtaining as much information as he could on the previous search attempts. He then interviewed Hedden, Hamilton, and anyone else he could find who'd worked on the island. And he naturally received a lot of valuable firsthand data from Chappell. He also researched the viability of many of the theories that had been advanced. In January 1968 he even attended a seance in Florida in which a spirit identified as Nojean explained that Oak Island was built by the surviving "sun people" of Atlantis following the destruction of their city.

But the real fruits of Dan's search came from his careful exploration of the island itself as well as from a systematic drilling program.

In 1966 he reopened and deepened the shaft (No. 28) that Dunfield had found earlier on the south shore. At about 60 feet down he found an ancient hand-wrought nail and a kind of nut or washer. The hole was dug to about 90 feet, where he encountered a layer of round granite rocks, all about the size of a man's head, lying in a pool of black stagnant water. Blankenship was sure he had intersected part of the south shore flood tunnel, and he spent several months trying to crib the shaft and excavate it even deeper. But even wood and steel casing couldn't hold back the collapsing earth, and the hole was eventually abandoned.

The following year Blankenship dug up parts of the Smith's Cove beach. This yielded more coconut fiber (confirmed as such by Canadian botanists) and the remains of the artificial drainage network. He also found a pair of wrought-iron scissors beneath one of the drains. These were submitted to the Smithsonian Institution in Washington, which found them to be Spanish-American in origin, probably made in Mexico. They were examined by Mendel Peterson, the former curator of the Smithsonian's Historical Archeology division. Peterson said the scissors were of a pattern that was being made as long as three hundred years ago in Mexico and they could be that old or they could be fairly recent.

Blankenship also found a heart-shaped stone about three feet under the beach at Smith's Cove. This too was submitted to Peterson who concluded that it had been chiseled with some sort of tool at an early though undeterminable date.

The most significant discovery made by Triton at Smith's Cove was in 1970 while Blankenship was building a 400-foot earth and rock cofferdam around the cove's perimeter. It extended about 50 feet seaward of the dams that had been built by searchers in 1850 and 1866 and was therefore well outside the low-tide mark.

This cofferdam, like the others before it, was eventually destroyed by storms. But during its construction a large U-shaped structure was found buried below the silt beyond the low-tide mark. It consisted of several huge logs about 2 feet thick and from 30 to 65 feet long. They were notched exactly every 4 feet along their length, and beside each notch was carved a Roman numeral, each number different from the others. The notched surfaces had been bored, and some contained the remains of 2-inch-thick wooden dowels. These presumably had been used to fasten crosspieces to the logs. In fact, several crosspieces and some handsawed boards were found buried in the mud in the same area.

Experts were brought in to examine the structure and it was concluded that it was an ancient wharf or slipway, or perhaps even the remains of the original cofferdam built to contain the sea while the flood tunnel was driven to the Money Pit. One of the investigators, Dr. H.B.S. Cooke, a geologist from Dalhousie University in Halifax, says, "I had no doubt whatsoever that it was an artificial structure, probably a cofferdam, with a well-built wall."

Blankenship believes it was more likely a wharf built by the original depositors, though it may have been a combination wharf and cofferdam that was purposely destroyed after the Money Pit and flood tunnels were completed. Possibly the smaller notched logs that Hedden found in the cove in 1936 were once part of this same original structure.

Triton had samples of wood cut from the logs and submitted for carbon-dating analysis. The wood was found to be approximately 250 years old. (Carbon dating involves measuring the amount of radioactive carbon-14 contained in organic matter such as wood. This isotope is absorbed by living organisms from atmospheric carbon dioxide at a fairly constant rate. After death, the isotope steadily decays and analysis can determine approximately how many years have elapsed since death. In the case of wood, this indicates the period at which the tree was cut down.)

Prior to that discovery, Blankenship had found two other crudely built wooden structures beneath the beach at the island's western end. These appeared to have been slipways used to haul out boats. Handmade wrought-iron nails and metal straps were also found in these areas, and a laboratory analysis determined the metal to have been forged sometime before 1790.

Blankenship has unearthed other strange artifacts scattered around the island. These include a pair of old leather shoes 9 feet below the island's western beach, and three drilled rocks north of the Money Pit that are similar to the two found by Hedden. He also discovered several rock piles under which were mounds of gray ash. The ash was later analyzed and found to be the remains of burned bones; how it got there isn't known.

Most of Triton's work, however, has consisted of drilling. And these probes have resulted in some of the most exciting finds made on the island, particularly because they have been well below previous digging or drilling or else under parts of the island where no other searchers had ever explored.

Between 1967 and 1969 some fifty holes were put down in and around the Money Pit area. The drilling programs were carried out by professionals, Becker Drilling Ltd. of Toronto and Warnock Hersey International Ltd. of Montreal.

They determined that bedrock in that area begins about 160 feet down, though in places it varies 10 feet either way. The bedrock is mostly anhydrite, with lesser amounts of limestone and gypsum in the upper layer. By this time the surface of the Money Pit area was about 12 feet lower in elevation as a result of the removal of much of the overburden in 1965. Thus, depths at which Triton's discoveries were recorded were that many feet lower from the surface than they would have been when the workings were originally built.

Triton disregarded anything that was found near the Money Pit above bedrock, since it conceivably could have been the result of early search work. But in several holes they brought up pieces of china, oak buds, cement, wood, and metal, anywhere from between 160 and 212 feet down.

Some of the holes hit tunnels or chambers that appear to have been cut through the bedrock. In these instances the drill went through about 40 feet of rock and then hit several inches of wood, a thin layer of blue clay, a few more inches of wood, and then dropped into a void 6 to 7 feet deep. Samples of this wood were sent to Geochron Laboratories Inc. of Cambridge, Massachusetts, for carbon-14 analysis.

The report dated the wood at A.D. 1575, plus or minus eighty-five years. Geochron also noted that the wood was definitely not part of a natural glacial deposit since that would have resulted in an age of ten thousand years or more.

Those findings have convinced Triton that there are man-made tunnels 200 feet and more below the island and that their ceilings are shored up with wooden planks or logs.

Triton also encountered the deep cavity that Dunfield found several years earlier, north of the Chappell shaft. In addition, the group discovered a depression extending from about 160 feet to 210 feet almost directly beneath the Hedden shaft. This hole was about 30 feet in diameter and appeared to have been naturally or artificially cut out of the bedrock. It was filled with a heavy putty-like blue clay in which layers of small stones were found regularly spaced approximately every 18 inches.

A Triton report on that finding states: "In the opinion of Major-General Colin Campbell, a leading mining engineer and consultant, this seems to indicate that the clay had been puddled on the surface and poured into the hole in layers. Under these circumstances the small stones present in the clay would sink to the bottom of each layer and produce the kind of stratification noted in the drill cores. General Campbell also pointed out that in the period before the development of concrete, clay was commonly used in underground workings as a water seal."

At 174 feet down in that clay-filled depression the drill chewed through metal and then brought up a piece of brass. This sample was submitted for spectrographic analysis. The results showed a high level of impurities, indicating that it had been smelted at an early but undeterminable date.

Samples of a bricklike material discovered at around 200 feet were also tested by mineralogists and were found to have been exposed to heat at some former time. This is seen by some investigators as further evidence that a primitive kiln had once operated below the island's surface to make and repair iron tools. A cementlike substance, analyzed by experts as being worked by man, was also brought up from cavities below bedrock.

One borehole in the Money Pit came to an abrupt halt at 198 feet. Blankenship and the professional driller operating the machine were positive, because of the high-pitched whining sound, that the drill was biting into hard metal. It required twenty-five minutes for the diamond drill bit to bore through a half-inch of this material. But the core sample was lost just before it reached the surface.

These drilling results prompted Triton to do even further underground exploratory work. In the summer of 1970 Golder Associates of Toronto, a leading geotechnical engineering firm, was hired to conduct the most complete study ever done beneath the island. They drilled a series of deep holes all around the island's east end, examined core samples, and ran seismic and other tests to measure the exact nature and porosity of the soil and the underlying bedrock. They also determined that the water under the Money Pit area was coming in at a rate of 600 to 650 gallons per minute. Based on this data, pumping holes were put down in spots where they would be most effective in holding the water down to below the bedrock level.

Triton has never released the details of the Golder report (rumored to have cost over $100,000 to prepare), but obviously the findings encouraged the syndicate to continue their search. The Golder engineers drew up detailed charts and cross-sectional drawings of the island's interior, and they reportedly found a combination of natural and man-made formations below bedrock.

Golder's work also indirectly led to Triton's most dramatic discovery in a test hole known as Borehole 10-X; a hole in which six years later Blankenship would come within thirty-five seconds of terminating his search.

Chapter Twenty-three

Even as Triton's work continues, there are others conducting their own investigations of the Oak Island mystery. Some have done a bit of work on the island in the past and are waiting for a chance to return if and when Triton gives up.

But Fred Nolan, by virtue of his land holdings on the island, has been able to carry out a simultaneous search. In fact, he has been at it on a sporadic basis for over twenty years, though most of his work has been limited to a surface investigation and relatively shallow excavations in the center portion of the island.

Nolan, a fifty-year-old land surveyor, is as determined as Blankenship to find the answer to the puzzle. Unfortunately, the property dispute has kept the two from working together or even sharing information, and the relationship is strained. In Triton's early years, however, Nolan did some surveying for the group in exchange for a couple of Triton shares. This cooperation ended in 1971 when Nolan succeeded in obtaining treasure trove rights over his own seven lots.

Beginning in the late 1950's, Nolan surveyed the island's east end and charted the various markers as Roper had done before him. Since then he has combed the entire island looking for other surface clues. He has found many that he is certain were left behind by the original depositors. He may be right. For example, he has located several drilled rocks similar to the ones found by Hedden in 1937. One of these, near Joudrey's Cove, has two weathered holes bored into it about 2 inches deep and 5 inches apart. And like the stone triangle, the line of the holes is on a true-north bearing.

Another item, which Nolan terms "a major discovery," is a large pointed stone that was half-buried near the center of the island. He found it while running a transit line from other markers and noticed that its sharp point jutting out of the ground was precisely on his survey line. The rock was inspected by a geologist who concluded that it had probably been artificially cut.

However, there are many other so-called rock markers that Nolan accepts as genuine but which on observation appear simply to have been chipped or fractured by frost or other natural causes. He also found imbedded in rock several iron ring bolts that he maintained were left there as survey markers by the treasure depositors. A more likely explanation, which Nolan now agrees is "a possibility," is that the ring bolts were inserted as guy-wire anchors to support the utility poles placed across the length of the island in 1931.

Nolan has accurately plotted all of his markers on a chart that he says shows the location of "a massive treasure" distributed in many separate caches all around the island. He has dug in about a dozen areas indicated by this map (which he keeps in a Halifax bank vault) but has so far come up empty-handed. He attributes this to the fact that the treasures were all buried at shallow depths and that apparently "someone got there before me and removed the treasure." He did find some old hand-cut wood in several of the holes he dug and is sure that the wood once formed part of a chest.

His largest excavation was made in 1971, an uncribbed shaft (No. 30) 650 feet northwest of the Money Pit. The location was picked on the basis of intersecting lines from certain markers found on the island. However, after digging down to 35 feet, Nolan concluded that he was in the wrong spot.

He is now convinced that the bulk of the treasure is buried beneath the swamp, most of which forms part of his property. He has done some drilling there and found bits of old wood and even metal. He has also encountered beach gravel below the bog. This would seem to confirm the opinion of some geologists that Oak Island was actually two islands three hundred or more years ago and the swamp began as a narrow channel between the two. Nolan hopes eventually to drain the swamp and completely explore its muddy depths.

As for the Money Pit, Nolan believes that Triton is on the wrong track and that the pit was originally constructed as a decoy to divert searchers from the real treasure locations. The theory of the Money Pit being a ruse has previously been suggested by a few other investigators, none of whom has been able to explain satisfactorily why such an elaborate decoy would have been necessary.

Nolan also has his own theory about who designed the workings. He is "absolutely convinced" that Oak Island contains the treasure of Havana, Cuba, and that it was deposited by "a secret organization" within the British military after that city was captured in 1762.

Havana had been a Spanish stronghold since 1511 and was the supply and communications base for the Spanish fleets sailing between Spain and the conquered territories of Mexico and Central and South America. The Spanish galleons loaded with gold and silver from the New World would normally assemble in Havana harbor and from there would be convoyed across the Atlantic. Sometimes these rich cargos would be temporarily stored in Havana while being transferred from one vessel to another. And the city itself was the home of many wealthy Spanish noblemen and ecclesiastics.

In June of 1762 a British naval force led by Admirals George Pocock and George Keppel, the Earl of Albemarle, attacked the heavily fortified city and captured it after a ten-week siege. The British occupied Havana until July 1763 when it was returned to Spain in exchange for the Floridas. During their year of rule the British extracted millions of dollars worth of gold in ransoms from the Catholic Church and from nobility in the city. The records indicate that these prizes of war were shipped back to England.

But Nolan believes that some of those involved in the Havana expedition worked in conjunction with British military leaders in Halifax to sneak much of the loot up to Nova Scotia and bury it on Oak Island. The theory has two heavy strikes against it. There is no known record or even rumor in British colonial history of the Havana gold being diverted from its destination in England. But even if that was the case, the Oak Island project could not have been undertaken in complete secrecy four years after Chester had been settled.

Still, Nolan has already built a museum at the mainland end of the causeway, where he expects to be able eventually to exhibit the treasure he uncovers.

Other current investigators aren't so physically close to the scene as Nolan is, but they too are sure they are on the right track. One of these is Lavern Johnson, a sixty-three-year-old power engineer from Vancouver. He is certain he has figured out how and where the treasure was deposited and how it can be retrieved.

He first visited Oak Island in 1959 and was intrigued by the stone triangle and the two drilled rocks that Roper had surveyed. He is positive they were laid out as part of the original work, though he doesn't place any significance in the bearings and measurements contained in the Mar Del map drawn by Harold Wilkins.

Johnson theorizes that the deposit was made sometime between 1650 and 1750 by the crew of a richly laden Spanish or other European vessel on its way home from the New World. Having arrived at Oak Island, either intentionally or as the result of being driven north by storms, the depositors set out to hide their treasure in such a way that it could be easily reclaimed at a later date.

According to Johnson, the Money Pit was dug to just over 100 feet deep. From there a tunnel was driven on a slight uphill gradient until it reached a point 20 or 30 feet from the surface. The treasure was placed at the end of this corridor. The workers then drove a flood tunnel from the Money Pit to Smith's Cove and used the earth from it to backfill the tunnel leading to the treasure vault. To hasten the work a separate crew dug another shaft (the Cave-in Pit) and drove a tunnel toward the Money Pit, meeting the tunnelers who were coming in the opposite direction. The Money Pit was filled in and the flood system opened up at the beach. But the treasure itself was high and dry above sea level hundreds of feet away from the Money Pit. Most important, the ground directly above the cache was virginal, giving no indication that anything lay below it. And any attempt to enter it via the Money Pit would of course be ruled out by the flood trap.

This theory is accepted by several other investigators, though with some technical variations. But the trick is to figure out exactly where the treasure vault lies. Common sense suggests that the depositors would have placed it a good distance from the Money Pit where evidence of their work might be discovered. And if they wanted the cache to be at least 20 feet deep and yet above sea level, the contour of the land in the Money Pit area would rule out going east, west, or south for any appreciable distance. But how far north and how many degrees off actual north did they go?

Johnson claims to have found that answer by studying the "code" contained in the triangle and drilled rocks. "The depositor," he says, "set up the necessary code to lead him to the correct spot to dig if and when he could return for his deposit."

Johnson got an opportunity to test his interpretation of the code in the summer of 1962 when he leased a section of land north of the Money Pit from Chappell. (Restall was then working in the Money Pit and Smith's Cove.) Johnson dug a shaft (No. 25) about 240 feet north of the Money Pit, a spot he selected on the basis of intersections of certain lines in his code as well as from a reading he got on a metal detector. But he abandoned the shaft after reaching 30 feet and finding nothing of interest. A short tunnel driven from the 25-foot level also proved fruitless.

Three years later he returned to the island and put down about forty drill holes in the vicinity of his shaft. He used a pneumatic drill, which forces air down into the ground in order to drive up the drilled material. In some of the holes between the Money Pit and his shaft the air traveled underground and was blown out many feet away through other drill holes and into the shaft itself. As the ground in that area is mostly solid clay, Johnson speculates that he may have intersected sections of the filled-in treasure tunnel. However, he ran out of funds before being able to complete his search.

Today Johnson is still sure he was in approximately the right area and would like to test his theory further. But Triton's lease has so far prevented him from doing so.

In case he gets another chance, Johnson is not about to publicize details of his code that's based on the triangle and drilled rocks as shown on the Charles Roper survey of 1937. Johnson believes that the easterly drilled rock may have been moved slightly prior to the survey, and says this could account for the failure of his 1962 excavation. (His shaft lies on a line that's 7° west of true north from the stone triangle; a compass bearing that appears to have been a significant part of Johnson's calculations.)

One of the few hints that Johnson does give about his theory is that "the treasure lies from the Money Pit the same distance that the Money Pit lies from the apex stone of the triangle." But this clue can mean different things to different people, as there is some debate over where the Money Pit was originally located. Chappell, Blankenship, and many other investigators place it about 10 feet west of the north end of the still-visible Hedden shaft; and therefore about 295 feet north of the apex stone. Johnson, on the other hand, believes the original spot was just south of the Hedden shaft. Those two suggested positions lie about 30 feet apart.

In the late 1960's and early 1970's many other would-be treasure hunters came to Oak Island, each with his own theory on what the deposit was and how to recover it. But they were usually prohibited by Chappell and Triton from doing any actual digging, and had to content themselves with snooping around and looking for surface clues.

One of these, Alarik Walton of San Diego, concluded that the project had been engineered in 1776 by the British during the American Revolution. This theory was later adopted by another investigator, Rupert Furneaux of England, who then went on to write a book on the subject. (But as has been previously noted, such chronologically late theories are insupportable given the total secrecy of the project.)

In March 1972 a man who described himself as a part-time archeologist and ornithologist arrived from Belfast, Northern Ireland, and informed the Nova Scotia press that he had the answer to Oak Island. He said the island's flooding system was similar to one developed in Ireland more than a thousand years ago and that he could reveal the location of the treasure. He tried to obtain a treasure trove license on the island in order to conduct his own search and announced that he would turn the wealth over to the "Boy Scouts Association and the Indian reservation at Wounded Knee, South Dakota." His license application was denied and he was eventually barred from the island, but not before locating a second triangle of stones (a crude one composed of five rocks) about 420 feet due east of the triangle Hedden had found. The man from Belfast also insists that according to his "calculations" a third stone triangle exists elsewhere on the island.

Another contemporary researcher who is positive he has the solution to the riddle is an ex-machinist from Chicago who first heard about Oak Island in 1968. Since then he has spent most of his waking hours deciphering a myriad of codes that he claims all relate to the island. He gets his information from the stone triangle, the symbols found on the inscribed rock in the Money Pit in 1803, as well as from several "pirate maps," including the Wilkins Mar Del map and the Palmer charts, which have long been regarded by many people as fakes.

By using mathematical wizardry and by turning numbers into letters and vice versa, he says he has pinpointed the locations of seven treasure caches beneath the island having a total value of $210,000,000.

He has long maintained that the pirate William Dampier, and not William Kidd, drew the original Mar Del map. Part of his "proof" lies in a small flag that is drawn in the lower right-hand corner of the chart. The code, he explains, is simple. There are four letters in the word "flag" and the fourth letter of the alphabet is "D" for Dampier. *Voila.*

Another clue lies in the numbers "44106818." By playing around with these figures he uses them to confirm the location of one of Oak Island's treasure vaults. The numbers were supposedly on a card that Kidd slipped to his wife just before he was hanged in 1701. Although he refuses to believe it, the ex-machinist is being taken in by one of the more celebrated hoaxes in the history of pirate lore.

Briefly, the practical joke began in 1894 when a Chicago industrialist wrote a pamphlet describing a fanciful lawsuit being filed against descendants of the John Jacob Astor family of New York. The "suit" alleged that the Astor wealth had originated from a Captain Kidd treasure supposedly found and illegally removed from Deer Isle, Maine. (The invented number code applied to Deer Isle's approximate latitude and longitude—44° 10′ N; 68° 18′ W.) The elaborate joke was taken seriously by some writers, and was often printed as fact in books and magazine articles during the early twentieth century.

But the ex-machinist is persistent, and in 1970 he managed to persuade Triton to use a bulldozer to excavate several spots where he was sure there were tunnels leading to a treasure cache. Nothing was found, and his agreement with Triton was terminated. But feeling that he had miscalculated slightly in his chosen locations, he insisted on another chance. When Triton refused, he kept pestering them with registered letters and even took his case to the Nova Scotia newspapers and radio.

He now spends his summers in a tiny coastal community 120 miles northeast of Oak Island and is continuing his research in hopes of again trying his luck on the island. He has created seven separate maps of the codes to the underground locations, all of them beautifully embroidered on large bedsheets.

Apart from the treasure locations, he also insists he knows where there are seven "death traps" below the island. On September 20, 1976, he asked this writer to "let me know the exact spot that the first person is killed or the first death trap is found. It is my belief that if anyone is trapped in the tunnels, I am the only one alive that might be able to rescue them."

He made this grim offer of assistance five days before Dan Blankenship and his son David were about to make a perilous journey deep into the heart of Oak Island.

Chapter Twenty-four

September 25, 1976. At 6:45 P.M. the sun is getting ready to slide below the tall pines on the mainland. A few hundred yards off Smith's Cove a small gaff-rigged schooner glides across the bay, its silent passage in sharp contrast to the monotonous roar of the pumps and compressor that sit on this hill at the east end of Oak Island.

The last few feet of cable creak over the drum, and David Blankenship emerges from the 237-foot tube of rusty steel that is Borehole 10-X. He looks discouraged, as do his father, Dan, and the half dozen other people who've been here for the past ten hours. Today was the first time searchers had been below ground in almost three years, and everyone had hoped this particular Saturday might prove a momentous day in the island's long history.

Using an acetylene torch, David had cut six holes, each about a foot in diameter, in the sides of the metal casing between 150 and 160 feet down. Sonar equipment had indicated the presence of cavities behind the casing at those spots, and there was a chance they formed part of the original underground workings. But David found they were just shallow voids that were probably created when the borehole was initially drilled.

Still, there were many other suspected areas left to check. Dan, David, and the other members of Triton Alliance had good reason to believe that someone had been down in that same spot long before them; and that someone certainly hadn't been a treasure hunter.

The investigation of 10-X was far from over. As David put it, "We're going to make that pipe look like a piece of Swiss cheese before we give up." But in two months time they'd have no choice in the matter.

Borehole 10-X is 180 feet northeast of the Money Pit and the same distance away from the center of the Cave-in Pit. Oddly enough, it falls exactly on the line of the two drilled rocks found by Hedden in 1937. This had nothing to do with deciding its location, though considering what was found there, maybe there was a connection in the scheme of the original designers of the Oak Island project.

It was drilled by Blankenship as a test hole in the summer of 1970 while the Golder engineers were conducting their geophysical survey of the island. Bedrock at this location begins about 180 feet underground, or at relatively the same level as under the Money Pit. (As a result of Dunfield's excavation in 1965 the current surface elevation of the Money Pit is 18 feet lower than the ground surface at 10-X).

The hole was bored with a 6-inch-diameter rotary drill. At approximately 140 feet down in the hard clay overburden, the drill dropped into a 4-foot cavity. A similar void was encountered 20 feet later. Bedrock was reached at 180 feet, and at 210 feet the drill hit a 2-foot cavity. Then at 230 feet a large cavity was found extending down to 237 feet.

The drill was pulled out and then later reinserted to blow up any loose material. At a depth of 165 feet, two handfuls of metal pieces were blown to the surface. When it came up, the metal was soft and the color of lead. But within minutes it began oxidizing and became brittle, indicating that it had been starved for oxygen for a long period.

Samples were sent to the Steel Company of Canada for analysis and it was determined to be a low-carbon type of steel smelted prior to 1800 and cold-worked or hammered after fabrication.

The existence of the metal and the cavities in an area where no previous searchers had ever dug or drilled prompted Triton to ream the hole large enough to permit cameras and searchers to be lowered into it. Borehole 10-X was to become a full-fledged shaft (No. 29), the deepest one ever sunk into the island.

Triton was approached by Statesman Mining Co. of Aspen, Colorado, which owned a piece of equipment that seemed perfect for the job. It was a cross between a hydraulic clamshell digger and a drill capable of scooping out a 27-inch-diameter hole. Blankenship and Tobias flew to California to meet with representatives of the company, and an agreement was signed. (One of the principals of Statesman, which has been defunct since 1975, was the actor John Wayne. There was some talk at the time of getting him to do a film documentary on Oak Island, but nothing came of it.)

The machine arrived in October 1970 and began redrilling 10-X. At a depth of 45 feet it brought up more of the metal that had been found earlier. But the machine soon ran into difficulties getting through boulders, and by the end of the year the drillers were only at 85 feet, still well above bedrock. So the machine was pulled off the job.

That winter Blankenship called up Parker Kennedy, an experienced professional driller from Halifax. Kennedy (whom Dan calls "the best damn driller I've ever had on the island") agreed to come out that spring and finish the hole with a large Bucyrus-Erie churn drill. The shaft was eventually completed, with a ¼-inch-thick steel casing put down to bedrock and the rest of the hole left uncased to 237 feet.

While it was being drilled, a large quantity of spruce was brought up from a depth of 155 feet. The wood, to everyone's bewilderment, was carbon dated to the future date of A.D. 3100. It was later theorized that this impossible reading was perhaps due to the wood's having at one time been coated with pitchblende (which centuries ago was often used as a preserving agent on ships' hulls). Pitchblende is a uranium ore and would render the dating process meaningless by affecting the radioactive carbon-14 content of the wood. Eight pieces of steel chain were also brought up from about 155 feet. These were analyzed and found to be hand-forged Swedish steel of a type made prior to 1790.

The drill also went through wood below 180 feet, and more metal was brought up from several levels above and below bedrock.

Another hole, of 20-inch-diameter, was put down several feet away from 10-X. This and several smaller holes were later used as pumping shafts to help drain 10-X, which is normally filled with water to about 44 feet from the surface.

The first investigation of 10-X was in August 1971 when an underwater television camera was lowered into its depths. The camera was sent down to the 230-foot cavity as Blankenship sat in a shack a few feet away watching the closed-circuit monitor. One of the first things he saw was what appeared to be a half-clenched hand still covered in flesh and severed (probably by the drill) at the wrist. Dan called the three other workers in one at a time and asked them what they saw. Each stated it was a human hand. It hung suspended in the water and remained in range of the camera for several minutes before the camera accidentally touched it and knocked it out of sight.

A later probe with the camera picked up what seemed to be three chests (one with a clearly visible handle at one end) and several large wooden logs or beams on the bottom toward one end of the cavity. A pickaxe and cut boards with spikes or dowels protruding from them also came on the screen. And then suddenly the camera focused on what appeared to be a human body slumped against one wall of the chamber.

Photographs were taken of all of these findings. But most of them lack clarity and are inconclusive; they were shot with a flash camera directly off the monitor screen.

The photo of the apparent corpse was studied by a Montreal physiologist who reported: "This is outline of a body. Jaw and mouth very realistic; perhaps too much so. No teeth in evidence. Suggests body in sitting position originally, then toppled over." And a leading Halifax pathologist agreed that it would be possible for human flesh to be preserved "over a long period of time" if it were buried in a moist and airless environment under the island.

The next step was to physically explore 10-X. At this time Blankenship had a pump that was capable of handling only 450 gallons per minute, enough to temporarily lower the water level but not to completely drain the shaft. So Atlantic Divers Ltd. of Brooklyn, Nova Scotia, was hired to send some professional divers into the bottom of the pit.

The first dive was made by Phil Irwin. Wearing a wet suit and a helmet through which he received air from a surface compressor, he was lowered by cable into 10-X. The pump was holding the water level down to 100 feet from the surface. At 170 feet Irwin radioed up that the water was starting to get murky. Then just past 180 feet (where the casing ended) he reported a current of water so strong that it was twisting the helmet on his head. He went lower, but the visibility was now so bad that he couldn't see his hand in front of his face.

He was hauled out and a check was made of Smith's Cove. In one section the water had been muddied up. "We had been doing that with our pumping," says Blankenship. "There's no question that we had stumbled on one of the flood tunnels." He theorizes that the tunnel passed by 10-X above bedrock and that the drilling had rerouted the flow down to where the casing ended at 180 feet.

A bulldozer was used to pile tons of clay on the suspected tunnel entrance, and a week later Irwin and other divers made separate descents into 10-X. This time there was no rush of water below 180 feet. At 200 feet the divers found the first bedrock cavity, describing it as 2½ feet high and loosely filled with smooth beach rocks. But the visibility was still bad. Because of the confined space, the divers' shoulders were rubbing on the soluble anhydrite rock walls, and this immediately clouded the water, turning it a milky color.

At the bottom of the hole, the divers were suspended in a large cavern. It was about 7 feet high, but even with strong underwater lights the lateral dimensions couldn't be seen through the murky water. They groped around the bottom but found nothing other than loose stone.

Later that year and again in 1972 Blankenship himself made several dives to the bottom. But he too encountered bad visibility and found nothing worth bringing to the surface. "This chamber is really big," says Dan. "You go down into it, and you're just hanging from the cable like a pendulum in this big void. But the things I'd like to get at are too far away; it's too dangerous to move away from the shaft opening."

He discovered in subsequent dives that the pumping had caused considerable erosion, and the original cavity had become a large bottle-shaped cavern about 15 feet high. Also, the bottom was filled with additional rubble that hadn't been there before, indicating that the chamber might be gradually caving in. So further diving was ruled out as too risky.

About this time Bill Parkin joined Triton. He was interested in the scientific possibilities provided by the search, and he began designing and adapting electronic equipment to be used on Oak Island. Among the gadgets he has made are one for measuring speed and direction of flow of underground water, a conductivity meter to record the depth and salinity of water, and a hydrophone unit to pick up and measure underwater sound and thereby determine the nature of the ground between the location of the hydrophone and the source of the sound. All this equipment is designed to be used in drill holes as small as 6 inches in diameter and to withstand water pressures below 200 feet.

But it was Parkin's sonar equipment that especially interested Blankenship. Encased in a 4-foot-long tube, it can detect the presence of cavities outside of steel-encased holes. It was used extensively in 10-X and located many possible voids above bedrock, the largest ones appearing to be east of the shaft and some of them seeming to end several feet away from the casing.

Triton decided to explore these areas to determine whether the cavities were natural or man-made. But first a pump had to be found that, working in tandem with the existing one, would be large enough to get the water level down to 180 feet in 10-X. A pump with a capacity of over 1,000 gallons per minute was eventually purchased in 1975, and the exploration of 10-X was resumed the following summer.

In the meantime, Blankenship had returned to his drilling program on other parts of the island. On the basis of drilled rocks and other surface markers, Dan put down a series of small boreholes several hundred feet north of the Money Pit in 1973. Core samples from a few of the holes yielded wood from almost 100 feet down.

At one spot, 660 feet north-northeast of the Money Pit, a 2-inch piece of wire came up from 110 feet underground. The drill also bit into what Dan was sure was a solid metal plate slightly lower down. The wire, similar to some pieces that had been retrieved from 10-X, was examined by the Steel Company of Canada. It was analyzed as "a corroded low-carbon material which has been drawn by cold workings, probably in the 1500's to 1800's."

Triton decided to put a cribbed 12-by-6½-foot shaft (No. 31) down in that spot. It was started in October 1973 and finished the following spring, all of it excavated by hand. Digging through firm clay was difficult, and large boulders had to be drilled and blasted apart. But at about 100 feet, the amount of fresh groundwater seeping into the pit from above the workers' heads became unmanageable and the project had to be abandoned until electrical submersible pumps could be brought to the site. The shaft has stood idle since 1974, though Blankenship intends to deepen it eventually and try to find how the wire that was brought up by the drill got there in the first place.

In the summer of 1976, Blankenship did some more drilling in the Money Pit area, again bringing up samples of wood from between 160 and 190 feet. Then in August he began preparations for an examination behind the casing of 10-X above bedrock.

Two pumps capable of drawing up to 2 million gallons a day were hooked to the bottom of two nearby pumping holes. They ran continuously for almost a week trying to get the water down to below 180 feet in 10-X. Bill Parkin was up from Boston running various tests in the hole. One interesting discovery was that the water being pumped out had a low salinity count, indicating that the water flowing into the area beneath 10-X was more fresh than salt. A check of the water levels in other open drill holes and in shaft No. 31 showed that the pumping of 10-X was apparently lowering the island's entire water table. Yet after several days, as the water level fell the salinity count increased until it was almost the same as the surrounding bay.

Just about the time the Triton workers had succeeded in holding the water to below 160 feet, the drive shaft on the large pump snapped. Within two days the level was again near the surface of the pit, and the descent into 10-X was put off for a month while repairs were made to the pump.

Finally, on September 25 the first observation holes were cut through the casing. The results were negative. But over the next two months Dan and David Blankenship made several more excursions into the shaft seeking evidence of artificial workings behind the casing.

Then one day in mid-November Borehole 10-X ceased to exist.

Dan was down at 145 feet in 10-X, while at the surface David operated the winch for the cable from which his father was suspended. A headset telephone kept them in constant touch with each other and (as was done in all their dangerous descents) a tape recorder kept track of everything that occurred. The following incident was recorded on that tape:

Dan had just started scooping clay out of the hole he'd cut. Suddenly there was a deep rumbling in the background, like something heavy crashing against a metal drum. Dan felt small pieces of debris falling on his head and shoulders. He realized what was happening, and shouted into his headset: "Bring me up; bring me up! Out, out, out, out!"

David ran the winch at full speed. But the sound of rock against metal got ominously louder, and Dan knew the noise was still well above him. His yelling got more frantic: "Keep bringing me out; don't stop! Bring me up! It's still over my head; over my head! Bring me up!"

Dan passed the 90-foot mark and looked down. The casing, designed to withstand thousands of pounds of pressure, was being crushed like an eggshell and thick wet mud was spewing in from outside. As he continued his ascent the thumping and crashing increased in volume. But now he was safely above the chaos.

Thirty-five seconds elapsed between the first warning at 145 feet and the time Dan passed the 95-foot level where the casing gave way. Had it taken five seconds longer he would have been entombed deep in the interior of Oak Island.

The next time Dan went into the shaft he could stand on firm ground 73 feet down. He later drilled through it to 95 feet where the drill met twisted steel, the former casing of 10-X. "There was tremendous pressure down there," says Dan, "and the break [at 95 feet] forced debris upwards for 22 feet." As of this writing, the hole has been abandoned.

Blankenship hopes that the rupture only bridged the pipe and that the hole isn't filled all the way to its bottom at 237 feet. Nevertheless, even if it can be reopened the shaft may never be safe enough to enter. For there was obviously a shift of tons of material against the side of the pipe, and the ground in that area is now highly unstable. Dan believes the collapse was indirectly caused by a man-made flood tunnel that he had always maintained passed near 10-X around 90 feet down. The continuous pumping of the bottom of the shaft could have washed away a large amount of earth outside the pipe, creating an artificial fault that finally collapsed downward and into the side of the casing.

Following that incident, Blankenship resumed his drilling program. By spring of 1977 he had put down several holes between 10-X and the Cave-in Pit, still looking for traces of the flood tunnels and any other underground work. He spent most of the summer and fall of 1977 redrilling the Money Pit area, but no unusual finds were made.

Triton's current plans call for an eventual major excavation of the Money Pit itself. The drilling results have proven to their satisfaction that there is definitely original work deep in that area. For several years they have discussed using large-capacity pumps and heavy open-pit mining equipment to excavate a huge shaft 100 feet across and gradually sloping downward to more than 200 feet. It would be carefully shored against erosion and crews of workers would use cement to seal off any flooding outlets that are encountered. All open tunnels would be strongly cribbed and followed to their source, and any artifacts would be carefully removed and analyzed by experts.

But Triton estimates the operation will cost over $2,000,000 to complete, and the group wants to raise at least a good part of that before proceeding. Many of the original members of Triton feel they've spent about as much as they can afford on the project, so the group would have to bring in new members to finance a major dig.

In the past few years Triton has looked into the possibility of a public share offering in Canada and the United States, and also considered running ads in national magazines to attract wealthy investors. However, both these plans were found impractical due to high underwriting costs and a potential maze of red tape to get them approved by the Securities and Exchange Commission and other regulatory agencies.

Nevertheless, most of Triton's members, particularly Chappell, Blankenship, and Tobias, aren't about to leave the island. In 1977 Chappell renewed his treasure trove license, and Triton signed a new agreement with him to continue the search. Both contracts are in effect until the end of 1981.

While Triton may be unified in its determination to solve the mystery, there is internal division over what they expect to find. Tobias has long maintained that the most likely originators of the underground workings were Caribbean buccaneers who banded together to hide their stolen loot when the navies of England, France, and Spain made a determined effort to stamp out piracy in the early 1700's.

According to this theory, the pirates combined their labor to build a large communal bank under Oak Island. The main shaft

(Money Pit) was first excavated. Then each group of pirates dug its own tunnel at a specific level and in a certain direction away from the Money Pit. A watertight vault was made at the end of each tunnel to contain the treasure. Only the pirate band using that particular tunnel would know the precise length and bearing of the corridor. Once they had buried their separate treasures, the pirates completed the flood tunnels, filled in the Money Pit, and then opened up the drains at the water's edge.

Neither the pirates nor any searcher who happened along would be able to get at the treasure caches via the booby-trapped main shaft. But each group of buccaneers could come back any time and retrieve its own loot by simply digging straight through virgin ground and into the vault, the depth and location of which would have been previously measured and recorded in relation to surface features.

The theory is a good one from an engineering point of view. But considering the mistrust that pirates had for one another, their combining forces to hide their valuables is difficult to conceive. Even harder to imagine is the idea that pirates would ever spend the time and energy required for such a complex project. And then, if a large group of buccaneers was involved, surely some rumors of the operation would have later circulated through the bars and brothels of seaports around the world.

Tobias says similar pirate communal banks have been constructed elsewhere, such as Haiti and Madagascar. But this writer has been unable to find any independent proof of this, at least not of a deep underground project similar to Oak Island. And the Haitian bank to which Tobias refers may well be a hoax or an exaggerated story.

In the late 1960's Tobias heard of Albert Lochard, a Haitian engineer who claimed to have uncovered a communal bank at a place he called Kavanach Hill in southern Haiti. Blankenship flew down to the island in 1970 to investigate the story, but after spending several days, he could find neither the site nor anyone who knew anything about it.

Following Dan's return, he and Tobias tracked Lochard down. He was living in the New York area under an assumed name, and explained that he was a political refugee and didn't want his whereabouts known.

However, without asking for or receiving any remuneration, Lochard described his discovery of the communal bank. He said he found the workings in 1947 and secretly explored them for three years, removing about $50,000 worth of coins (dated 1725 to early 1800) from the site. He added that he and a friend fled Haiti by private plane in 1951 when "government pressure" forced him to leave the island before he could complete the examination of the underground workings.

He also showed Triton a diagram of the Haitian project. It included a dome-roofed chamber that extended from 140 to 180 feet underground and was 35 feet across. Leading out of this chamber were five main tunnels; three of them were 10 feet wide by 15 feet high, and the other two were 3 feet by 5 feet. Numerous small flood tunnels designed to channel underground watercourses into the chamber were at regularly spaced intervals. The flood tunnels were apparently plugged with clay, and Lochard said he was able to investigate the workings without being hampered by water.

Lochard said the coins were found on the floors of the chamber and the three large corridors. One interesting coincidence is that Lochard described a heart-shaped rock, which he said he found in one of the tunnels. It was similar to the rock Blankenship had discovered (though Lochard didn't know it) under Smith's Cove beach in 1967.

The problem with Lochard's story is that there doesn't seem to be anyone around who can verify it. Some news articles about Oak Island have stated that the Smithsonian Institution had confirmed the existence of the Haitian communal bank. But Mendel Peterson, the Smithsonian expert who examined some of Triton's finds, says the first he heard of it was from Tobias' report on Lochard. He adds that he has seen no proof that workings similar to Oak Island exist in Haiti or anywhere else. Peterson also doubts that pirates would have gone to such elaborate lengths to bury their money. Other Smithsonian experts also say they have no independent evidence of the Haitian discovery.

In addition, several prominent persons who were in Haiti at the time of Lochard's alleged exploration express strong disbelief in the story.

Paul Magloire was head of the Haitian army and Minister of the Interior from 1946 to 1950 and then President of Haiti from 1950 to 1956. Magloire, who now lives in exile in New York (he was ousted by a coup in 1956, shortly before "Papa Doc" Duvalier came to power), says he certainly would have known about it had someone fled the country under government pressure after finding a hidden treasure. He acknowledges that if such a discovery was made, the treasure by law would have to be turned over to the state, which would then decide how much of it the finder could retain. Lochard would therefore have had good reason to be secretive about his work. But then why, if the government knew nothing about it, would he have left without fully exploring the workings?

Max Bissainthe, who was head of Haiti's National Library from 1942 to 1956, also discounts the story as "legend, complete legend." In addition, several journalists who operated out of Haiti's capital, Port-au-Prince, in the late 1940's and 1950's say they never heard so much as a rumor of such a story.

In fact, none of the Haitians interviewed by this writer know of any such place as Kavanach Hill. Moreover, they say the only treasure that has ever been discovered on the island has consisted of small deposits of French or Spanish coins, usually found in chests or boxes buried no more than a few feet underground.

If Lochard actually found underground workings (he did show Blankenship photographs of himself in some sort of cave or stone room), they probably weren't as elaborate as he described. And he has yet to prove that he discovered treasure in Haiti or anywhere else. (This writer's efforts to locate him and hear his story first-hand have been unsuccessful.)

Tobias is one of the few Triton members who believes that pirates were responsible for the Oak Island project. Most current investigators find that the depth and magnitude of the workings suggest an operation undertaken by a highly intelligent, ambitious, and coordinated people. And the purpose of the project was surely greater than to hide a few chests of coins and trinkets. Only an enormous treasure would be worth the work and masterful engineering that went into Oak Island.

Dan Blankenship, for one, is certain that the answer is "going to be incredible." He resists discussing his own personal theory, but he believes the project was probably built "in the late 1500's or anytime in the 1600's." And, he adds, "There was one great source of wealth during that period—the Spanish and the people they took it from."

In the writer's opinion, there is good reason to believe that Oak Island's secret is linked to the Spanish conquest of the New World.

Chapter Twenty-five

One school of thought that ties Oak Island in with the Spanish New World dates the project in the first half of the sixteenth century. And perhaps the depositors were not the Spaniards, but the Indians during the time of their conquest.

Several theories have been developed along these lines by Oak Island investigators.

The first was in 1931 when John Wicks of Saginaw, Michigan, wrote Fred Blair informing him that the workings had been constructed by the Incas of Tumbez, Peru, around the year 1530. He told Blair that the bulk of the Inca treasure lay in a Gothic-domed chamber 175 feet below the Money Pit. Wicks also supplied a few details concerning Oak Island that Blair knew he couldn't have gotten from newspaper articles about the treasure hunt.

Blair was curious, especially since Wicks and his brother, William, were wealthy and offered to put $30,000 into the search to prove their theory. The following February, Blair and Mel Chappell went to Saginaw to hear more about the treasure of Tumbez. They were astounded by Wicks' source of information.

The factual background to the theory is intriguing. Tumbez (now Tumbes) was a city of the Incas, about six hundred miles north of modern-day Lima. It was first visited by Europeans in 1527 when the Spanish conqueror Francisco Pizarro sailed down the Pacific coast from Panama with a small band of explorers. They were amazed by what they saw: a fortified city where vessels of gold and silver were common utensils, emeralds as large as pigeon's eggs, a temple lined with plates of gold, and a palace filled with gold and silver ornaments.

Pizarro, in true conquistador style, coveted everything he saw and decided to return to Spain to raise a force large enough to loot Tumbez and the rest of the Inca empire. He left at least two of his men, Alonso de Molina and a black servant, Gines, at Tumbez and sailed home. (Some accounts indicate that other unidentified members of his group may also have been left behind.)

But to have his petition to return as conqueror of Peru approved by King Charles V and Spain's Council of the Indies took time. Finally, in the spring of 1531 Pizarro and a force of 180 soldiers arrived in Tumbez. What they found was a city almost in ruins, completely ransacked of its wealth. And there was no sign of Molina, Gines, or anyone else who had been left behind.

Pizarro was told by the Incas that the city had been plundered during a recent battle between the armies of the Inca king Atahualpa and Huascar, his half brother and pretender to the throne. That may have been the case, as an Inca civil war was indeed under way. But it was also suspected that the inhabitants of Tumbez had stripped the city of its precious ornaments and hidden them, guessing Pizarro's plans. What actually happened is unknown, but the treasure of Tumbez was never found.

Blair and Chappell were to hear an interesting sequel to this piece of recorded history on their visit to Saginaw. John Wicks was an automatic writer, a psychic who claims to have an involuntary power to scribble down messages from the netherworld. He had been "contacted" by a certain Menzies, a Spanish priest, who said he had remained in Tumbez when Pizarro left in 1527.

According to Menzies' story, he told the Inca leaders what Pizarro's intentions were and urged them to hide their valuables and religious ornaments as far away as they could. The city's riches were then carried overland to the Darien Gulf in the Caribbean Sea, and there the Incas built ships on which they loaded the treasure. With the seafaring and navigational aid of Menzies and other sympathetic Spaniards, they set out to find an uninhabited eastern Caribbean island to use as a repository. But they were driven northward by a series of violent storms and finally landed in a desolate region (Nova Scotia) thousands of miles from home. They selected an island and built a complex underground cache to store their treasure.

If Blair and Chappell found the story farfetched, they were nevertheless impressed by Wicks' automatic writing abilities. Chappell recalls that the process was "absolutely fantastic." He, Blair, and the two brothers were in the room. John did the writing on rolls of wallpaper while William sat opposite him reeling out the paper across the table.

Through John's hand, Menzies and an Inca priest, identified as Circle, repeated the tale to the two observers. Most of the writing was in English, though some was also in Spanish. "There seemed to be some power behind it," says Chappell, "because I know no one could by physical effort alone write as fast and as clear as he did. It was amazing."

Chappell brought several rolls of the paper home with him, but unfortunately they were destroyed in a fire at his office ten years later. And the Wicks brothers, now both deceased, never did come to the island to locate the treasure.

One of the last communications from them was in 1937 when John Wicks wrote Gilbert Hedden warning him that "the time is not yet ripe" to solve the mystery of the missing treasure of Tumbez.

The next Spanish New World theory began with a Halifax newspaper advertisement in December of 1960. It requested trained scuba divers to come to a meeting where they would hear about an important underwater expedition planned for the following spring.

Eric Hamblin, who now lives in Chester, was one of about forty divers who answered the ad. The meeting was at the home of Brian Backman, a young college student. He explained that the purpose of the expedition was to solve the mystery of Oak Island by approaching it from the water rather than by futile digging. Backman had previously studied air photos of the island and was certain there was something unnatural under the water off the south shore. He was sure it was the entrance to the Money Pit.

Hamblin was interested, and he was among a group of nine persons selected to join the search. They expected that if the tunnel entrance was found it would lead them to a point 170 feet under the Money Pit. So that winter was spent practicing deep dives into sunken wrecks off of Halifax.

In April 1961 the team explored the waters off the south side of Oak Island. Hamblin recalls that "we found it was basically a sand bottom, but we found rock outcroppings that appeared unnatural. They were in an area and shape that could have corresponded to the remains of a cofferdam; in sort of a bow shape. These were huge rocks that went down below the silt." But apart from a few old rusty anchors, they found no other artifacts or any evidence of a tunnel.

The group tried to raise money to get silt pumps, magnetometers, and seismic equipment with which to continue their work. They were unsuccessful, and the members eventually lost interest. The group was disbanded.

But during their research, they developed what to them was the most plausible explanation of the origin of the workings: that they had been engineered by either the Mayan or Aztec Indians of Mexico and that it had been done voluntarily or under the direction of Spanish masters.

Hamblin, who introduced the idea to the group, says he had never been able to accept pirates as the source of the project. "So I looked for something that fit in with the known facts. And that's the answer I came to and I still believe it."

In 1961 he wrote a brief thesis outlining the theory. Some of its more interesting points are:

"The oak platforms [in the Money Pit] were set at a common distance of ten feet apart. Why ten feet? It is not a convenient height to climb in and out of or to pass things up and down from. Nor was it, prior to the 17th century, a 'normal' measure. Who might use ten feet as a standard measure? To date research has uncovered only one possible group. The Maya, praised above all things for the perfection of their systems of measurement, had a linear measurement similar to the Royal cubit of ancient Egypt of 20.68 inches. In their system the next standard length was equivalent to six such cubits, or 10 feet four inches, which, allowing for the thickness of the logs, could account for the spacing of the platforms with a precision and regularity not characteristic of Europeans of former days.

"Oak Island in its southeastern end overlies a limestone deposit. The Maya and Aztecs both were well aware of limestone's capabilities; both as an ideal substance for tunneling operations and as a building material. Much evidence remains today of its use by those people in their native Mexico.

"More important is the method used for more than 2,000 years by the Maya to manufacture their lime from raw limestone. Briefly, a circular pile of logs was raised to a height of about four feet. On top of this were placed small pieces of limestone. Then the wood was lit through a hole in the center and allowed to burn through. The Maya have always believed that is was essential for a successful kiln to have absolutely no wind and a fire that burned evenly on all sides. To such people, needing to make a cement vault at the bottom of a pit, what would be more logical than to avoid all wind by placing it within the pit? Here may well lie the mystery of the layers of ash or charcoal [found in the Money Pit]."

Hamblin concluded that "the complexity and permanence" of the workings are similar with respect to the "strength, thoroughness and details of construction" of the "drains and buildings uncovered in Mexico."

Currently, a similar though much more elaborate theory is being advanced by a trio of men in Phoenix, Arizona. This group claims to have solved the Oak Island mystery through the use of ciphers, mathematics, and research.

According to their calculations, an intricate network of tunnels and chambers was built beneath the island by the Mayan Indians sometime between 1520 and 1540. Their purpose was to hide not just gold and silver, but also Mayan codices relating to the history of their culture prior to the beginning of the Spanish conquest under Hernan Cortez in 1519.

Such a discovery would certainly be astounding, as the few codices that exist today relate only to the Mayan calendar, astronomy, and religious divinations. Most of the Mayan hieroglyphic manuscripts, written on reams of bark coated with plaster, were destroyed in the sixteenth century by zealous Spanish priests who regarded the codices as evil. Apart from these, many Mayan glyphs (primarily dealing with religion and astronomy) are found carved into rock in the Mayan pyramids and temples of Mexico's Yucatan Peninsula. Similar Mayan ruins have also been uncovered in Guatemala and Honduras.

An engineer and spokesperson for the Phoenix group explains that the Mayan theory was the result of six years of research which has "established with very little doubt" the layout of the underground workings and the identity of the people who constructed them. The group has drafted blueprints of the interior of the island showing the approximate locations of vaults, passageways, flood tunnels, and even underground living quarters used by the Maya who designed and built the project.

Some of the group's underground designs incorporate data from the drilling and digging results of Triton Alliance and other searchers. And in a couple of cases the group's "knowledge" of what's under Oak Island seems incomplete and based on false information. For example, one of their charts places the large cavern that is 230 feet down in Borehole 10-X a good distance away from the actual location. In their chart it's in a position that was erroneously reported by a Halifax newspaper article in 1971 and then picked up (with the same error) by a later book on the subject.

But most of the Phoenix group's drawings involve subterranean workings at depths and locations on the island that haven't yet been explored. And in that respect the validity of their theory hasn't been proven or disproven. But where did all this information come from?

They are not about to reveal the details, for the group has been trying for several years to get Chappell, Triton, or Nolan to allow them on the island to prove their theory. So far they have had no luck, even though they claim they could verify some of their findings within a couple of months. They still hope to do that eventually, and they are therefore cautiously guarding most of their data.

Their work began in 1972 when two Phoenix steel workers read about the island for the first time. They began investigating possible solutions to the riddle and concluded it was an Inca deposit. The following year the engineer and other researchers were brought into the group, and by 1975 they had modified their hypothesis to the present one.

The basis of their theory lies in the symbols on the inscribed rock found in the Money Pit in 1803 (see p.25) and those on the rock Hedden found in 1936 (see p.115). One of their members says these symbols "must be used in conjunction with some very important factors, which I'm not at liberty to disclose, or else they are totally meaningless." He adds that the group has traced these characters back to a "Mayan with Spanish influence" source (though they look nothing like Mayan glyphs) and that by using these and other items they have formulated "mathematical proof" of how the project was constructed.

As for the possibility that the original inscription might have been incorrectly copied or is even a fake, he says this is ruled out by the fact that the group's measurements based on these symbols "work out to the inch" with what has already been found (by drilling) under the island. (But, as can be seen on their charts, this is not always the case. In addition, their source for the symbols on the Money Pit's inscribed stone wasn't the earliest and probably most authentic account.)

Nevertheless, he says, "We have cracked the Mayan code of measurement, and it fits in with what is known" about Oak Island.

While the Phoenix group is certain the Maya engineered the Oak Island project, they can only speculate on why it was done.

They theorize that perhaps an intelligent Spanish priest recognized and appreciated the enormous achievements of the Mayan people and organized an expedition to save some of the artifacts and historical records from the advancing Spanish conquistadors. Ships were built on the coast of the Yucatan and the Indians then sailed across the Gulf of Mexico and up the eastern United States coast until they came to an area they were sure was safe from the Europeans.

They dug the Oak Island workings over a period of a year or more, depositing their treasures and codices in waterproof vaults of cement. They later perished on the island or else they sailed home, certain that they had preserved a time-capsule record of their culture in a place that wouldn't be found by the Spanish predators.

The hypothesis seems incredible, yet there are no known facts about either Oak Island or Mayan culture that can totally rule it out.

The Maya were a sophisticated and highly intelligent people. By the tenth century they had developed a calendar more accurate than the Julian, and had precisely plotted the movements of the stars and planets. They were masters of mathematics, engineering, and architecture. They used stone and mortar construction extensively, and built concrete tunnels, water drains, and bridges. Oddly enough, they didn't use the wheel; perhaps because they had no beasts of burden.

And the Maya were capable of extensive sea travel. Columbus, on his second voyage to the Indies (1493–95), came across Indians who said they were from the "land of the Maia" sailing large canoes off the south coast of Cuba. In recent years Mayan glyphs have been discovered by archeologists on cave walls on the Caribbean island of Bonaire, fourteen hundred miles southeast of the Yucatan.

Whether the Phoenix group will get an opportunity to test their findings remains to be seen. If their theory turns out to have been correct, Oak Island would be the site of one of the most significant archeological discoveries ever made.

There are other related theories that point to the disappearance of several famous Mayan or Inca treasures during the sixteenth century.

For instance, the Inca king Atahualpa was taken prisoner by Pizarro in 1532 and, in order to secure his release, was told to have his subjects fill a 17-by-22-foot room once with gold and twice with silver artifacts as high as he could reach. Within eight months more than 24 tons of treasure (worth about $75,000,000 today) had been collected. Pizarro expressed his gratitude by having Atahualpa garroted, and most of the ransom was melted down and sent back to Spain.

But some legends insist that many of the artifacts intended for the ransom disappeared before they reached the Spaniards. One was supposedly a 300-foot chain fashioned from ten tons of gold that had surrounded the square in the Inca capital of Cuzco.

Other Inca cities like Tumbez were also stripped of their wealth before the arrival of the conquistadors. One of these was Pachakamak, a few miles from Lima. However, its treasures are thought to be buried in the nearby valley of Lurin.

And in the early eighteenth century, a 7-foot-tall solid gold statue known as the "Golden Virgin" disappeared from Panama just before it was to be shipped to Spain.

These and other "missing" Central and South American treasures are occasionally rumored to be below Oak Island. But as with the many other theories, this one is only speculation.

Chapter Twenty-six

What, then, is the answer to the riddle of Oak Island?

I have been caught up in this fascinating mystery for the past seven years, the last two of which have been spent doing little else other than researching and writing this book. In the course of interviewing, corresponding with, or examining the records of every person who has been closely associated with the search, I have heard every conceivable guess as to the origin of the workings. Each theory has been subsequently checked against findings on the island and known historical facts.

No one who has ever investigated Oak Island has come across any firm documentary evidence identifying the originators of the project. So solving the mystery becomes a matter of deduction; weighing all the possibilities in the light of known facts, valid assumptions, probability, and logic.

The established facts about Oak Island are:

1. The underground workings exist.
2. They are man-made, though they may also incorporate some natural cavities and watercourses.
3. At least one artificial flooding system was designed to protect the deposit, and others probably exist.
4. The workings extend well below the 160-foot bedrock level in

the Money Pit area and cover much of the eastern end of the island.

5. The designers of the project arrived by ship from a tropical area where coconuts are plentiful.

6. The work was done after 1500 (according to carbon-dating results) and before 1750 (when the Mahone Bay area was first being settled).

7. Depending on the number of workers involved, the project took anywhere from a few months to several years to complete.

Those, as far as I'm concerned, are irrefutable facts. In addition, some highly supportable assumptions can be made:

1. The project was designed to hide something that was of enormous value to the depositors and which was intended to be left there for some time.

2. It was not the work of pirates, privateers, French or British military forces, or anyone known to have inhabited Nova Scotia.

3. The project was not organized by any government or other large group that had an opportunity to record it or discuss it.

4. Whoever did it probably perished while they were on the island or shortly thereafter.

5. The chances are good that whatever was buried is still there. At least, archeologically significant artifacts will eventually be uncovered.

Personally, I would date the operation at somewhere between 1550 and 1700, with perhaps a few years leeway on either side. In my opinion there is a Spanish New World connection to Oak Island and whatever was buried there originated from Mexico, Peru, or some other part of South America. The depositors might well have been the Spanish, the Maya, or a combination of the two.

Blankenship and other current investigators also believe there is a connection between Oak Island and the Spanish conquest of the New World during the sixteenth and seventeenth centuries. The engineering and labor that went into the project suggest that a treasure of immense value was deposited there. And Mexico and Central and South America were the source of incredible wealth—virtually all of it being looted or mined by the Spaniards.

In the early years of the conquest (till about 1550) the riches consisted mainly of gold and silver artifacts as well as pearls and emeralds stolen from the Incas of Peru and the Maya and Aztecs of Mexico. The artifacts were usually melted down and returned to Spain in the form of bullion. Beginning in the latter half of the sixteenth century, the Spaniards went straight to the Indians' source—the rich gold and silver mines. For the next two centuries they bled the mines of billions of dollars worth of valuable ore, all of it smelted on the spot into Spanish coins or ingots.

The cargos were usually loaded on the galleons at Caribbean ports in Colombia, Panama, or Mexico. From there the ships sailed to the Spanish stronghold of Havana where they were assembled into convoys for the voyage back to Spain. This measure was taken primarily to protect the vessels from pirates and from English, French, and Dutch naval squadrons. Convoys were also a safeguard against possible embezzlement by a single ship's captain or crew.

Until about 1545 the route home was approximately due east across the Atlantic from Cuba to the Canary Islands. But the accepted course was soon changed to the easier one following the Gulf Stream up the southeast coast of America and then turning east at about latitude 38 degrees on a heading for the Azores and Spain. On this route the fleets would pass within six hundred miles of Nova Scotia.

These treasure expeditions were normally private ventures, often underwritten by the merchants and exporters of Seville. Provisions, munitions, and settlers were transported to the New World, as were tons of mercury, used for extracting silver from its ore. The same ships would return laden with gold and silver, tobacco, indigo, and other goods from the colonies. The Spanish crown was entitled to one-fifth of all the treasure brought back, though in the early years of exploration the crown's share was sometimes as much as half.

There is no reason why the project might not date back to the 1500's. Those who argue against such an early time period usually maintain that the large red oak tree found by the Money Pit in 1795 couldn't have lived that long. The tree with its cut-off limb had apparently been used as a hoisting support to excavate the pit, and it was therefore a mature tree when the project was created.

According to Harvard University's Harvard Forest division at Petersham, Massachusetts, Nova Scotia red oaks commonly live for three hundred years. And at an age of approximately seventy years the tree would have an 18-inch-diameter trunk and branches stout enough to support hoisting equipment. If, for argument's sake, the tree in question was at or near the end of its life span in 1795 and had been employed at the age of seventy, the project could date back to 1565. But that is not even the optimum case since, according to the experts, it's "quite possible" for a red oak to live 350 years. So even a date as early as 1515 can't be ruled out.

One case for a possible Spanish deposit is advanced by Ross Wilhelm, an economics professor at the University of Michigan Business School. He notes that on the homeward voyage the treasure-laden galleons ran the risk of encountering severe southerly gales on their way up the American coast and then across the 38th parallel. Ships that were damaged might have used Nova Scotia as a landfall where repairs could be made.

Wilhelm suggests that the Spanish crown under Philip II (1556–98) may have built the Oak Island workings as a "bank" in which to store the valuable cargos of damaged or totally crippled vessels. The bullion would remain there until it could be picked up by another vessel. Thus, he sees it as a repository that may have been used many times over a long period of years and consequently there had to be a way to reopen the vault under the Money Pit without springing the flood trap.

The key to this, according to Wilhelm, lies in the inscribed stone found in the Money Pit by the 1803 searchers. In 1970 Wilhelm noticed that many of the symbols (see p.25) that supposedly were on the rock were similar to ones used by Giovanni Battista Porta, an Italian cryptologist of the sixteenth century. Porta had designed several cipher disks, consisting of a ring of symbols surrounded by an outer ring bearing the letters of the alphabet. By following a specified procedure, the inner ring is turned so many spaces until a particular symbol is aligned with a letter.

Using one of Porta's disks, Wilhelm translated the symbols into a Spanish plaintext message: "A ochenta gui(a) mij(o) r(i)a sumideq(o). F." The letters in parentheses were added by Wilhelm, who says they were probably left out of the original message for security reasons. Similarly, the last word is supposedly an intentional misspelling of "sumidero."

Translated into English it reads: "At eighty guide maize or millet (into the) estuary or drain. F."

Wilhelm says this means that the inscribed stone offered instructions on what to do before digging into the vault. That is, pour maize or millet into the drainage system at Smith's Cove to plug it up. The grain would swell and halt the flow of water. Then the wooden platform, or air lock, below the stone in the Money Pit could be removed, the shaft bailed out, and the vault entered. After the Money Pit was resealed, the grain would eventually rot and the trap would again be set.

Wilhelm adds that the reference to "eighty" indicates the level at which the stone was found (although almost all early accounts say it was discovered 90 feet down), and that the "F" stood for King Philip (Filipe in Spanish).

This interesting theory has a few bugs in it. First, there's no proof that those characters were the ones originally seen on the stone. In fact, Wilhelm uses symbols that are slightly different from the ones reported by the Mahone Bay schoolteacher in his 1909 essay.

Second, if the Spanish government intended to have a temporary repository for disabled ships, why should they go to all the trouble of digging an underground bank? The area was uninhabited then, and a small armed garrison could have been built far more easily on the island to serve the same purpose.

The theory also runs into the same problem as do all others that seek to describe Oak Island as an "official" project planned and executed by a government and therefore known to many people. How could it have been kept such a total historical secret? Moreover, it implies that at least each captain of every Spanish vessel using that route would have had to be aware of the island and the purpose it served (as well as be armed with the appropriate Porta cipher disk). If a ship ran into trouble, the captain would have to know where to go and what to do to hide his cargo. And then, of course, the entire crew of any vessel that had occasion to use (or to empty) the repository would subsequently know the secret as well.

Yet no word of it seems ever to have leaked out. And the many historians who've pored through the official records and firsthand written accounts of Spain's New World activities have yet to find any mention of such a project.

In any case, Wilhelm is sure the vault has long been empty; that it was cleaned out one last time and the pit refilled in case of possible future use. This would obviously be true if it was used in the way he believes it was. The Spanish crown certainly wouldn't have abandoned a treasure on Oak Island forever.

A more logical argument could be made for Oak Island's having been used as a repository by chance and not by design.

The Spanish fleets were often scattered apart during bad weather and a single ship would sometimes straggle home days or weeks after the others. And if the ship and her crew were unlucky, they wouldn't get home at all. Records in the Archive of the Indies at Seville list hundreds of vessels that disappeared during storms on their way to or from the New World. In many cases the approximate location is known (from the accounts of other ships in the convoy) but in others it is simply stated as "*en el Golfo*" (in the deep part of the Atlantic).

Some of those sunk carried incredible wealth to the bottom. The 600-ton galleon *Atocha*, for example, had approximately $100,000,000 worth of gold and silver aboard when she went down in a hurricane off Florida's Marquesas Keys in 1622. (Treasure hunter Mel Fisher found the wreck in 1971 and is still recovering the coins and ingots from beneath the sandy seabed.)

Consider the following scenario: In late spring sometime in the 1630's, a fleet sails from Cuba on its way back to Spain via the Gulf Stream route. Hundreds of miles south of Nova Scotia a severe storm is encountered, and a richly laden ship is separated from the rest of the fleet. The vessel is badly damaged, and the captain has no choice but to run before the storm. Two days later the winds subside. But the ship has lost most of her spars and is taking on water. A decision is made to find a sheltered area in which to make repairs, and Mahone Bay is selected. The bay is uncharted, and on the way in rocky shoals do more damage to the hull. But the ship is safely run aground off the east end of Oak Island. The crew, numbering more than a hundred, wade ashore, and a camp is established on the island.

Over the next few days the damage is inspected and the Spaniards learn that extensive repairs to the hull and rigging will be required before the boat is seaworthy. The ship's carpenters have all the tools they need, including a forge for shaping iron fittings. But they estimate the repairs will take several months to complete, and that even then it will be a patch-up job.

The ship's commander tells them to do the best they can, and then decides on a course of action. When the repairs are done, he may attempt to sail to the nearest Spanish colony—Florida. Or he may decide that a better plan would be to rejoin the Gulf Stream and sail downwind to the Azores.

Also on board are an auditor representing the Spanish crown and agents of the Seville merchant who owns most of the cargo (their presence aboard was common practice). Their particular concern is for the tons of gold and silver bullion and coins in the ship's hold. They and the commander agree that transporting such wealth on a damaged ship through waters infested with pirates and enemy corsairs would be foolhardy. Leaving the treasure here and returning for it later under the protection of a convoy would be safer. A secondary reason is that the patched-up ship will be that much lighter and have a better chance of making it to a Spanish port.

The uninhabited island they are on is ideally suited for their stay. It is tucked in behind the outer islands and they can't be spotted by any enemy ships that might be crossing the mouth of the bay. Moreover, it contains fresh water, game, hardwood for repairs and accommodations, and is a natural fortress against any Indians that may be in the area. It is also suitable as the repository for the treasure they intend to leave behind.

Perhaps also on board is a mining engineer, on his way home after supervising the opening of a new silver deposit in Mexico. (Or substitute for him any intelligent officer or passenger with basic engineering knowledge.) The repository is designed to be completely tamper-proof should anyone stumble across it before the Spaniards can return. They have the manpower (besides the crew there may also have been black slaves aboard) to make it deep enough and large enough to contain a treasure that occupies most of the ship's hold. Digging tools are fashioned on the ship's forge from scraps of iron, and the clay ground is firm enough to excavate without the need for cribbing.

The Money Pit is dug first. Separate work crews then tunnel out from it at various levels and directions, and large chambers are made at the end of each corridor. The treasure is distributed throughout these vaults, sealed perhaps with crude cement made from the island's limestone. At the same time at least two flood tunnels are dug, one toward Smith's Cove and the other to the South Shore Cove.

Other crews have been constructing cofferdams at mean low tide in both these locations. The one at Smith's Cove also serves as the outer wall of a huge dry dock containing the galleon that's being repaired. The stone drains are built and covered over with the ship's fiber dunnage, eel grass, rocks, and sand.

Each vault has been carefully measured and mapped with respect to its position directly below the island's surface. The ship's commander has the valuable map, for it shows precisely where to dig through virgin soil to enter each watertight vault. Alternatively, his chart may simply indicate exactly where the drainage systems are and how to plug them up so that the seals in the Money Pit can later be safely removed. The pit could then be bailed and the vaults entered by way of the tunnels. The stone triangle and drilled rocks are set into place and are keyed to the captain's map.

Four months have elapsed. The entire crew has put in ten hours a day to repair the ship and build the cache. The galleon is riding at anchor now, and they are ready to leave. Every precaution is taken to clear up any evidence of their stay. Their living quarters are dismantled and burned. Any garbage or other residue has been taken well offshore by the ship's longboats and dumped overboard. The cofferdams are dismantled and the flooding system becomes operational. The many tree stumps and the disturbed earth in the Money Pit area might indicate that something happened here. But should any chance discoverer attempt to dig into the refilled shaft, he'll get no farther than 90 feet before being flooded out.

The galleon sets sail and leaves Mahone Bay. The Seville agents are anxious to get to Spain to organize an expedition to return to Oak Island for the treasure. But they are satisfied with the project and know their money will still be there when they get back.

Three days out at sea. The weather has turned nasty, and the pumps have to be manned around the clock. The makeshift clay-and-fiber caulking is not holding up as well as the carpenters had hoped. Worse still, there had been no time to properly season the new planking in the hull, and the wood is swelling and buckling in places. How long the patched-up hull will be able to withstand the pounding of the rough seas is uncertain.

The captain is considering heading back to the Nova Scotia coast. He is examining his chart of the coast when suddenly the ship's garboard springs loose. No amount of pumping can check the rush of water into the bilges. Within twenty minutes the galleon is on her way to the bottom of the North Atlantic, and within an hour the last of the crew members perishes in the icy waters.

Included in the wreck some 2,500 fathoms down on the ocean floor is the commander's strongbox. Inside it there is a carefully drawn map showing the location of Oak Island, what is buried on it, and how it can be retrieved.

Back in Seville the ship and her cargo of bullion had already been written off several months earlier as having disappeared *en el Golfo.*

This chain of events is hypothetical. But who can say it couldn't have happened? Spanish treasure ships *did* disappear without a trace, and something *was* buried on Oak Island. Could there have been a connection?

The final answer awaits further discoveries. And they will come in time; for too many enigmatic clues have been found to expect that the mystery will be left unsolved. As one search group gives up in frustration, another will always be eager to jump in.

But Oak Island is more than a treasure hunt. It's a challenge to twentieth-century technologists to outwit the mastermind who designed the workings several hundred years ago. As the Canadian *Consulting Engineer* magazine stated in 1973, the island has "emerged as a threat to the reputation of the engineering society as a whole."

It has also emerged as one of history's most bewildering riddles. The answer will surely be worth the almost two hundred years that have been devoted to the search.

Money, technology, and careful digging will eventually bring the search to its conclusion. However, there are two persistent legends concerning the preconditions under which Oak Island's secret will finally be disclosed: One states that all of the island's large red oak trees must first die; the other is that the search will end after it has taken seven lives.

As of this writing, a few red oaks remain, and six men have been killed.

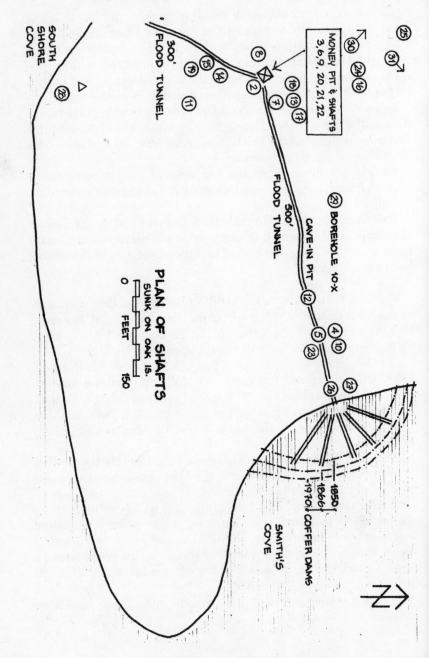

PLAN OF SHAFTS
SUNK ON OAK IS.

Appendix

Number:	Year:	Depth:	Location:
1	1795	30 ft.	Money Pit (MP)
1	1803	93	MP deepened
2	1804	110	14' SE of MP
3	1850	109	10' NW of MP
4	1850	75	100' W of Smith's Cove
5	1850	35	12' S of No. 4
6	1850	112	Just W of MP
1	1861	88	MP reopened
7	1861	120	25' E of MP
8	1861	118	18' W of MP
9	1862	107	Next to MP
1	1862	103	MP deepened
10	1862	50	25' NE of No. 5
11	1863	120	100' SE of MP
1	1863	108	MP deepened
12	1894	55	350' E of MP (Cave-in Pit)
13	1894	43	30' ENE of MP
4	1896	88	No. 4 deepened
3	1897	110	No. 3 reopened
1	1897	113	MP deepened
14	1897	105	45' S of MP

15	1898	160	30' SW of No. 14
16	1898	134	150' N of MP
17	1898	90	45' E of No. 3
18	1899	116	30' E of No. 3
19	1899	144	Near No. 15
20	1900	113	Along W side of MP
1	1909	113	MP reopened
21	1931	163	15' S of MP (Chappell Shaft)
21	1936	168	Chappell Shaft deepened
22	1937	125	10' E of MP (Hedden Shaft)
10	1939	50	No. 10 reopened
4	1939	82	No. 4 reopened
23	1939	63	30' S of No. 10
22	1942	168	Section of 22 deepened
21	1942	176	No. 21 deepened
24	1950	50	150' NNW of MP
25	1962	30	240' N of MP
26	1964	24	Smith's Cove beach
27	1964	27	30' N of No. 26
28	1965	45	South shore beach
1	1965	140	MP reopened
12	1966	108	No. 12 deepened
28	1966	90	No. 28 deepened
29	1971	237	180' NE of MP (Borehole 10-X)
30	1971	35	650' NW of MP
31	1974	100	660' NNE of MP

Bibliography

Baxter, James Phinney. *The Greatest of Literary Problems.* New York: Houghton Mifflin Company, 1915.

Bell, Winthrop Pickard. *The "Foreign Protestants" and the Settlement of Nova Scotia.* Toronto: University of Toronto Press, 1961.

Bird, Will R. *These Are the Maritimes.* Toronto: The Ryerson Press, 1959.

———. *This Is Nova Scotia.* Toronto: The Ryerson Press, 1950.

Bowen, Catherine Drinker. *Francis Bacon: The Temper of a Man.* Boston: Little, Brown and Company, 1963.

Brebner, John Bartlet. *The Neutral Yankees of Nova Scotia.* Toronto: McClelland and Stewart Ltd., 1969.

Caso, Alfonso. *The Aztecs: People of the Sun.* Norman, Oklahoma: University of Oklahoma Press, 1958.

Clark, Andrew Hill. *Acadia: The Geography of Early Nova Scotia to 1760.* Madison, Wisconsin: The University of Wisconsin Press, 1968.

Clarke, George Frederick. *Expulsion of the Acadians.* Fredericton, New Brunswick: Brunswick Press, 1965.

Creighton, Helen. *Bluenose Ghosts.* Toronto: McGraw-Hill Ryerson Ltd., 1957.

———. *Bluenose Magic.* Toronto: The Ryerson Press, 1968.

————. *Folklore of Lunenburg County, Nova Scotia.* Ottawa: National Museum of Canada, 1950.

DesBrisay, Mather Byles. *History of the County of Lunenburg.* Bridgewater, Nova Scotia: The Bridgewater Bulletin Ltd., 1967.

Driscoll, Charles B. *Doubloons.* New York: Farrar & Rinehart Inc., 1930.

Fraser, Mary L. *Folklore of Nova Scotia.* Antigonish, Nova Scotia: Formac Ltd., 1928.

Freidel, Frank. *Franklin D. Roosevelt: The Apprenticeship.* Boston: Little, Brown and Company, 1952.

————. *Franklin D. Roosevelt: The Ordeal.* Boston: Little, Brown and Company, 1954.

Furneaux, Rupert. *The Money Pit Mystery.* New York: Dodd, Mead & Company, 1972.

Gage, Thomas. *A New Survey of the West-Indies.* London: 1677.

Godwin, John. *This Baffling World.* New York: Hart Publishing Co., Inc., 1968.

Griffiths, Naomi. *The Acadians: Creation of a People.* Toronto: McGraw-Hill Ryerson Ltd., 1973.

Haring, Clarence Henry. *Trade and Navigation Between Spain and the Indies.* Boston: Harvard University Press, 1918.

Harris, R.V. *The Oak Island Mystery.* Toronto: McGraw-Hill Ryerson Ltd., 1958.

Helps, Arthur. *The Life of Pizarro.* London: Bell and Daldy, 1869.

Hoffman, Birney. *Brothers of Doom.* New York: G.P. Putnam's Sons, 1942.

Howard, Cecil. *Pizarro and the Conquest of Peru.* New York: American Heritage Publishing Co., 1968.

Kaulback, Ruth E. *Historic Saga of Leheve (La Have).* Nova Scotia: Published by the author, 1970.

Kennedy, B.F. *Buried Treasure of Casco Bay.* New York: Vantage Press, Inc., 1963.

Leary, Thomas P. "The Oak Island Enigma." Omaha, Nebraska: Published by the author, 1953.

MacMechan, Archibald. *Old Province Tales.* Toronto: McLelland & Stewart Ltd., 1924.

MacNutt, W.S. *The Atlantic Provinces.* Toronto: McLelland and Stewart Ltd., 1965.

McLennan, J.S. *Louisbourg from Its Foundation to Its Fall 1713–1758.* Sydney, Nova Scotia: Fortress Press, 1969.

Nesmith, Robert I. *Dig for Pirate Treasure*. New York: The Devin-Adair Company, 1958.

Paine, Ralph D. *The Book of Buried Treasure*. London: William Heinemann, 1911.

Parkman, Francis. *A Half-Century of Conflict* (Vol. 2). Boston: Little, Brown and Company, 1892.

Quarrell, Charles. *Buried Treasure*. London: MacDonald & Evans Ltd., 1955.

Snow, Edward Rowe. *Mysteries and Adventures Along the Atlantic Coast*. New York: Dodd, Mead & Co., 1948.

Spedon, Andrew Learmont. *Rambles Among the Blue-Noses*. Montreal: John Lovell, 1863.

Thompson, John Eric S. *A Catalog of Maya Hieroglyphs*. Norman, Oklahoma: University of Oklahoma Press, 1962.

———. *Maya Hieroglyphic Writing Introduction*. Washington, D.C.: Carnegie Institution of Washington, 1950.

———. *The Rise and Fall of Maya Civilization*. Norman, Oklahoma: University of Oklahoma Press, 1954.

Vaillant, George C. *Aztecs of Mexico*. New York: Doubleday, Doran & Company, Inc., 1941.

Verrill, Alpheus Hyatt. *Lost Treasure: True Tales of Hidden Hoards*. New York: D. Appleton and Company, 1930.

———. *They Found Gold*. New York: G.P. Putnam's Sons, 1936.

Von Hagen, Victor Wolfgang. *The Ancient Sun Kingdoms of the Americas*. London: Thames & Hudson Ltd., 1962.

Wilkins, Harold T. *Captain Kidd and His Skeleton Island*. New York: Liveright Publishing Corp., 1937.

INDEX